William Charles Newbolt

Counsels of Faith and Practice

Being sermons preached on various occasions

William Charles Newbolt

Counsels of Faith and Practice
Being sermons preached on various occasions

ISBN/EAN: 9783337087852

Printed in Europe, USA, Canada, Australia, Japan

Cover: Foto ©Lupo / pixelio.de

More available books at **www.hansebooks.com**

COUNSELS

OF

FAITH AND PRACTICE

BEING SERMONS

𝔓𝔯𝔢𝔞𝔠𝔥𝔢𝔡 on 𝔙𝔞𝔯𝔦𝔬𝔲𝔰 𝔒𝔠𝔠𝔞𝔰𝔦𝔬𝔫𝔰

BY THE REV.

W. C. E. NEWBOLT, M.A.

CANON AND CHANCELLOR OF ST. PAUL'S CATHEDRAL
SELECT PREACHER BEFORE THE UNIVERSITY OF OXFORD, AND
EXAMINING CHAPLAIN TO THE LORD BISHOP OF ELY

NEW IMPRESSION

LONGMANS, GREEN, AND CO.
39 PATERNOSTER ROW, LONDON
NEW YORK AND BOMBAY
1899

TO

THE RIGHT HONOURABLE

FREDERICK EARL BEAUCHAMP,

LORD-LIEUTENANT OF THE COUNTY OF WORCESTER,
AND ONE OF THE COUNCIL OF KEBLE COLLEGE, OXFORD,

AT WHOSE REQUEST THESE SERMONS HAVE BEEN PRINTED,

𝕿𝖍𝖎𝖘 𝖁𝖔𝖑𝖚𝖒𝖊 𝖎𝖘 𝕯𝖊𝖉𝖎𝖈𝖆𝖙𝖊𝖉

BY

THE AUTHOR,

AS A SLIGHT ACKNOWLEDGMENT

OF THE KINDNESS OF MANY YEARS.

PREFACE TO THE FIRST EDITION

THE dedication prefixed to this book will sufficiently explain the reason why these sermons appear in their present printed form, and must serve as the author's apology for intruding himself into a field already fully occupied by those best entitled to speak on the holy subjects herein treated. It is a commonplace, in issuing volumes of sermons, to say that they were never intended to be printed—a mode of expression which bears witness to the extreme difficulty which an ordinary preacher of parochial sermons must feel in adapting sermons, which were preached to congregations whose needs were presumably known, and requirements to a certain extent gauged, to an unknown, uncertain, miscellaneous audience, in a mode of address in which he loses all the adventitious helps of his personality and living voice, and must depend on the sheer force of the expressions used as set forth in the passionless evenness of printers' type. In the full consciousness of these difficulties, the author puts forth these sermons, claiming for them no literary merit, for they have none; advancing no new theological speculation, of which he is incapable; but asking those who read them to remember, that they were each of them preached with a definite object, to meet the needs of those to whom they were addressed as far as lay within the preacher's power; and that if, in aiming wider, he is drawing his bow at a venture, no longer with a definite range and aim, it is in the hope that God may find a place for them between the joints of the harness, in appealing to the heart, where they have not force enough to strike home to the intelligence, of the reader.

The author wishes to express his thanks to those who have so kindly helped him in preparing these sermons for the press; and especially his thanks are due to a kind friend, who prefers to remain anonymous, for his careful supervision, and for several valuable notes to the text which he has contributed.

October, 1883.

PREFACE TO THE SECOND EDITION

THESE sermons are reprinted in consequence of a certain demand for them, without any alteration, except one or two trifling corrections. Three new sermons are added, the nature and occasion of which are explained in the note which is appended to each of them respectively.

W. C. E. N.

3, AMEN COURT, ST. PAUL'S,
    July 1894.

CONTENTS

SERMON I.
Our Ghostly Enemy.
No. I.

PAGE

"And the devil said unto Him, If Thou be the Son of God, command this stone that it be made bread."—S. LUKE iv. 3 1

SERMON II.
Our Ghostly Enemy.
No. II.

"And the devil, taking Him up into an high mountain, shewed unto Him all the kingdoms of the world in a moment of time. And the devil said unto Him, All this power will I give Thee, and the glory of them: for that is delivered unto me; and to whomsoever I will I give it. If Thou therefore wilt worship me, all shall be Thine. And Jesus answered and said unto Him, Get thee behind Me, Satan: for it is written, Thou shalt worship the Lord thy God, and Him only shalt thou serve."—S. LUKE iv. 5-8 17

SERMON III.
Our Ghostly Enemy.
No. III.

"And he brought Him to Jerusalem, and set Him on a pinnacle of the temple, and said unto Him, If Thou be the Son of God, cast Thyself down from hence: for it is written, He shall give

His angels charge over Thee to keep Thee; and in their hands they shall bear Thee up, lest at any time Thou dash Thy foot against a stone. And Jesus answering said unto him, It is said, Thou shalt not tempt the Lord thy God."—S. LUKE iv. 9–12 33

SERMON IV.
The Tree of Life.

"*In the midst of the street of it, and on either side of the river, was there the tree of life, which bare twelve manner of fruits, and yielded her fruit every month: and the leaves of the tree were for the healing of the nations.*"—REV. xxii. 2 . . . 50

SERMON V.
Night.

"*And there shall be no night there.*"—REV. xxii. 5 62

SERMON VI.
Faith in the Holy Trinity.

"*With the heart man believeth unto righteousness; and with the mouth confession is made unto salvation.*"—ROMANS x. 10 . 69

SERMON VII.
Clerical Assumption.

"*And they gathered themselves together against Moses and against Aaron, and said unto them, Ye take too much upon you, seeing all the congregation are holy, every one of them, and the Lord is among them: wherefore then lift ye up yourselves above the congregation of the Lord?*"—NUMB. xvi. 3 77

SERMON VIII.
Sunday.

"*The same day at evening, being the first day of the week, when the doors were shut where the disciples were assembled for fear*

CONTENTS.

of the Jews, came Jesus and stood in the midst, and saith unto them, Peace be unto you."—S. JOHN xx. 19 86

SERMON IX.
The Saviour of them that believe.
"*For therefore we both labour and suffer reproach, because we trust in the Living God, Who is the Saviour of all men, specially of those that believe.*"—1 TIM. iv. 10 94

SERMON X.
The Holy Innocents.
"*Suffer the little children to come unto Me, and forbid them not; for of such is the kingdom of God.*"—S. MARK x. 14 . . . 104

SERMON XI.
Religious Indolence.
"*Not every one that saith unto Me, Lord, Lord, shall enter into the kingdom of heaven; but he that doeth the will of My Father Which is in heaven.*"—S. MATT. vii. 21 114

SERMON XII.
Now!
"*Behold, now is the accepted time; behold, now is the day of salvation.*"—2 COR. vi. 2 123

SERMON XIII.
The Religion of the Body.
"*I beseech you therefore, brethren, by the mercies of God, that ye present your bodies a living sacrifice, holy, acceptable unto God, which is your reasonable service.*"—ROMANS xii. 1 135

SERMON XIV.
The Creature.

"*For the earnest expectation of the creature waiteth for the manifestation of the sons of God. For the creature was made subject to vanity, not willingly, but by reason of Him Who hath subjected the same in hope.*"—ROMANS viii. 19, 20 . . 144

SERMON XV.
Church Restoration.

"*The glory of this latter house shall be greater than of the former, saith the Lord of Hosts: and in this place will I give peace, saith the Lord of Hosts.*"—HAGGAI ii. 9 152

SERMON XVI.
Care.

"*Casting all your care upon Him; for He careth for you.*"—1 S. PETER v. 7 161

SERMON XVII.
The Broken Net.

"*And when they had this done, they inclosed a great multitude of fishes; and their net brake.*"—S. LUKE v. 6 169

SERMON XVIII.
The Joy of the Holy Ghost in the Saints.

"*The Lord thy God in the midst of thee is mighty; He will save, He will rejoice over thee with joy; He will rest in His love, He will joy over thee with singing.*"—ZEPH. iii. 17 . . . 179

SERMON XIX.
The Following Rock.

"*They drank of that spiritual Rock that followed them: and that Rock was Christ.*"—1 COR. x. 4 190

CONTENTS.

SERMON XX.
The Saints.

"*Grace and mercy is to His saints, and He hath care for His elect.*"—WISDOM iii. 9 199

SERMON XXI.
The Angels.

"*For this cause ought the woman to have power on her head because of the Angels.*"—1 COR. xi. 10 207

SERMON XXII.
Fasting.

"*Whosoever doth not bear his cross, and come after Me, cannot be My disciple.*"—S. LUKE xiv. 27 217

SERMON XXIII.
Almsgiving.

"*Lay up thy treasure according to the commandments of the Most High, and it shall bring thee more profit than gold. Shut up alms in thy storehouses: and it shall deliver thee from all affliction.*"—ECCLUS. xxix. 11, 12 227

SERMON XXIV.
Prayer.

"*Lord, teach us to pray.*"—S. LUKE xi. 1 238

SERMON XXV.
The Sword of the Lord.

"*The days shall come upon thee, that thine enemies shall cast a trench about thee, and compass thee round, and keep thee in on every side, and shall lay thee even with the ground, and thy children within thee; and they shall not leave in thee one stone upon another; because thou knewest not the time of thy visitation.*"—S. LUKE xix. 43, 44 247

SERMON XXVI.
Wisdom and Folly.

"*Ye suffer fools gladly, seeing ye yourselves are wise.*"—2 Cor. xi. 19   256

SERMON XXVII.
The Rejected of Men.

"*And one shall say unto Him, What are these wounds in Thine hands? Then He shall answer, Those with which I was wounded in the house of My friends.*"—Zech. xiii. 6 . . . 264

SERMON XXVIII.
The Proportion of Faith.

"*Whether prophecy, let us prophesy according to the proportion of faith.*"—Romans xii. 6 273

SERMON XXIX.
The Physician of the Body and the Physician of the Soul.

"*Honour a physician with the honour due unto him, for the uses which ye may have of him; for the Lord hath created him.*"—Ecclus. xxxviii. 1 281

SERMON XXX.
The Valley of Decision.

"*Multitudes, multitudes in the Valley of Decision: for the day of the Lord is near in the Valley of Decision.*"—Joel iii. 14 . 291

SERMON XXXI.
The Enthusiasm of the City.

"*In that day shall this song be sung in the land of Judah; We have a strong city; salvation will God appoint for walls and bulwarks.*"—Isa. xxvi. 1 305

SERMON I.

Our Ghostly Enemy.

No. I.

"*And the devil said unto Him, If Thou be the Son of God, command this stone that it be made bread.*"—S. LUKE iv. 3.

ANY account which could be given of the *way of salvation*[1] would surely be inadequate and incomplete which did not take true and faithful notice of this fact, that the way of salvation is not the popular way; that it is not thronged by rejoicing crowds, with glad footsteps and easy progress; that it is not the broad road, the easy road of sunshine and of song, but that it is strait and narrow and steep—and, beyond all this, the road of the minority.

And, further, he who would speak of the way of salvation must give some account of these phenomena of daily experience. What is the burden of those groans, which ascend up to God from the travailing creation?[2] What is the meaning of that mute,

[1] These three sermons formed part of a course, on "The Way of Salvation," preached in Worcester Cathedral, during Lent, 1881, on Thursday evenings, March 24, March 31, and April 7.
[2] Rom. viii. 22. See remarks in sermon No. xiv., "The Creature."

upturned head of the longing creature? What is the meaning of its subjection to vanity, failure, and unfulfilled hope? What means death? What is the mystery of pain? Why does Christ reign from the tree, instead of from the throne prepared for Him beyond the stars?

There is only one answer that can be given to these questions. There is a stumbling-block laid across the way of salvation; it matters not that it is known and marked; it matters not that God in His Word, and in His Church, has never ceased to warn men night and day of the terrible obstacle. Woe unto the world because of offences, for, alas, it must needs be that offences come.[1]

Human language has gathered together all its force to express the malignity of the evil and the magnitude of the danger. While it speaks of "*sin*,"[2] that little word contains within it the testimony of experience, crystallized in language to the "*hurt*," the "*damage*," the "*injury*" inflicted upon the soul. Or when the word "*offence*"[3] is uttered, we see the blow struck at the Majesty of God, as men blindfold that awful face that they may smite Him the more with their rebellion. Or if it is *wickedness*,[4] we are reminded of the association with what is evil and bad because the soul is shut out from God's presence. Or else we speak of the "*fault*,"[5] the error, the mistake, the missing the end

---

[1] S. Matt. xviii. 7.   [2] Sin, from the Greek σίνειν, to injure.

[3] *Offence*, Latin *offendere*, to strike a blow.

[4] Wickedness probably = *witched*, allured, led astray by enticement of evil.

[5] *Fault*, from the Latin *fallere*, that into which any one is deceived.

of life; or the *crime*,[1] that which will be gathered up so as to form a subject of accusation and reproof. God in the warnings of His Holy word, man in the accumulated experience of generations stamped upon his language, both agree in this: that no one looking God in the face, or with his eyes fixed upon the fearful consequences before him, or even in view of his own interest, could openly and deliberately and of free choice stumble at that stumbling-block and commit sin.

But facts are against us; sin goes on, it baffles religion, civilization, progress, all prudential considerations. Why is it? What is the secret of its malignity and power? And here God lifts the veil which hangs over the spiritual world. It is not only that man is weak, frail, and rebellious, that he carries about with him a body prone and liable to fall, a weak will and a guilty desire; but rather that man is not left to himself in this matter, but that all this delicate and complicated machinery of will, desire, and motive, is acted upon from without—that there is a tempter who, as the *devil*,[2] the accuser, is anxious to promote a crime or subject of accusation; as *Satan*,[3] is desirous to stop the Christian in his path; as the *serpent*,[4] lies in wait to deceive him; as the *roaring lion*,[5] terrifies him by his boldness; as the *father of lies*,[6] alienates him from God; as the *murderer*,[7] seeks his death here and hereafter by working on those

---

[1] *Crime*, Latin *crimen*, an indictment, charge.
[2] Rev. xii. 10. [3] Zech. iii. 1. [4] Gen. iii. 1.
[5] 1 S. Pet. v. 8. [6] S. John viii. 44. [7] S. John viii. 44.

principles and motions of death which war in the members of sinful man.

I. And this, if you will, shall shape our thoughts during this Lenten season, this strange and awful mystery of temptation, which lures so many Christians to perish on the rock of sin. And at the outset we are met with several difficulties, which need to be cleared away before the subject can be adequately considered.

Are you sure, some say, that you are not being misled by the vivid imagery of Scripture poetry? Is it not rather true, that where a more scientific age would speak of an evil principle working mysteriously in the hearts of men, a less precise but more graphic age would invest this principle with a personality, a body with attributes, out of which an age of uncritical belief has evolved a personal agent called the devil?

Perhaps it will be sufficient to say now in answer to this, that any theory which represents the devil as only an impersonation of evil, cannot be entertained without doing violence to plain and unambiguous statements of Holy Scripture, not here and there, but running throughout the Bible, either explicitly or implicitly, as part of its revelation of the mystery of life.

And, further, that it seems clear and important to maintain that the devil is a spirit, not omnipotent, not himself[1] omnipresent; that his aim and object is,

---

[1] *Cf.* Mill on "The Temptation," Sermon iii. p. 58; Moberly, Bampton Lectures, No. i. p. 25.

It would appear that the devil is certainly not himself omnipresent, for omnipresence is an attribute of Almighty God, but that

as described in the book of Job,[1] "Going to and fro in the earth, and walking up and down in it," that he may minister not good but evil to those who are heirs of salvation.

Having said thus much let us hasten to disentangle another difficulty. There is a confusion often made —to the great disquiet of a man's soul—between temptation and sin. Temptation and sin are two distinct things. Every one is *tempted*; the bad *sin*. Sin is a sign of alienation from God; temptation rather a sign of His presence. Temptation does us real good[2]—sin does us actual harm. We ought in this connection always to distinguish three stages in the growth of a sin: first, the suggestion of evil; second, delight in the temptation; third, the consent of the will.

In the first suggestion of evil, there is not, there cannot be, any sin: every one is exposed to it; no age, no position of life so holy and separate as not to have brought before it the suggestion of evil. It is alarming, it is disquieting, it is a subject for anxious watchfulness, as the little cloud arises in the horizon of a life no bigger than a man's hand,[3] as we are conscious of some one busy at our thoughts with suggestions of evil, but as yet there is no sin; or if something is flashed before our eyes as the devil draws us beneath the fruit tree,[4] or throws down the

in some inexplicable manner, either of himself or by his evil angels, he is possessed of the tremendous power of simultaneously assailing all men with temptation.

[1] Job i. 7.
[2] S. James i. 2, 3.
[3] 1 Kings xviii. 44.
[4] Gen. iii. 1, etc.

golden apple[1] to stop us in the race. But as yet there is no sin.

Or it may be something is whispered into the ear, and enters through that door; as the voice of the mob came once surging up to Pilate, "If thou let this man go, thou art not Cæsar's friend;"[2] but as yet there is no sin. But one step more; the thought is encouraged. Eve sees the tree that it is "good for food, a tree to be desired to make one wise."[3] If Pilate hastens to recognize the importance of the cry, if he closes with the threat, as Tiberius, lust-consumed, suspicious and hateful, comes before him, the temptation is admitted, delighted in, assimilated; then sin is conceived. The next step is but a question of time. The consent of the will is given and a sin is born, "a sin pregnant with death."[4] Yes, in suggestion, in temptation, in the involuntary seeing and hearing, there is no sin; sin lies in the will. A man has sinned—whether he has taken action or not—at least before God, when he wills to sin.

II. And it is only natural in considering this subject that our thoughts should turn to that terrible scene of deep and awful mystery, about which so much has been carelessly and irreverently said, the temptation of our Lord and Saviour Jesus Christ; a subject, which in His tender mercy He willed to have recorded, that we poor sinners, as we come before the throne of justice clasping the sword to our

---

[1] *Cf.* the Fable of Atalanta.   [2] S. John xix. 12.   [3] Gen. iii. 6.
[4] S. James i. 15. "Peccatum morte gravidum nascitur." Bengel, *in loc.*

hearts, praying with an intensity which we dare not give up, "Wash me more and more from my wickedness,"[1] may be able to say, yes, "in all points tempted like as I am, yet without sin."[2] It is a subject round which gathers so much which is strange and terrible, a subject in which it is so easy to be presumptuous and irreverent, and yet a subject of such intense helpfulness, that again and again the soul must return to it for comfort, instruction, and help; here are the devil's tactics, here is the devil's masterpiece, here is one tempted who could not sin. Away, then, for ever, with the horrible thought that the suggestions of evil are mine, that the thoughts and motives, and the phantoms of evil, all come from within. If the Holy One of God could be tempted without sin, so I may hope yet for my weary life, that when the day of reckoning comes, something may be disentangled out of the black mass; this came from without, this never entered in, this was temptation, but not sin.

Yes, as we enter upon this mysterious scene, two things are stamped upon it—a warning and a consolation. No one is exempt, every one shall be tempted. Not the age of Job, not the position of Judas, not the past innocence of David, not the spotless holiness of our Blessed Lord Himself shall be spared; but at the same time as we get to be like Him, temptation shall be more external, the sentinels shall be more trustworthy, there shall be no fear of treachery from within. Temptation may be seen,

[1] Psa. li. 2. "Lava me amplius." Vulgate. [2] Heb. iv. 15.

may even be recognized in its specious promises, but a stronger man reigns within and sin lies chained at the door; and although Satan desires to have you "that he may sift you as wheat,"[1] yet from the guarded citadel of a pure life, with untouched desire, and unbroken will, thou shalt rule over him.[2]

III. In considering the temptation of our Blessed Lord then, we are probably contemplating a pattern temptation, a typical temptation, a masterpiece of Satan, whereby he hoped to overthrow One Whom, with imperfect knowledge, he thought might be Divine,[3] but probably did not fully recognize as being the Son of God. And we all are aware that the first temptation, which is all that is possible to consider at this time, was addressed by Satan to the most obviously weak part of human nature, the appetite, the scene of his most ordinary and coarsest victories. It was ably and subtly and skilfully conceived. The circumstances were favourable—the hunger of a prolonged fast without any apparent limit imposed by a resolution; the possession, on the other hand, by the very hypothesis that He was the Son of God, of miraculous power; the fact that the temptation apparently was to break no *moral*[4] law, but only to satisfy a legitimate hunger. All this lent point and significance to the words of the temptation, "If thou be the Son of God, command this stone that it be made bread."[5]

[1] S. Luke xxii. 31.   [2] Gen. iv. 7.
[3] *Cf.* Mill on "The Temptation," p. 63.
[4] *Cf.* Hutchings, "Mystery of the Temptation," Sermon iv.
[5] S. Luke iv. 3.

But he altogether miscalculated his power of temptation, and the force of the suggestion. The temptation to Jesus Christ meant nothing short of this: that He who had been driven by the Spirit into the wilderness, must hasten out of it without the bidding of God; that He who had urged Him thither was yet unable to protect Him. "Man shall not live by bread alone, but by every word of God."[1] Feeding the body is not the first thought, but life— as afterwards He said, "My meat is to do the will of Him that sent Me, and to finish His work."[2] There were other ways of supplying life, and other means of life than the life of appetite. As has been well pointed out, "the righteousness of Christ consisted not in doing nothing against the will of God, but in doing nothing without it. He could have no doubt about His Father's faithfulness, no suspicions that He had forgotten Him. He knew that He could send manna as to Israel of old, or send His angels to minister unto Him, as He did. The idea of doing anything without His Father's will was not to be entertained for one moment. 'Man shall not live by bread alone.' His Father had brought Him into the wilderness, as He had brought the children of Israel before, in order to try Him and prove Him; and His purpose was to show that man is not to live by bread alone, for there was none in the wilderness, but by whatever other food the Lord would provide, whether that might be manna or angels' food ministered by angels. In any circumstances His duty was to wait

[1] S. Luke iv. 4. [2] S. John iv. 31.

upon God and do nothing without His guidance and direction."[1] And Satan fell back baffled from the attack.

IV. Whatever view we may take of the mystery of the first temptation, whatever may have been the precise sin to which the devil tried to allure our Blessed Lord, one thing is clear, that Jesus Christ here touched the edges of one of our most awful temptations; that is to say, He felt the force with which the devil could attack our weak appetites. He felt the full force of the temptation without the sin-induced weakness of the tempted. He felt that suggestion with no delight, but with horror, which makes men's appetites overwhelm their great and noble destiny. Here was the breath of that maddening suggestion which rouses the latent beast within man, and excites those slaves of his necessities to an open servile war. Here was the invitation to revolt; the summons to that good, that useful, that splendid servant, the body, to be the terrible despot and awful master. Here was the germ of that monster intemperance, in its fullest, deepest meaning, the inverting the due proportion of the mixture of life,[2] whether in the sin of drunkenness, as it has settled down on mankind, and crushed out reason by the dead weight of criminal self-indulgence, or whether it be in that even more deadly and terrible sin of lust, which, like "the pestilence that walketh in darkness,"[3] blights

---

[1] "Primæval Man," p. 252. Hamilton, Adams, and Co.
[2] *Temperance*, from the Latin *temperare*, to mix, to moderate.
[3] Isa. xci. 6.

so many homes, and ruins so many hopes, which spares sometimes not even the young and tender, which lingers with its smouldering fires in the hearts of so many. There are few passages of more awful significance in Holy Scripture than this; when that angry crowd surrounding the woman taken in adultery, asked our Blessed Lord, "What sayest Thou?" You remember the answer. "He that is without sin among you," or, as His words would suggest, he that is without sin *in this matter*, "let him first cast a stone at her."[1] They all went out—that short sermon sent away a whole congregation conscience-stricken.

Oh, let not our Blessed Lord appeal to us in vain, by appetite conquered in the region of things lawful, against *sinful* appetite unresisted, unguarded, unsubdued; against suggestions of Satan, welcomed and approved. The conceiving lust bringeth forth sin, "and sin, when it is finished, bringeth forth death."[2]

Oh, praise and thanks be to our Blessed Lord in this His temptation for His sympathy with man in the terrible rebellion of passion against the will! Praise to Him that here, too, blood-stained and weary, after what seems almost a Pyrrhine victory no better than a defeat, the weary combatant can drink of "the rock that followed him"[3] in the sympathizing heart of Christ, Who, while knowing nothing of that deadly

---

[1] S. John viii. 7. *Cf.* Westcott, *in loc.* Bishop Ellicott, Hulsean Lectures, lecture vii. p. 311, note.
[2] S. James i. 15.   [3] 1 Cor. x. 4.

weakness, felt in His strength, as God made man, the force of those blasts of passion which sweep across the world.

V. But the temptation of Satan goes further, and the blow which Christ gave him with the sword of the spirit cuts deeper still. The life of appetite in its grosser form, whatever it leads to, for whatever cause it is pursued, palpably and clearly and openly brings forth death. But surely we may trace a subtle and more insinuating poison in the suggestion, "If Thou be the Son of God, command this stone that it may be made bread;" it is a cunning, a more deliberate attack on life still. It is the invitation to all of us from our ghostly enemy to misuse life, to misuse our real powers, to take the body as the thing to live for, to make "a man's life consist in the abundance of the things which he possesseth."[1] A boy's first idea of happiness is plenty, and a man's last idea of happiness is too often comfort.

Have we any temptation to put *comfort* first? The devil seemed to think that the first thought of the fasting Christ must be to appease the pangs of hunger. And very often this question does materially influence the view which men take of things, how does it affect my comfort? We wish to turn everything around us into bread—to make everything comfortable. Religion must be comfortable, duties must be comfortable, home-life must be comfortable. But what a hold does this give Satan over us. As the prophet of God comes to the modern Sybarite, padded with

[1] S. Luke xii. 15.

comfort and cushioned in case, with the roll of God's wrath in his hand, he cuts it with his penknife, he casts it into the fire that is on his hearth, and none are afraid or rend their garments.[1] The everlasting punishment of hell must be cast out; it interferes, as he pretends, with the mercies of God, but really it disquiets the uneasy conscience. The plain commands of God as to divorce are put on one side, and burnt as interfering with modern laxity. The strict rules of the Church, which she has based on our Blessed Lord's precepts in his Sermon on the Mount, are tossed contemptuously away. Fasting is not tolerated, almsgiving is almost gone, prayer must be kept in its place. It penetrates deeper and deeper; it shows itself in that want of strictness with ourselves and others, in that easy-going careless religion; it shows itself in that grinding selfishness—bread out of everything; it gives the devil a great hold over us; and this is why perhaps our Blessed Lord did not think it necessary to say any more about the rich man than that he "was clothed in purple and fine linen, and fared sumptuously every day,"[2] *i.e.* he lived a life of selfish comfort. Life was given us for something more than as a time in which to make ourselves comfortable. It is written, "Man shall not live by bread alone."

And then, lastly, it is a subtle appeal to give way to human weakness.

The appetite is strong — here is something to work upon; man naturally likes comfort—here is a

[1] Jer. xxxvi. 23.   [2] S. Luke xvi. 19.

predisposition to temptation; but also man is naturally very weak—forty days' fast might be an excuse for a trifling deflection from the higher life.

No doubt our Blessed Lord must have been hungry. He knew in the days of His flesh what it was to sit weary by the well in the noontide heat, and to beg for water from an unwilling hand. He knew what it was to fall beneath the weight of the cross, and to feel the agony of the fever of death. He has bound Himself to suffering humanity by no tenderer tie than when in the agony of His perfect manhood He cried, "I thirst;" yes, He hungered. And we are apt to pity ourselves very much. We say, "Youth must have its pleasures," or, "We are all liable to fall," or, "Why should life be all labour?" and that "we are all frail." But our Blessed Lord here showed that a man's will can never be forced without his consent. A man *can* resist self-indulgence; he *can* resist evil lusts and passions; he *can* resist evil thoughts. Plenty need not be luxury, nor riches love of money. To waver is to be lost. "Man does not live by bread alone;" it is not a question of weakness, but of God's grace. Our nature, our weak points, overwhelming temptations, have nothing to do with it; man is free. "My grace is sufficient for thee."[1] Do not let us be frightened into sin by the persistency of the temptation or the treachery of our hearts. There are within us slumbering fires, those great forces of the lower nature, which the will holds in check and trains to the service of the man. Suggestion plays on these;

[1] 2 Cor. xii. 9.

it tries to make the will take pleasure in its wiles, to relax the bit and bridle and consent to be subdued. But we know whither it leads. The flesh is a tyrant which leads strong men captive. The flesh is a siren which lures men to throw themselves out of the good ship of the Church. The flesh is a bullying braggart which trades upon our weakness. But Christ has conquered, and we must conquer too. Oh, as we beseech Him this week, for the defence of the right hand of His Majesty,[1] let us remember that His right hand is pierced, "that henceforth there should be no condemnation to those that are in Christ Jesus;"[2] let us remember that that right hand is full of gifts, that it contains the two pence and the provision for us in His Church until His coming again;[3] let us remember that that right hand contains a crown for all those who strive lawfully.[4] "They shall receive a glorious kingdom and a beautiful crown from the Lord's right hand."[5] Thy right hand, O Lord, shall indeed teach Thee terrible things.[6] Thy pierced right hand shall teach Thee the malice of sin, which wounded Thee in the house of Thy friends.[7] Thy uplifted right hand shall show Thee a world gasping unto Thee as a thirsty land[8] for the continual dew of Thy blessing. Thy bountiful right hand shall teach Thee the needs of man. "The eyes of all wait upon Thee, O Lord."[9] Thy absolving right hand shall show

---

[1] Third week in Lent. See Collect.
[2] Rom. viii. 1.
[3] S. Luke x. 35.
[4] 2 Tim. ii. 5.
[5] Wisd. v. 16.
[6] Psa. xlv. 4.
[7] Zech. xiii. 6.
[8] Psa. cxliii. 6.
[9] Psa. cxlv. 15.

Thee the depth of sin; Thy crowning right hand the greatness of the struggle; Thy right hand of wrath the vengeance which has inverted mercy. O terrible "wrath of the Lamb"![1] "They shall look on Him whom they pierced,"[2] each for himself shall see the malice of rejection, and wasted love,

> "And feel as though thou could'st but pity Him,
> That one so sweet should e'er have placed Himself
> At disadvantage such, as to be used
> So vilely by a being as vile as thee."[3]

Oh, let us enter boldly upon the combat, and meet Satan as our Master met him before us; let us be firm about one thing—that our flesh shall be subdued to the spirit, that the will shall be master. For my own sake, for His sake, for very shame's sake, "I keep under my body, and bring it into subjection: lest that by any means, when I have preached to others, I myself should be a castaway."[4]

[1] Rev. vi. 16.   [2] Zech. xii. 10.
[3] "Dream of Gerontius," Newman, p. 43.   [4] I Cor. ix. 27

SERMON II.

Our Ghostly Enemy.

No. II.

"*And the devil, taking Him up into an high mountain, shewed unto Him all the kingdoms of the world in a moment of time. And the devil said unto Him, All this power will I give Thee, and the glory of them: for that is delivered unto me; and to whomsoever I will I give it. If Thou therefore wilt worship me, all shall be Thine. And Jesus answered and said unto him, Get thee behind Me, Satan: for it is written, Thou shalt worship the Lord thy God, and Him only shalt thou serve.*"—S. LUKE iv. 5-8.

THE devil, baffled in one point, now tries another. He had failed where he had seldom failed before. The temptation which had led strong men captive, which had beaten down the gate of Paradise, and brought death and sorrow and sin into the world, and armed the earth with thorns and thistles, and the curse against man who tilled it; the temptation which had ruined David, and laid Solomon low, glanced off blunted and pointless from the impenetrable armour of righteousness which enveloped David's greater son. This was useless. It was a defeat, utter and overwhelming; there was "a decision so complete as to leave no suspicion of a hankering after the other alternative."[1] "Man shall not live by

[1] Kinglake, "Crimea," iv. p. 57.

bread alone, but by every word that proceedeth out of the mouth of God."[1] But the devil, beaten in one point, has his "then" and his "again." He tries another bait. Beaten in the region of stones beneath the feet, in grovelling and carnal sins, he betakes himself to the mountain top, to the more refined and spiritual sins—those sins with which, as a spirit, he is most familiar, the temptation which he himself swallowed with fatal eagerness when, clutching at the suggestions of pride, he fell "as lightning"[2] from Heaven.

Oh, let us remember this. The devil has more than one temptation. When the fiery heat of youth is passed in safety he lays wait for middle age in ambition, for old age in false confidence. He stands by the sick bed of death; he does not despair even when the words of the priest are falling on the ears of the dying man, when the words of the Creed are being uttered for the last time, while the soul is being commended into the hands of God Who gave it; even at the last hour Satan hides himself among the curtains of death, and tries to make the soul in that last extremity fall away from God.[3] "It is the greatest temptation," it has been said, " to be without temptation." Beware of a false security. Perhaps the strong temptation, that temptation which is to try you to the very quick, is yet to come. As it came to Job, while he was easy and comfortable, apparently in the

---

[1] S. Matt. iv. 4.   [2] S. Luke x. 18.
[3] *Cf.* Burial Service, "Suffer us not, at our last hour, for any pains of death, to fall from Thee."

evening of life; as it came to S. Peter, at the end of his close companionship with our Blessed Lord; yes, as it came to Jesus Christ Himself during the last and great three years of the finish of His work on earth. Oh, beware of a security which thinks the devil has gone when he has only shifted his ground.[1]

I. And here we must notice that S. Matthew and S. Luke, who alone have preserved for us the record of them, differ in the order of the sequence of the temptations. In S. Matthew our Blessed Lord is led on from the stones of the wilderness to the pinnacle of the temple, and *then* to the mountain top. In S. Luke He is led through the temptation from the mountain to the temptation on the pinnacle. This, we may be sure, is not without a reason, nor is it without significance.

In S. Matthew, as is usual in his graphic and systematic account, marked by the different adverbs of time, we probably have the account of the temptations in the exact order in which they occurred; while in S. Luke a more artificial and ethical sequence is followed, according to a division which we are cognisant of in other parts of Holy Scripture, "The lust of the flesh, and the lust of the eyes, and the pride of life,"[2] or proceeding in converse order, "The devil, the world, and the flesh," the world—temptation occupying the middle place in each.

Nor is this without its significance. "While the

---

[1] It is said by Kingsley, that the devil's great device for ruining souls, in these days, is "shamming dead."
[2] 1 John ii. 16.

sense is necessarily the first avenue of temptation, Satan may have his different order with the two remaining temptations, according to the temperament of different subjects, with some proceeding by way of pride to ambition, with others from ambition to pride."[1]

Having said thus much, let us go on to consider the temptation, the second in order according to S. Luke, the third in order according to S. Matthew, when the devil takes our Blessed Lord up into an high mountain and shows Him all the kingdoms of the world in a moment of time, promising to Him all this power on one condition: "If Thou wilt fall down and worship me, all shall be Thine."

II. Our Blessed Lord, then suffers Himself, in meekness, to be led by the devil to the top of an exceeding high mountain, such an one as is now pointed out to travellers, rising twelve or fifteen hundred feet above the plain. Before them stretched out a great landscape, containing much within view, suggesting even more; stretching out on one side into the far distance beyond Jordan to the old scenes of Oriental empire, on another touching with the vision the distant coasts of the Mediterranean;[2] opening up suggestions of the imperial power of Rome, of the bright glories of Greece, with its sun of glory and learning and poetry and art now almost set; perhaps to the foreseeing eye of Christ, illuminated by His

---

[1] See Mill on "The Temptation," iv. p. 85; Hutchings' "Mystery of Temptation," Sermon v. p. 144.
[2] Mill, Sermon iv. p. 104.

Godhead, carrying beyond its vanishing distance the advancing wave of that civilization which should lap up to the very shores of distant Britain, reaching out to empires as yet unborn, to peoples and kingdoms and powers yet to be.

With this view before them, as from a model, or a reduced plan of the world, the devil lays down the extent of his offer and the condition of its fulfilment. He brings the map of the country before the eyes of a possible conqueror, and tries to make terms at an apparent loss, in the hope of either gaining a treacherous advantage, or of averting a certain calamity. "If Thou, therefore, wilt worship me, all shall be Thine."

Was this a lie? Was this a vain empty boast? Was it the impotence of despair, which had forgot its cunning, and could only show its malignity? No, we cannot believe that. There was a *substratum* of truth, we cannot doubt, in the statement—"For that is delivered unto me, and to whomsoever I will I give it."

Satan certainly, before our Lord's coming, would seem to have wielded some mysterious power in the world. He was "The prince of this world,"[1] "The prince of the power of the air."[2] In the mutterings of the oracle, in the shriek of the possessed, in the shadow of Nemesis, in the dark and hideous vices of the empire, in the settled gloom and the terrible despair which brooded over the world, we can trace the marks of the powers of darkness, a power, alas!

[1] S. John xii. 31.   [2] Eph. ii. 2.

which still prevails where men have driven out God or where the devil reigns supreme in the blacker forms of heathenism.

Look at the awful state, the dark shadow of death which hangs over the devil worshippers of Africa, the religion of abject fear, the religion of hatred, the religion of death. Look at the awful possession of sin in souls now bound fast to Satan by the bonds of vice. We can trace by the mischief he now does, fettered by Redemption, the force of his empire while yet free. And all this Satan offers to give up, to retire from the seat of the scornful, to evacuate his throne in the hearts of men, to leave his poor victims, to renounce his tortures, to transfer his kingdom; to be the suzerain perhaps, and Christ the ruler, if Jesus Christ will fall down and worship him; if He will recognize him, that is, as a power; if He will recognize him as having a position in the world; if He will treat with him. Oh, it was the Gibeonites [1] of old coming to deal with Joshua and the advancing hosts of God, that they might dwell in the land even in a maimed condition, rather than be exterminated. It was an offer to give up his free power, in order to save himself from destruction. But if He is, at the same time, the real Christ, whom he is tempting, it is something more; one sin would wreck the work, one sin would stop the conqueror; therefore he offers all that he has, to bring Christ but to one sin,[2] that so he

---

[1] Josh. ix. 3, etc.
[2] See Ellicott, Hulsean Lectures, iii. p. 113; Hutchings' "Mystery of Temptation," Sermon vi. p. 221.

might retard redemption. He offers to give Him all that He sees, that he might stop the unknown and dreaded future. And to Jesus Christ it was an offer that might well have staggered one who was not God. To give up that awful power; to resign that bondage over the hearts of men; to renounce that terrible sovereignty of evil; that Jesus Christ should be seen and known as the great world-king; that the longing of the Jews should be satisfied, that a king should rule once more over the house of David, instead of the gradual progress and development of the kingdom, through opposition, despitefulness, and loss; to grasp the power at one blow, instead of by the slow process of a hard struggle, in greatness instead of poverty.

Oh, we can trace the nature of the temptation in the vehemence of the answer, "Get thee behind Me, Satan." Once again these words fell from our Blessed Lord under the force of a similar temptation when S. Peter would dissuade Him from His passion and cruel death—"Get thee behind Me, Satan; thou art an offence unto Me;"[1] a blight, a blot upon the

---

[1] S. Matt. xvi. 23. It has been suggested, as softening the apparent harshness of our Blessed Lord's reply to S. Peter, and illustrating the constancy of the struggle between the Power of Evil and Incarnate Good, that this rebuke was addressed, not to S. Peter himself, but to Satan present, though invisible to all but the All-seeing Christ, using the apostle as his unconscious tool, and seeking through the loving, albeit blind, tenderness of S. Peter—appealing to the shrinking from suffering inherent in our Lord's humanity—to divert Him from the world's redemption by His Cross and Passion. This idea is found in sermons by the late Rev. Edward Millee, of Bognor; first series.

glorious view, when the kingdoms of this world shall become the kingdoms of our Lord and His Christ[1]— a stumbling-block in the royal road of the cross.

Nothing may shake that purpose, nothing may alter that fixed determination. He shall reign indeed, all the power shall be His. His kingdom shall have no end. "His dominion shall be also from the one sea to the other, and from the flood unto the world's end."[2] But first He shall suffer; first, He shall be "rejected of men; a man of sorrows and acquainted with grief."[3] First, He shall kneel on the ground in agony, and feel the weight of that burden which Satan had bound upon the world, until the blood shall leap from His veins, and the humanity seem well nigh to break beneath the load. He would first mount the royal throne of the Cross, and grasp the sceptre which alone could pardon man. Not till He had tasted of death for every man[4] would He utter that triumphant cry, "It is finished."[5] Redemption, sanctification, the emancipation of the world, all is finished. Then He would seize hold of the two pillars of Satan's temple, Sin and Death, and bowing Himself with all His might, would bring low, and lay even with the ground, the tottering fabric which Satan had reared,[6] and take to Himself the great power and reign. There could be no terms with him, whom He had come to destroy; no change in the fixed purpose of redemption. It was a suggestion of Satan. The destroyer stood unmasked. The time would come

[1] Rev. xi. 15.   [2] Psa. lxxii. 8.   [3] Isa. liii. 3.
[4] Heb. ii. 9.   [5] S. John xix. 30.   [6] Judges xvi. 29.

when He would say, not, "I have received all the kingdoms of the world, because they have been delivered unto me," but, "Be of good cheer; I have overcome the world."[1]

III. And Satan still pursues his course, and, alas! with no inconsiderable measure of success. It is not every one whom he needs to take upon a mountain.[2] Even the view from their own doorstep is enough, the view which offers present gratification, in the place of the promises of God yet to come, or that portion of good things which God in His goodness has thought fit to provide.

But the high mountain plays a considerable part in the temptation with most people. Men still exalt themselves in the magnificent contempt of the Epicurean poet.

> "But naught is sweeter, than to hold the towers
> Well-fenced, serene, built up with wisdom's lore,
> From which thou mayest, looking down below,
> See others here and there around thee stray,
> And, erring, seek the mazy paths of life."[3]

A high mountain is a dangerous elevation, if the devil places us there. It is dangerous to look down from; it was meant to look up from. Christ led His disciples into the mountain to see His glory, or to

[1] S. John xvi. 33.
[2] Bishop Andrewes' Sermons, vol. v., vi. p. 546.
[3] "Sed nil dulcius est, bene quam munita tenere
    Edita doctrinâ sapientum templa serena;
    Despicere unde queas alios, passimque videre
    Errare atque viam palantes quærere vitæ."
                                        Lucretius, ii. 7

receive His instruction, or to witness His ascension, and to receive His blessing. The devil leads his disciples up into the mountain to look down on others, to build castles in the air of "empty happiness,"[1] to drink in the lust of power, of getting, and of supremacy. And the price paid for the view, the reward which he asks, is too often, the worship of "the creature more than the Creator, Who is blessed for ever. Amen."[2] Yes, pride, ambition, the idolatry of covetousness,[3] these are the sins which we bring down with us from the mountain.

(1) "All this power will I give Thee." He comes with this offer to the Church, the bride of Christ. Do you not see your splendid national position, with a recognized place in a great nation, which boasts of some of the highest intellects, the proudest fortunes, the most distinguished ancestry in the world? What prevents you from extending your influence? Why are not more young men attracted to the ministry? Why is it always to be "not many wise men after the flesh, not many mighty, not many noble, are called?"[4] The Church is wasting her opportunities by living in the straitened *formulæ* of a dead past. Cut away the trammels of a mediæval creed, which offends the more liberal mind of a purer Christianity. Preach philanthropy, and kindness, and the religion of love, rather than the stern doctrine of a strict retribution. Do not frighten back the rising youth of science, flushed with those victories over

---

[1] κενή μακαρία. Quoted in Trevelyan's "Life of Macaulay," ii. 451.
[2] Rom. i. 25.   [3] Col. iii. 5.   1 Cor. i. 26.

matter snatched by the long struggle of a patient philosophy, by exacting dogmas, and a parade of the supernatural. Preach the freedom of truth, the universal comprehension under one fatherhood of all who strive after truth, and the world is at your feet. Oh, the temptation is subtle, it is dazzling, as some poor steward of God's mysteries feels that the reckoning is coming, when he must give an account of his stewardship, as having wasted his master's goods.[1] It is a temptation to make friends with his Lord's debtors at the expense of his Master. To say to one, "How much owest thou unto my Lord?"—"I owe a wasted life, misused opportunities, carelessness, sin; I dread the future, and the world beyond the grave."—"Take thy bill, then, sit down quickly, and instead of everlasting punishment, write universal restitution."—To another, "And how much owest thou?"—"I owe a stubborn, rebellious heart of pride; I do not believe, I cannot believe, I will not believe."—"Take thy bill, then, sit down quickly, and write, instead of the Bible, God's inspired word, an ancient document of doubtful authority, full of legendary matter."—To another, "And how much owest thou?"—"I owe deliberate disregard for the Church of my youth, for her orders, her discipline, her sacraments."—"Take thy bill, then, sit down quickly, and write the simple belief of an enlightened civilization."

This may be popular, but is it honest? This may open up a great view of power, but whose suggestion is it? No, there is no shorter road to power for the

[1] S. Luke xvi. 5.

Church than the royal road of the Cross, by the foolishness of preaching,[1] by evil report, as well as good report;[2] yes, even the rich young ruler[3] must go away, rather than the Gospel standard be lowered. The Church must indignantly refuse any compromise with error. If right is right, then she will follow right, and scorn the consequence. The power she seeks is not the power of toleration, but the power which she wins for herself, by the conquest of the world.

(2) And the same offer is put before man at different stages of his existence. "All this power will I give thee." What is dishonesty in many cases, but the clutching at some immediate profit, which the slow revolving wheel of the course of God's providence seemed to withhold? Is it unnecessary, dear friends, to speak of dishonesty at this time? Would to God it were! Is it true that in some cases, the commercial fame of England is ruined, in some places severely damaged, by a wholesale policy of dishonest trading? Is all the depression, in all branches of trade, due entirely to home influence? Is there anything in it of retribution, is there anything of retaliation from foreign lands, for fraud and dishonesty in commercial England?

These are voices which cannot be ignored. These are indications which must make any Englishman anxious. Certainly, again and again, the temptation comes to every one, "All this power will I give thee, if thou wilt fall down and worship me."

The temptation is great, it is a real one, in this

---

[1] 1 Cor. i. 21.   [2] 2 Cor. vi. 8.   [3] S. Matt. xix. 16.

hungry, bustling, realizing age, to snatch at the prize, without considering the giver, or the conditions of the gift. Oh, beware of the first beginning, beware of the first mutterings of discontent, the first symptoms of covetousness. The money taken from the bag is the beginning of betraying Christ.

Has not Satan been found out yet? Can any worldly pleasure compensate for the loss of a quiet conscience? Can any position, however honourable, minister comfort if its supports are rotted through and through with dishonesty? Can any power, or any influence, minister happiness which has been won at the cost of the loss of self-respect?

"All this power will I give Thee." Oh, bid Satan take back his power, his victory, his throne, his dominion, if the price to be paid for them is discontent, dishonesty, or covetousness. "Better is a dinner of herbs where love is, than a stalled ox and hatred therewith."[1]

(3) And then, lastly, with the devil it is always "look down;" with Christ it is always "look up."

There is much to dazzle us all around, much to captivate, much to charm; but what does Satan promise for the future? He can offer a great deal: it is astonishing what men can attain to, who give themselves to his work and service. They *have* their reward.[2] All their energies and powers and intellect are devoted to one object, and it is attained. *What*

---

[1] Prov. xv. 17.
[2] S. Matt. vi. 2. απέχουσι τοὺ μισθοὺ ἀυτῶν. They have it, *i.e.* to the full, there is nothing more to come.

then? What is there for the future? What is there for the soul as it stands trembling and empty and naked? It brought nothing into this world, and it is certain it can carry nothing out. "He shall carry nothing away with him when he dieth, neither shall his pomp follow him."[1] Oh, our Lord asks with startling earnestness, "What shall it profit a man, if he shall gain the whole world, and lose his own soul? Or what shall a man give in exchange for his soul?"[2]

Satan offers us what we can see; well and good. But, if we could only see God's offer, as Moses and the patriarchs endured, "as seeing Him who is invisible,"[3] there would be no comparison between them. Is it possible that we can go on and on, through the world, without stopping to satisfy the craving of our immortal soul? "We are not children of the bond-woman, but of the free;"[4] we have a loving mother, and a blessed home, here in this world. Here we were born again of water and the Holy Ghost. Here we were confirmed, and made strong by the Holy Ghost. Here we may be nourished and sanctified by the blessed food of the Body and Blood of Christ.

Yes, the view that is open to the eye of faith here —here in this world—far eclipses the most glorious view which even Satan can gild for us with artificial light, and present to the eye of sight! The call to live only for this world is a deliberate call not only to our future and eternal, but to our present and temporal loss. The far-sighted and the keen-eyed eagle,

---

[1] Psa. xlix. 17. [2] S. Mark viii. 36, 37.
[3] Heb. xi. 27. [4] Gal. iv. 31.

permitted by God to gaze into the very sun of His mysteries, will not be drawn down by the purblind, near-sighted tempter, to the little vision which lies at his feet. The light will soon fade out of that landscape, and the world's power turn to dust—and what have we done for the soul?

Yes, any one who is scorning the royal road of the Cross, who is casting away the glorious destiny which God provides for him, who snatches at this world's good, or this world's opinion, or this world's profit, and forgets his own soul—yes, he is losing. Every time we turn from God we are losing. Every Lent we neglect, we are losing. Every Holy Communion we turn from, every prayer we omit, every duty we leave undone, we are losing. Every act of unfaithfulness is a loss, a distinct and awful loss—as was his:

> "Seven days, we read, a Saint of old
> Dreamed on in doubt alone;
> Seven days of hope and joy untold
> For evermore were gone."[1]

We must work on, and not gaze at the view beneath, but ever look upwards to the eye of Christ. Let us go with Him into the mountain. There is an ambition, a noble pride, which He alone can fill. Let Him tell us of those nights spent in prayer on the mountain-top—of the sweetness, the force, the power of prayer. Let Him tell us of the transfiguration which turns our dull lives into the silvery light of peace, and transforms us into children of grace. Let Him tell us of those words of love and wisdom

[1] "Lyra Innocentium," poem v.

which held the multitudes entranced, and brought the rocks and the trees to listen to His voice. Let us bend our heads to receive His blessing, which falls from those uplifted hands, and strain our eyes to catch the receding glories of heaven, which the jealous cloud of sight would snatch from the eye of faith. Above all, let us linger with Him on that mount of sacrifice. Let us see the price which he paid for the world, to spoil the spoiler of his prey. Let us "make a covenant with Him with sacrifice."[1] And if there is a pride, if there is an ambition, which comes to us on that mountain-top, let it be the pride of being good, the ambition to be heirs of that kingdom which shall last for ever, which shall help us to spurn, once for all, all low and discontented and covetous desires beneath our feet.

Men shall take knowledge of us that we have been with Jesus.[2] Our faces shall shine with supernatural glow. The deaf and dumb devil shall yield to our touch; we shall return to Jerusalem with fear and great joy, and be continually in the temple praising and blessing God.[3] For we look for no earthly power, no bewildering, dazzling fruits of covetousness, but "for a city which hath foundations, whose builder and maker is God."[4]

[1] Psa. l. 5.
[2] Acts iv. 13.
[3] S. Luke xxiv. 52, 53.
[4] Heb xi. 10.

SERMON III.

Our Ghostly Enemy.

No. III.

"*And he brought Him to Jerusalem, and set Him on a pinnacle of the temple, and said unto Him, If Thou be the Son of God, cast Thyself down from hence: for it is written, He shall give His angels charge over Thee to keep Thee; and in their hands they shall bear Thee up, lest at any time Thou dash Thy foot against a stone. And Jesus answering said unto Him, It is said, Thou shalt not tempt the Lord thy God.*"—S. LUKE iv. 9-12.

WHEN the enemies of the prophet Daniel, weighing well his integrity, and despairing of any loophole of attack in a life so well-ordered and righteous, cast about for some mode of approach for their machinations, which were to work his ruin, they said, "We shall not find any occasion against this Daniel, except we find it against him concerning the law of his God."[1] And so the devil—failing in the region of sense, failing even more conspicuously in the soul, the region of the imagination, the seat of the empire of the will, where covetousness and ambition and love of power are generally found to exercise some sway—tries yet one more region, as yet unexplored, higher up, and

[1] Dan. vi. 5.

therefore with a greater fall—the region of the spirit, the higher portion of our purely human nature, the medium of our cognisance of the Divine nature, the temple within the little city of a man's life, the place of his meeting with God;[1] and there tries what presumption will do, where appetite and ambition had failed; whether he could strain those relations (how intimate he knew not) between the Divine and human nature; to see if he could enter within the Paradise of the soul; to see if there was any forbidden tree to be tasted, any limitation to that perfect walking with God, any possibility of introducing his "Yea, hath God said?"[2] any room to graft presumption upon that trust which refused to gratify even hunger without the clear and directing will of God.

It is not unknown, alas! It is a common recognized battlefield with Satan. When all else fails—the Spirit. If I can find it in nothing else, I shall find occasion against him concerning the law of his God.

Ah! well did the builders of our old cathedrals and churches carve their grinning fiends and hideous demons, clustering round the roofs and towers of the holy places. The Church and holy things are the scenes of the devil's greatest victories. When men have escaped him everywhere else, in appetite, in the glittering world; when they have crushed out lust from the body and ambition from the soul, he has

---

[1] See Bishop Ellicott, "Destiny of The Creature and other sermons."
[2] Gen. iii. 1.

met them in the path of their God; he has laid wait for them between the pages of the Bible; he has met them on the steps of the altar; he has come to some Moses, even as the water of the Sacraments was about to gush from the rock; he has pillowed the bed of death with a false assurance, which is not the comfort of the rod and staff of the Cross.[1]

Cast your eye down that weary page of history, the history of heresy and schism; whence is this sad scene of bitterness and division? What mean those names cropping up here and there where Christ should be all in all? "Was Paul crucified for you? or were ye baptized in the name of Paul?"[2] What mean those distorted doctrines, upsetting the proportion of faith?

Trust in God, so holy and so noble as it is, has become presumption. Some one has tried to steady the ark with unhallowed hands;[3] and those who by splendid self-denial and noble self-restraint have conquered appetite and ambition, lie, like Dagon, prone before the ark of God—beaten in the spirit.

Oh, it is a temptation, so easy, so insinuating, so fascinating, that its danger is intense. Nowhere is there safety, not within the circle of our own life; a man is not safe even by himself; not in the world— its tempting, dazzling view may shut out God; and, alas! not even in the temple. "Even in harbour ships are broken,"[4] says S. Augustine. In heaven there

---

[1] Psa. xxiii. 4.   [2] 1 Cor. i 13.   [3] 2 Sam. vi. 6.
[4] St. Augustine on Psa. xix. "Nusquam est securitas fratres, neque in Cœlo, neque in Paradiso, multo minus in mundo; in cœlo enim

was war, and the devil was cast out.[1] In paradise the serpent coiled himself round the tree of God's planting. In the very school of the Saviour, under the eye of His presence, taught by His lips, helped by His grace, Judas fell away. Presumption must make us all tremble; the sin of good men, the sin of Paradise, the sin in the Holy Place, unlooked for, unsuspected, and sometimes, alas! unrepented of.

I. Perhaps, then, we may venture to say—on a subject in which, alas! it is only too easy to go wrong—that it was with some such intent that the devil carries our Lord away to a lofty eminence of the temple, unresisting, in obedience to the will of the Holy Spirit, Who drove Him into the desert, that He might test here, too, the force of that terrible temptation—the temptation of saints. Our Lord was led to the top of some eminence in the temple; perhaps the gilded dome of the sanctuary; perhaps the roof of the royal porch, looking down from a dizzy height over the valley of Kidron beneath; perhaps the top of Solomon's porch, looking down into the court of the Israelites, from which afterwards S. James was hurled. Taking his stand here, the tempter commences his last effort.[2] "If Thou be the Son of God, cast Thyself down from hence, for it is written, He shall give His angels charge over Thee, to keep Thee, and in their hands they shall bear Thee up, lest at any time Thou dash Thy foot against a stone."

---

cecidit angelus sub præsentiâ Divinitatis; Adam in Paradiso, in loco voluptatis; Judas in mundo de scholâ Salvatoris."

[1] Rev. xii. 7.   [2] Farrar, "Life of Christ," vol. i. p. 133.

There are several points in this temptation which require our very earnest and serious attention. It has been well pointed out[1] that the temptation was complex in its character and happy in its opportunity; and whether He were God, or only a Divine man, charged on either hypothesis, with sufficient ruin and destruction. And, first of all, what did the devil want? What *was*, in fact, the temptation? Gratified appetite we can understand as a loud clamorous prompter to rebellion. The surrender of His power, and a world-wide empire without the Cross, were a sufficiently tempting bait to conceal the barb of sin. But what was to be gained by a sudden fall from the temple? What would Satan gain? What would Christ gain if the offer was closed with and the suggestion carried out?

"*If Thou be the Son of God.*" As far as Satan was concerned, it may well be there was a double end to be secured. Our Blessed Lord might be God. He might be only man. If, stung by his taunts, He would try to prove His Godhead, which did not really belong to Him, by an act of this sort—death was certain; and the prophet of Nazareth was removed for ever from his path. If He were God, on the other hand, then, in the first place, He would be obeying his command; and in the second place, acting contrary to the whole tenor of God's dealing with man, which—as Satan himself must have known—protects trustfulness in danger, but not presumption. He asked Him, in

[1] Hutchings' "Mystery of the Temptation," sermon v. p. 159. Mill, sermon v. p. 119.

short, to destroy Himself if he were man; to sin if He were God.

But was there nothing to point the temptation? nothing to recommend this violent course?[1] As hunger transformed the shape of the stones into soft and welcome bread; as the view melted into the kingdoms of this world, surrendered without a battle, lying at the feet of Jesus—a worthy price for the adoration of a moment—so, was there nothing here to take the roughness from suicide, the guilt from presumption? Yes, beneath them were spread out the courts of the temple, where the priests were offering the victims, and the smoke of incense was ascending, and the chaunts of psalm and thanksgiving were mounting up in waves of sound, as they passed before the throne of God. Here would be a fulfilment of prophecy, more real and more complete than heretofore. Not Simeon and Anna, a few faithful souls, should see the Lord, whom they sought, suddenly come to His temple.[2] Here would be no lowly procession on an ass, and a colt the foal of an ass; but He should appear, upborne by angels, coming on the clouds of heaven[3] as the long looked for Messiah. Every eye should see Him—the outpost of the Roman power from the tower of Antonia, the superstitious Pharisee, the sceptical Sadducee, the Erastian Herodian—all should be convinced. The victory of the Messiah should be won by sight, without that hard discipline of faith. That heartfelt cry would no longer be realized,[4] " O Jerusalem, Jerusalem,

[1] See Mill on "The Temptation," sermon v. 117, 118.
[2] Mal. iii. 1.   [3] S. Luke xxi. 27.
[4] See Hutchings' "Mystery of the Temptation," lecture v.

thou that killest the prophets, and stonest them which are sent unto thee, how often would I have gathered thy children together, as a hen gathereth her chickens under her wings, and ye would not!"[1] Faith would be lost in sight, and the reservation of His glory withdrawn—"Cast Thyself down, and the angel-guard shall bear Thee up." The temple suggests this, and Holy Scripture endorses it. Angels will always protect the Son of God. Their hands will always bear Him up. His foot, even, shall not be dashed against a stone.

But where? "In all Thy ways."[2] We must be careful when the devil quotes Scripture. God's angels will protect confident obedience, but will not protect rebellious presumption. This way was not one of the ways of God. There were no angels around this path; but the angel of God with a drawn sword to resist. But, no. His way was different. His hour was not yet come. I, if I be lifted up from the earth, not if I cast Myself down, will draw all men unto Me.[3]

No will shall be forced, no ear shall be strained, no eye dazzled. By parables veiling truth; by miracles worked before a few, and carefully concealed; by the words spoken to them that had ears to hear; by the slow education of faith—"here a little, and there a little"—His sun of truth was to burst upon the world.

A vain display was not a way of God. The

---

[1] S. Matt. xxiii. 37.
[2] "Ut custodiant te in omnibus viis tuis, numquid in præcipitiis?"
—St. Bernard. Quoted by Dr. Mill *in loc.*
[3] S. John xii. 32.

principle was wrong, and the Scripture that supported it was garbled. If Scripture he wanted, Scripture he should have. It was to presume on God in a path which God had not chosen, to expect a miracle where no miracle was needed. "Thou shalt not tempt the Lord thy God."

II. "If Thou be the Son of God, cast Thyself down." It is the peculiar temptation of a son of God, to think that he can walk alone, here in the infancy of his life, without God to support his trembling footsteps; to think that he can soar out into space on unfledged wing, forgetting the pride of the children of God. "As an eagle stirreth up her nest, fluttereth over her young, spreadeth abroad her wings, taketh them, beareth them on her wings: so the Lord alone did lead him, and there was no strange God with him."[1]

Looking at God, we are all tempted, all too ready to presume on that wondrous tender love; looking at man, we are too apt to take to ourselves the strength and glory which come from God. "He was marvellously helped, till he was strong. But when he was strong, his heart was lifted up."[2]

The Son of God must never cast Himself down. The height is dizzy, the wind of the world battles it, the flesh trembles and quivers at the fall beneath it, Satan shakes, and grapples, and wrestles to loose our hold. But the Son of God must never cast *Himself* down, despising the mercy of God, underrating the depth of the fall, and the danger of the descent.

Ah, many a child of God who has been carried by

[1] Deut. xxxii. 11, 12.   [2] 2 Chron. xxvi. 15, 16.

God to a pinnacle far above the black and surging waves of this world's crime, through the tender love of a good father and mother, by the dutiful care of the Church, by prayer and sacraments—protected in every stage, sheltered, and kept from ill, favoured by God with some especial blessing—ah, too often we see him listening to this temptation, "Cast thyself down;" and if saved from destruction, only to climb again, by slow and painful steps, the pinnacle of *penitence*, and that a lower eminence than that of *innocence*. For the devil, like Herod of old, if he cannot slay Christ, will slay innocence. It takes the form of superiority to temptation, it will not hurt *me*; *I* am proof against such temptations, *I* am a son of God. So Balaam the prophet came before God in prayer, went to his rest in security, with the messengers of Balak in his house. A trifling declension from the high and rigid line of pure spirituality could not hurt a prophet of the Lord. He cast himself down. There were no angels to support him, only one to resist him; —his foot was dashed against the wall, and he perished at last on the hard rocks of avarice, an apostate to his God, and a traitor to his conscience.[1]

David again—the man after God's own heart—what could hurt him? What temptation need he fear? He cast himself down upon temptation—deeper and deeper, through murder and adultery he fell—to be arrested only at the voice of the prophet announcing his pardon, while he proclaimed his broken life, "The sword shall never depart from thine house."[2]

[1] Numb. xxxi. 8.   [2] 2 Sam. xii. 10.

Nothing could ever be wrong in a loyal patriotism, thought Jonah; and he cast himself down upon the temptation of self-will, to dash his foot against trouble, sorrow, peril, and almost death.[1]

And day by day, as men taste more and more of the fruit of the tree of knowledge of good and evil, and stretch out their hands in presumption, where God has told them not to eat, saying, "I am safe, it will not hurt me"—more and more, we are surprised at the falls of good men. A S. Peter is seen in the high priest's palace at one moment in bravery, at another he is laid low in a terrible denial through cowardice. A Judas, but now the almoner of Christ Himself and the apostles, is dashed to pieces by an impious treachery. Faithful Abraham sins through want of faith, meek Moses in passion, wise Solomon in idolatry.[2]

Oh, let us beware how we cast ourselves down! Let us beware lest we turn dizzy on a pinnacle where we thought ourselves safe! So many bribes are held out to us that we may cast ourselves down. There are some people, we are told, who are alienated by our over-strictness;—let us break down the rigour of our will, that we may make ourselves "all things to all men,"[3] and attract by a shaded light, where the full blaze of truth would repel. There is that companion whom we might elevate, if we would descend

[1] See for this explanation of Jonah's conduct, Oxford Lent Sermons, 1869, p. 106.
[2] Dr. Newman, "Paroch, and Plain Sermons," vol. i. p. 41.
[3] 1 Cor. ix. 22.

to his level, and wean him by degrees from evil influences, and win him to ourselves. The growing vigour of intellect cannot be kept in swaddling bands. If unbelief publishes its assaults upon Revelation—is it not the duty of the believing Christian to read it, that he may the better refute it? If certain amusements and scenes are frequented by the careless and wicked, is it not the duty of the Christian to mix with evil that he may counteract it and purge it? Is he not the salt of the earth? the city set on an hill, which cannot be hid?[1] Ah, beneath it all—listen! listen well! and you will hear, "cast thyself down." There is no angel to meet thee in the poison of the fool's folly, who would corrupt thy mind against God. There is no angel to uphold thee, if thou losest the vantage ground of a high life, and triest to meet sin on its own dead level. There is no angel to purify thee, as the leaven of evil spreads its corruption over the whole lump of thy goodness. He who would grapple with sin must elevate the sinner, from the high level of the rock of holiness, not in the same quicksand of engulfing temptation.

The Son of God must never cast himself down. "For we wrestle not against flesh and blood, but against principalities, against powers, . . . against spiritual wickedness in high places."[2] O set me up upon the rock that is higher than I, for Thou hast been my hope, and a strong tower for me against the enemy."[3]—" He shall give His angels charge over thee,[4]

[1] S. Matt. v. 14. [2] Eph. vi. 12.
[3] Psa. lxi. 3. [4] S. Luke iv. 9, 10.

to keep thee." Men are only too glad to shut their eyes to the full truth of Holy Scripture, to presume on half truths, and to expect angels to uphold them in the air, instead of meeting them on the steps.[1]

We must look for stairs, not angels. God does not work a miracle without a reason, or allow us to dispense in presumption with the natural laws of His appointing. There is the orderly, stately ladder of the Church's life reaching up to heaven. Angels of God are ascending and descending on it. Passing through the cleansing laver of baptism to the confirming grace of the Holy Spirit, with the heavenly food of the Body and Blood of Christ—the manna in the wilderness to support us; passing through the cleansing Blood of Christ in prayer, in sacraments and ordinances, with the lantern of God's word, with the warning voice of His ministers, the dizzy descent into the grave is safely passed, the corn of wheat falls into the ground and dies,[2] sown by the careful hand of the Church, that it may rise into the full fruit of eternal life. But it is more easy to cast oneself down, to wait to the last, to spurn the warning voice of the Church, to shut out the guiding light, to decry sacraments, to refuse ordinances, to slumber and sleep, and say "the Lord is merciful, and throw ourselves down upon God's mercy, and expect that the fiery chariot that took up Elias is to come and fetch us up."[3]

Oh, if God has spoken, if He has said, "Now is the

---

[1] See Bishop Andrews, "Sermon on Temptation," vol. v. p. 512, etc.
[2] S. John xii. 24.　　[3] Bishop Andrews, vol. v. p. 321.

accepted time; behold, now is the day of salvation:"[1] —if He has said, "Work out your own salvation with fear and trembling,"[2] He will not be asked twice. There is no fresh warning for disobedient Balaam. God may cease to strive, conscience may cease to warn, but no angels are there to break our fall. If God has said, "Arise and eat; because the journey is too great for thee,"[3] it is idle to expect an angel to stay up our fainting life, when we have refused the cake and the cruse to which he pointed. If God has said, "the wages of sin is death,"[4] it is idle to expect an angel to come between us and the master whom we have served.

Oh, that men were wise, that they would understand this. Whose interest can it be? whom can it profit? whom can it serve? to drive away men from the Word and Sacraments and the Church of God, unless it be him, who lies in wait to deceive,[5] and who is ever whispering, "*because* thou art the Son of God, cast thyself down."

III. And surely, gathered together as we are at the end of Lent, as those who have been striving to serve God, and to be near Him, and to continue with Him in His temptations, it would be unwise on our part if we did not notice, and notice well, how familiar the devil is with the pinnacle of the temple. He knew his way there, and is not frightened away by the sanctity of the place, or the apparent security of the worshippers. He knows no law of sanctuary, he despairs of no victim.

---

[1] 2 Cor. vi. 2.   [2] Phil. ii. 12.   [3] 1 Kings xix. 7.
[4] Rom. vi. 23.   [5] Eph. iv. 14.

Is there any danger to us from our very familiarity with the high places of the sanctuary? If others err in the presumption of contempt, are we in no danger from the presumption of familiarity? Not without reason was it that "in the year that *King Uzziah died*,"[1] the king that profaned the temple by undue familiarity with holy things, the prophet Isaiah saw that wondrous vision of God—high and lifted up, with His train filling the temple, with the seraphim in adoration before Him, each with his six wings, with twain covering his face, with twain covering his feet, with twain poising himself in mid-air before the awful Presence of God, proclaiming once for all, as with a trumpet, those bounds which must be set around the Mount of God. Holy, holy, holy, is the Lord of Hosts. Separate, separate, separate, consecrated off from all that is unworthy of that presence, from all which that Majesty would burn up, as a consuming fire.

Oh, is there not a danger, as has been said, of "tripping in and out" before that awful Presence, of casting oneself down from that pinnacle of reverence, to let angels supply our lack of service towards Him? Oh, let us never forget the six wings as we come before God. "With twain he covered his face."[2] They fear to look upon God. "With twain he covered his feet"[3]—they fear that piercing eye of God, lest it should look upon *them*.[4] "With twain he did fly"—the gentle upbearing of their wings, by

---

[1] Isa. vi. 1, etc. [2] Ne videant.
[3] Ne videantur. [4] See Delitzsch; Is. vol. i. p. 191.

an effort, real yet imperceptible, keeps them in His presence. Oh, wondrous type of reverence for all who stand on high places before God. Alas! alas! we have not the eye of the eagle; we cannot gaze at the full sun. Let us veil our faces in reverence of the mystery of the Godhead. Alas! we dread that voice as we stand before Him. " Whence comest thou, Gehazi, to stand before Me?"[1] We veil our feet, our erring feet, in penitence. Our service flags, our devotion is faint; we need that constant rousing of our wills, and affections, and understanding, in the flapping wings of prayer.

Oh, we must fear lest, in an age of increased outward reverence, of multiplied services and enlarged devotion, the devil accustom us to the pinnacle where we stand before God, and bid us err by presumption, where angels fear to tread; fear, lest we offer the incense which was for our High Priest, and carry away with us only the leprosy of a curse, because we entered before God, untouched by the coal of fire, without repentance and without love.

Surely this holy season, within whose most sacred recesses we have now entered, will be our safety and our comfort. We see Jesus Christ once more passing through the tabernacle to go within the veil, with the blood of atonement and the incense of intercession in His hands. We know that "He ever liveth to make intercession for us"[2] there; we know that while we are struggling here below that there is One Whose

[1] 2 Kings v. 25.   [2] Heb. vii. 25.

"hands are steady until the going down of the sun."[1] We know that the blood which He pleads has taken away all power from sin, and has robbed Satan of his empire. Can it be that we shall refuse so great a salvation offered to us? Can it be that we shall follow Satan rather than the gracious pleading of our loving High Priest?

Oh, when temptations come to annoy us, and distress us, even when they have ceased to harm, let us see that His presence is with us, His grace to protect us! "Thou shalt prepare a table before me *against* them that trouble me."[2] He offers to strengthen us against the temptation, so that Satan when he comes to the house from which he was driven out in baptism, with original sin, may not find the house empty, and prepared for the sevenfold possession of actual sin. "Blessed is the man that endureth temptation, for when he is tried, he shall receive the crown of life, which the Lord hath promised to them that love Him"[3]—the crown, the symbol of victory; the crown, the symbol of sovereignty and well-ordered sway; the crown of the ten cities of heaven, which is promised to him who can administer the one pound of this life.[4] But if Satan seizes the pound here, take care lest he snatch from us the cities hereafter.

So shall Lent have been a blessed time to us, if we have learnt to tread the way of salvation. The perils of the way passed do but add joy to the safety of home. The husks of the swine, and the nakedness

---

[1] Exod. xvii. 12. [2] Psa. xxiii. 5.
[3] S. James i. 12. [4] S. Luke xix. 13.

of the prodigal, do but increase the comforts of his father's house. If the conflict is fierce and long, "They that be with us are more than they that be with them."[1] And "where are conflicts there are crowns also."

[1] 2 Kings vi. 16.

SERMON IV.

The Tree of Life.

"*In the midst of the street of it, and on either side of the river, was there the tree of life, which bare twelve manner of fruits, and yielded her fruit every month: and the leaves of the tree were for the healing of the nations.*"—REV. xxii. 2.

BEFORE entering upon this great subject, to which we have ventured to draw your attention this Advent, perhaps some word of explanation is necessary.[1]

[1] This sermon forms the first of a series, which was preached during the Advent of 1881, on the subject of the east window, lately presented to the church of S. Matthias, Malvern Link. The following description of the window by the artist, Mr. C. E. Kempe, will perhaps serve to make what follows more intelligible.

"The east window of the church is filled with stained glass, showing the somewhat unusual subject known among art students as the 'Tree of the Cross.' A tree of fine white foliage, of the nature of a vine, fills the whole surface of the window, and in its centre, the figure of our Lord crucified is shown, not a figure hanging helplessly in death, but alive, with open eyes, and His arms stretched voluntarily on the boughs, and with a crown on His head, indicating the Royal nature of the Sufferer, Who by His own Will humbled Himself to the death upon the Cross, and thus voluntarily perfected the great act of Atonement. Among the vine branches appear half-length figures of the principal Prophets, who foretold the mystery of the Atonement, each bearing his scroll in relation to that doctrine. Of these we read from Isaiah, 'Surely He hath borne our griefs;' from Jeremiah, 'I am the Man who hath seen affliction by the rod of His

In the first place, just as Christian architecture is meant not only to please the eye, by symmetry and beauty of form, but also to teach us lessons, by the poetry of its symbolism, so art, whether in glass, painting, or sculpture, when it is introduced into our churches, would fail in its object, if it were merely a decoration; it should elevate, it should teach.

And the first step to profit by its teaching, is clearly to understand what is meant by the lesson; and therefore, we thought it would surely be helpful to try and draw out the meaning of those beautiful forms and conceptions constantly before our eyes, in the east window of this church; that the sun shining through those colours, with its breathing light, may be only a symbol of the meaning which lies beneath

---

wrath;' from Zechariah, 'What are these wounds in Thine hands?' from Ezekiel, 'The leaf thereof for medicine;' from Hosea, 'O death, I will be thy plagues;' and from Malachi, 'I will come near unto you to judgment.' A scroll also on the Tree describes it in the words of the Apocalypse, 'The Tree of Life, which bare twelve manner of fruits, and yielded her fruit every month: and the leaves of the tree were for the healing of the nations,' in illustration of which, labels appear attached to the grape-clusters, named with Christian virtues, the results of the Atonement. Under the Tree stand the following figures, witnesses and confessors of the doctrine:—SS. Mary and John; S. Matthias, holding a Church in his hand; S. Augustine of England, carrying the banner of the Cross, with which he presented himself before King Ethelbert: S. Oswald of Worcester, and S. Eadburga. These latter have a local interest. S. Oswald is said to have died singing the 'Gloria Patri,' and he is accordingly represented holding the Doxology a'tached to his staff, as well as Worcester Cathedral in his hand; S. Eadburga, a granddaughter of Alfred the Great, was in old days commemorated at Pershore, and the church of Leigh was dedicated in her honour; having despised the wealth of a Court, she is here shown treading on a crown."

its beauty, of the teaching which it might convey to our understanding and imagination. And you will have noticed, that the subject which is there set before us is what is called a mystical subject; *i.e.* it is not a representation of the Crucifixion as it really took place, in fact it is not the Crucifixion at all; but it is an attempt to attach a mystical and symbolical meaning to this verse of the Book of Revelation, "The tree of life, which bare twelve manner of fruits, and yielded her fruit every month: and the leaves of the tree were for the healing of the nations."

And here again it is necessary to make a further digression. Is it right to treat Holy Scripture in this way? Is it not fanciful? Is it not playing tricks with it? Might not Holy Scripture be mystified in this way into meaning anything or nothing?

And here, at all events, as many of us know already, we can start with a clear conscience. Not only is it edifying and beautiful in itself to detect these mystical deeper meanings in Holy Scripture, as we hold it up to different lights, and in different angles, to catch the rays of the sun; but also we have the very highest authority for this devotional use of Holy Scripture.

S. Paul, you remember, uses the precept given by God in Deuteronomy, "Thou shalt not muzzle the mouth of the ox that treadeth out the corn,"[1] as conveying the mystical meaning that "the elders who rule well should be counted worthy of double honour." "Out of Egypt have I called my Son,"[2] is another

---

[1] 1 Cor. ix. 9; 1 Tim. v. 17, 18. [2] S. Matt. ii. 15.

instance of a passage of Holy Scripture, spoken in one sense and applied, in a higher and mystical way, in another. So are many passages of the Psalms, as used by our Blessed Lord and His Apostles. So, you remember, the elaborate allegory in the Epistle to the Galatians, of Agar and Mount Sinai.[1]

It is an interpretation of Holy Scripture recognized in Holy Scripture itself, it is edifying and instructive, it provokes thought and research, and has the sanction of the Church in the writings of her Doctors and Divines. And, therefore, we may without hesitation devote ourselves to drawing out this treatment of that passage from the Book of Revelation, which is portrayed for us in the east window of this church.

I. And you will notice, first of all, that the great Christian idea is represented as a large tree, with spreading branches, reaching through the earth and up to heaven itself. By its name, "The Tree of Life," we are bidden to carry back our thoughts to that time when, guilty, sorrowful, condemned, our first parents, who had tasted of the tree of *knowledge*, were driven out of the garden lest they should put forth their hands and take also of the tree of *life*, and eat, and live for ever.

And we are reminded that there was one bright spot in the gloom which overshadowed them, and that was the promise mingling almost with the words of the curse, that the seed of the woman should bruise the head of the serpent.[2] Here was a tree, which already began to grow; here was the Tree of Life,

---

[1] Gal. iv. 21.   [2] Gen. iii. 15.

replanted. Ezekiel had a vision of it, and S. John saw it in the garden of Paradise, so multiplied that it stands on either side of the river of life; so fruitful that it bears every month; so versatile that it produces twelve different sorts of fruit; so accessible, that, instead of being protected by a flaming sword, it stands in the very street, and whoever will, may freely pluck off, and eat its fruit.[1]

The window, then, sets before us, first, the gradual growth of this Christian idea, this Tree of Life.

It is the custom sometimes to speak of Buddhism, and other heathen religions as older than Christianity. Christianity is as old as the world, perhaps older. Certainly it is as old as the Fall.[2]

---

[1] See Dr. Vaughan, "Lecture on the Revelation," vol. ii. p. 300.

[2] From one point of view it may be said that the Old Testament is full of Christ, the New of God the Father. "No man hath seen God at any time" (*i.e.* hath seen the First Person of the Holy Trinity). Our Blessed Lord is the Word of God, and the Express Image of His Person.

Therefore every appearance of God, in anthropomorphic or other forms, and every audible voice of God recorded in the Old Testament, may well be taken as the appearance of God the Son,—not yet Incarnate, but assuming a human form by anticipation, and for a season,—or manifested in some other manner, and speaking to the children of men. What man yearned after, however, was the knowledge and the assurance of his filial relation to his Maker. The Old Testament revealed Him as the Creator, the King, the Judge. It said but little of Him as the Father. "Lord, shew us the Father, and it sufficeth us," was the cry, not only of Philip, but of mankind. And our Lord's answer to the cry is the keynote of the Gospels, "Have I been so long time with you, and yet hast thou not known Me, Philip? he that hath seen Me, hath seen the Father; and how sayest thou then, Shew us the Father?"

The New Testament is essentially the Revelation of the Fatherhood

As soon as man had tasted of the Tree of Knowledge, and had fallen, a seed from the Tree of Life was planted in the world; it grew, and germinated in the soil; the sacrifices of patriarchal times were its first "two little leaves, unlike that which the plant would have, extended like two little hands to heaven;"[1] then its leaves were unfolded in grace, the nearness of God, the freshness of His presence, the Revelation of His will. Then great flowers began to appear upon it one by one; the *prophets*, as they grew upon the branches, all indicating the character of the tree; all pointing on to what the fruit would be, as we may tell the character of the fruit by its precedent flower. And so the tree spread, without men understanding it; until when the fulness of the time was come the form of the Son of God became visible on the branches. The clusters of grapes shot forth thick and heavy. "Twelve manner of fruits:" fruit for every season, for every month; fruit for winter and summer, for spring and autumn; in scorching sun, in biting frost, in growing vigour, in "calm decay." Men tasted of that fruit and lived again, in the fisherman's boat, by the receipt of custom, at the feet of Gamaliel, in the Roman cohorts, in the palace of the Cæsars, among the ranks of slaves, on the thrones of kings. "Twelve manner of fruits:" fruit for every month—suitable to every condition, suitable to every rank. Each and all of that "great

of God. Compare it with the Old, and this truth will be readily recognized.

[1] Baring Gould, "Sermons to Children," p. 147.

multitude which no man could number,"[1] who follow the Lamb whithersoever He goeth, have tasted of that Tree of Life—of each of its fruits—of that noble elevation of character, that faith, that valour, that piety—of those grapes filled with the blood of Jesus, whose form enriches and ennobles, and ripens the tree.

And to teach us this lesson, we have gathered before us, beneath that tree, certain typical characters taken from among those who have tasted of its fruit and virtue.

First, we have an example of those who have filled difficult posts of responsibility, near to God, before their fellow-men, who have drunk in their strength from the pure blood of those heavenly grapes.

Then, we have an example of those who, in the great hierarchy of the Church, have used the office of a Bishop well, and who have chanted in death their "glory to God" as the worthy finish of a life of praise; whose strength has been this glorious fruit, in the place of the vineyard which God's right hand hath planted,[2] which they defended against the breach of the enemy.

Further, we have an example of those who, impelled by that haunting voice, "Go ye, therefore, and teach all nations, baptizing them in the name of the Father, and of the Son, and of the Holy Ghost,"[3] have left home and friends, carrying their lives in their hands—facing unknown dangers, and braving all terrors—that they might plant the banner of the Crucified on the

---

[1] Rev. vii. 9.   [2] Psa. lxxx. 15.   [3] S. Matt. xxviii. 19.

ramparts of heathendom—pioneers of the great missionary band, "who have bound their foal unto the vine and their ass's colt unto the choice vine, who washed their garments in wine, and their clothes in the blood of grapes;"[1] "whose eyes are red with wine, and their teeth white with milk."

Or, lastly, we have an example of those who, like Moses of old, have in all ages esteemed "the reproach of Christ greater riches than the treasures in Egypt,"[2] who have refused to be called the child of Pharaoh's daughter, who having overcome have been allowed "to eat of the Tree of Life, which is in the midst of the Paradise of God."[3] Such as these stand beneath the tree, as the fowls of the air lodge beneath the shadow of the branches of it;[4] with her, from whom sprang the human nature of the Divine fruit-bearer; with him, whose keen eagle eye typifies all who desire to penetrate the mysteries of God, and who study the inner meaning of that great Christian Revelation, that mighty growth of the Christian Religion, here called *the tree of life*; which has grown until it has become a mighty tree, first flowering with prophets, then ripening into its glorious fruit; attracting to itself all who hunger and thirst after righteousness, giving fruit to the Israel of God, and healing with its very leaves the Gentile world. These things the angels[5] desire to look into, as they cluster round the Majesty of God. These things holy souls desire to contemplate,

---

[1] Gen. xlix. 11. [2] Heb. xi. 26.
[3] Rev. ii. 7. [4] S. Luke xiii. 19.
[5] 1 S. Pet. i. 12.

who stand, like S. John, gazing at the mystery unfolded before them.

II. But it is time that we should try and gather up some practical lesson, on this Advent Sunday. And surely it is this:—Most of us have tasted of the tree of knowledge of good and evil; have we yet tasted of the Tree of Life?

As we gradually are being drawn nearer and nearer to the end, and the sentence of death which has been passed upon us becomes more imminent, have we yet tasted of the Tree of Life? Ah, we shall be asked before we enter Paradise again, not what riches we have, not what knowledge, nor what intelligence; but what life? whether our soul is alive unto God? whether we have known Him? whether we live by Him? whether our thoughts, words, and actions have been filled by Him? whether we dwell in Him, and He in us?

Oh, when hundreds and hundreds are tasting of the tree of knowledge, when the world is so clever, so eager, so wicked, would that more tasted of the Tree of Life, of religion, of holiness, of God! And, thank God, the Tree of Life is open, accessible to all; multiplied it stands on each side of the river, in the wilderness and in the promised land. There is an open Church, and an open Bible, and open privileges for every one. God is very near to all: "Where sin abounded, grace did much more abound."[1] And let me point out that there is fruit to be found on that tree for all, not only fruit for the good and religious,

Rom. v. 20.

but twelve manner of fruits; fruit for every month, fruit for this hard, weary life, fruit for the tempted, fruit for the penitent, fruit for the occupied, fruit for every one. Jesus Christ well nigh exhausts the power of language, to say, that the cherubim's flaming sword is lowered, and that He would have all come to him: "Come unto Me, all ye that labour and are heavy laden,"[1] ye whose burden would seem most to press you to the earth. The Holy Feast is open to all; He longs to welcome all who will come prepared. His Church is for all, His Holy Word for all. Twelve manner of fruits;—is there none to suit my taste? Is weariness, and worldliness, and controversy, and trouble, and want of appreciation, to be a perpetual barrier?

Shall I not find refreshment in each and all of these troubles? Twelve manner of fruits; fruit every month, fruit for all, fruit all through life, from the cradle to the grave. Oh, blessed are they who go up to the tree, and take hold of the branches thereof, and ask for fruit. Think how He bends the branches down to us; how He extends to us the very virtue and fruit of His Incarnation. "Solomon had a vineyard at Baal-hamon, he let out the vineyard unto keepers; every one for the fruit thereof was to bring a thousand pieces of silver."[2] But now it is, "Ho, every one that thirsteth, come ye to the waters, and he that hath no money; come ye, buy, and eat; yea, come, buy wine and milk without money, and without price."[3]

[1] S. Matt. xi. 28. [2] Cant. viii. 11. [3] Isa. lv. 1.

If the fruit of the land is so beautiful on this side of Jordan, which the spies bring to us, what must it be on the other side in the better land, where we shall see the king in His beauty, where we shall see Him as He is?

At least, despise not *the leaves*. The leaves which are "for the healing of the nations." For those who despise the fruit, for those who fear to crush these grapes in defiled and hard hands—still for them there are the leaves. Yes, the very outskirts of religion are blessed; yes, even to linger in these courts, to hear the voice of God speaking in the psalms, "to go with the multitude, and bring them forth into the house of God,"[1] even in the scanty service, the cold devotion, the imperfect knowledge, there is a leaf from the Tree of Life; there may be healing in it. It was such a leaf from this tree that healed the fevered soul of S. Augustine, fluttering to his feet charged with power and virtue. Many an old wound has been healed over by the buried leaves of early training; many a chance word which has winged its way from the Bible, or some good book or sermon, has proved to be a leaf from the Tree of Life.

Ah, yes, if you need healing, if you are full of wounds and bruises and putrefying sores, if you shrink from the fruit, still there is healing in the leaves. In the very outskirts of religion there is *healing*, but not *satisfaction*. Medicine is not food, but also food must sometimes be preceded by medicine.

So, while the Church this Advent reminds you of

[1] Psa. xlii. 4.

the approach of death, she holds in her hands the branches of the Tree of Life. Here is life for all; *Fruit* for those who press to the heart of the Church's Sacramental life; leaves, healing leaves, for those who linger on the outskirts; life to all who put forth their hand to take of the Tree of Life, multiplied in its growth, versatile in its fruits, accessible in its position, whose very leaves are medicine.

SERMON V.

Night.

"*And there shall be no night there.*"—Rev. xxii. 5.

WHEN Adam first saw darkness creeping up over the newly created world, as the sun sank beneath the horizon, and the blue left the sky, as the flowers closed their petals, and the grey hue of advancing night spread itself over the face of the bright earth, and the stars came out, and the moon shone, and that solemn hush of deep stillness fell like a solemn pall over the joyous youth of creation, fresh in all its beauty from the hand of God, surely to him night was but another change of a glad experience, a time of rest and repose, of closer undisturbed union with Him to Whom "the darkness and the light are both alike."[1] There was surely no terror in night, no gloomy surroundings, no loneliness and dread. Innocence had no enemies, and a clear conscience no fears.

But to us, centuries and centuries of guilt and unfaithfulness have fastened on to night other and more terrible associations. The night has blindfolded

[1] Psa. cxxxix. 12.

the sun, it is the hour for the murderer, the descendant of Cain. The night is a cloak to throw over our fellow-men; it is the hour of the thief who digs through houses in the dark.[1] The night shuts off the visible, the seen, the knowable, and fills the guilty conscience with weird shapes and strange visions. It is the punishment of the God-hating Egyptians. The night puts an abrupt stop to the labourer's toil; it is the symbol of the sudden arrest of vitality in the grave. "The night cometh, when no man can work."[2] Looking at the stillness and the blackness, the stagnation of visible, audible life, the strange drowsiness and loss of power which night brings, it is the symbol of death, of trouble, of gloom, of doubt and difficulty in a fallen world. And so the apostle, in his description of the "there," which needs no further designation, the opposite to the "here" of trouble, gloom, and uncertainty, says, "There shall be no night *there;* and they need no candle, neither light of the sun."

I. We may not be wrong, then, in taking night first of all as a symbol of *sorrow*. In Heaven above there will be none of that strange withdrawing of the sun, that hiding of God's face from us, the beauty vanishing out of life, the departure of joy from the earth, as the cold grey cloak of some heavy sorrow is thrown over our life with its deep and gloomy folds. Men shrink within themselves as the sun goes down, the sun of joy and prosperity, and the cold dark night of some sorrow comes upon them. And yet the night

---

[1] Job xxiv. 16.   [2] S. John ix. 4.

is useful, it is blessed. We could not do without it. And some day we shall see why God sends us nights to our days, sorrows upon our joys. It is to give us rest, it is to draw us from our work, our toil and labour, and our pleasure, that we may be alone with Him.

Dear friends, have you ever had any great sorrow? any dark night? God sent that night for the growth of your soul. "Before I was troubled I went wrong, but now have I kept Thy word."[1] David was in the full burst of a bright sun of successful vice; God sent him a night in Nathan and his message; the child whom he loved, the child of his sin, died. S. Peter was ablaze with the lurid light of a threefold denial of his Lord; God dashed down the light; he went out into the darkness to weep himself into the light. S. Paul, blinded, and groping in darkness, was turned round by his night to be an apostle and servant of God. And these nights which God sends to us are charged with blessings. Perhaps it is that there has been sin in early youth, or some alienation from God in the past. It has all gone by, a bright noon has succeeded the storms and tempest of the morning, and all is bright; and then there comes a night, so cold and chill, and dark. Oh, dear friends, let us remember these days of darkness; they will be, they must be, many, if we are to grow.[2] But "there is no night there; there probation and chastisement will have done their work, and sorrow and sighing will have flown away for ever.

[1] Psa. cxix. 67. [2] Eccles. xi. 8.

II. "There shall be no night there." Men stumble in the night, and grope their way in the night; familiar objects are indistinct and confused. It is a symbol of *doubt* and evil.

"Ah, this night is self-caused; it is the thick darkness coming up, while it is yet day, because we have crucified our Lord. It is the wilful rejection of the light, that we may sin in the night. There is the sun of God's truth shining in the Heavens, there is the candle of the Spirit's guidance in the conscience. But men shut up the windows, and put out the light, and there is darkness. Think of those horrible deeds of sin, those works of darkness, beginning in darkness, done in the darkness, producing darkness— the drunkenness, the lust, the violence, the crime. Open the windows, light up the candle ; give us light.

Or look at the trembling, the uncertainty, the hesitation, the doubt, the feeling which makes men shrink when they hear it said, "And thou also wast with Jesus of Nazareth."[1] Let in the sunlight, let the candle of conscience give us light, let us do what is right and true "in scorn of consequence"; let us drive away that "halting between two opinions," the uncertainty whether to serve God or mammon. God has called us out of darkness into His marvellous light;[2] let us not go back again into Egypt, and in our hearts turn away from God. Let His word be "a lantern unto our feet, and a light unto our paths,"[3] and the night of doubt and difficulty shall roll away; we shall hear a voice behind us saying, "This is the

[1] S. Mark xiv. 67.   [2] S. Pet. ii. 9.   [3] Psa. cxix. 105.

way, walk ye in it, when ye turn to the right hand, and when ye turn to the left."[1] "Then shall thy light break forth as the morning, ... the glory of the Lord shall be thy rereward,"[2] leading you on step by step to heaven, for *there* is no evil, and no doubt; "there is no night *there.*"

III. And then night is the symbol of death. You have stood by the side of the dead, and have seen all the vital forces stilled and paralyzed—the scheming brain, the busy hand, the active mind, all arrested in death. Death is very awful, it is a night with its cold grey hue cast over nature.

It is terrible even to the best of us, as it comes creeping on, so certain that no one will be found to doubt its approach, so uncertain that no one will venture to say when. It draws near with all its separation from everything that a man holds dear; its gloomy mist envelopes one familiar object after another, until it forces itself upon us in all its solemn meaning, "I die alone."[3] Terrible in its loneliness, terrible in its irreparable nature, terrible in the immensity of its issues, death comes creeping towards us. It has hung like a great pall over all the earth, weighing down the life of man, and causing him to shudder, even while it is yet day. But we know what our Blessed Lord has done for us: "There be some standing here that shall not taste of death;"[4] although all must drink of that cup, yet those who follow Him and love Him shall not *taste* of it. "I

[1] Isa. xxx. 21.
[2] Isa. lviii. 8.
[3] Paschal.
[4] S. Matt. xvi. 28.

am the Resurrection, and the life,"[1] saith the Lord; to us who believe death is but "a shadow cast upon nature."[2] Already light breaks in upon those who wait close to the gates of Paradise, light from that joyous dwelling of which we read, "there is no night there."

IV. And yet once more; there is a night, through which His Church is even now bidding us pass, the night of Advent before the dawn of Christmas. The Church, our kind mother, knows that we fear the darkness, and she darkens the room while it is yet day to accustom us to the darkness which we dread. She knows what death is to us with its gloomy terror; she knows how we shrink from judgment, that terrible time, when the Judge shall sit, and the books be opened, and the accuser do his work, and the sentence be awarded; she knows how little we can see of heaven in the bright glare of this world; she knows how we are afraid to look into hell. And Advent, therefore, is a sort of rehearsal, in which we may bring up before us all the gloom and terror of death; it is a night of concentration, in which we may shut out the world and see more of heaven; it is a night of sorrow, of godly sorrow for sin, of "repentance to salvation not to be repented of;"[3] it is a night of repose, in which our souls may grow, under the rest and discipline and shadow of the Church's life. Oh, what do we shrink from *now?* we shall shrink from

[1] S. John xi. 25.
[2] Speech of Archbishop Laud. Quoted in Dr. Neale's "Psalms." Psa. xxiii. 4.
[3] Cor. vii. 10.

the same *then*. Is it the sight of our sins, in all their blackness and guilt? We must face them in the terrors of the last day. Is it the meeting with our Saviour, in the sacrament of His *love*, here in the quiet morning, here at the peaceful altar of our church, surrounded by friends and companions? We must meet Him *then* in unveiled glory, seated on His throne, with saints and angels around Him. Is the love of the world strong within us? Do we shrink from *loneliness* or retirement? There is nothing we can carry away with us when we die, and no one but our Saviour may hold our hand as we enter that dark valley.

Truly Advent is a blessed time of preparation, that we may not enter upon these awful moments unprepared. But Advent, too, will some day have done its work; probation and trial and times of penitence will cease in the eternal feast-day of the Lord. There will be no Advent in heaven, no probation, no trial in our heavenly home. For we know of a truth that "there is no night there."

SERMON VI.

Faith in the Holy Trinity.

"With the heart man believeth unto righteousness; and with the mouth confession is made unto salvation."—Rom. x. 10.

ON Trinity Sunday we are in the region of pure faith. We start from what could not be known by man, and we end in what is unknowable. We contemplate a mystery, and not only a mystery, but a mystery of such a kind, that we see at once our human faculties supply us with no instruments whereby we can comprehend it; we can simply receive it, and believe it, adore and worship, when we are told that God is One and yet Three, Three and yet One; Three Persons and One God, in the Unity of the Holy and Ever Blessed Trinity.

I. And there rise up before us at once all the guesses after truth, all those " feelings after God," all those endeavours to realize his Maker, which have perplexed the heart of man.[1] Man has gone out into the world around him, seeking to penetrate the awful veil of stillness, which envelopes the Being of God,

[1] Acts xvii. 27.

and as he saw the sun rise in its splendour, or the stars moving in their courses, or the moon riding in her glory, or the manifold powers of life and fertility all around, he has worshipped them and called them God. Or the pleasures of life, as he deemed them pleasures, have stood up before him; he has elevated ease, or lust, or his lower passions, and has personified them, and called them God. Or the evils of life have frightened him. He has traced God's ways in misfortunes, His envy in life's difficulties, His malignity in the venom of reptiles, or the teeth of ravenous beasts. He has made images of those things which he feared, and has called them God. Or their great men investigated, their vigorous intellects pushed their discoveries further and further, until cause and effect, cause and effect, led them by stepping-stones to the gates of heaven, and in a great first cause, passionless, immovable, unalterable, they recognized God.

But in the meantime, there had been growing up a more distinct knowledge of the true God. God revealed Himself to a few chosen men, to Enoch, to Abraham, and the patriarchs. He revealed Himself, again, to a chosen nation. The knowledge of His power and goodness became wide-spread and developed, and even if it faded away, it still lingered as a beautiful tradition. Once more he revealed Himself in a Revelation unknown before in the Person of His dear Son; and He caused that men should commit to writing what may be known of Him, what is good to know, what is possible to know, what is right to know. And God now remains for us, the centre, the author, the finisher, the beginning and the ending of all that is good and holy; Three Persons and One God revealed to us in a Mystery.

II. And can we return? Can we be now as if God had never spoken? Can we make our God a first cause again, and nothing more? Can we say that the doctrine of the Holy Trinity is based on one text which is cut out of the Bible by a scholarly revision, and there leave it? No, if our Creed be true, based, as it certainly is, on Holy Scripture, the heartfelt assent to that Creed is the door of righteousness, and the confession of that Creed is salvation.

We cannot be, on Trinity Sunday, as if God had never spoken, as if God had never revealed Himself; and this for several reasons. First of all, if we believe in the Bible as the Word of God, and in the Church as the keeper and interpreter of Holy Writ, it cannot be consistent with the dignity and power of Almighty God, that we should treat as open questions, or even worse, what He has willed to reveal. In an age sensitively alive to all injunctions of morality, keenly jealous of innovation, it seems to be at the same time forgotten, that it is possible to *reject* God's teaching, to do despite to the Spirit of grace, to refuse His counsel, and further, that it is possible, that a wrong belief or wilful unbelief may be just as serious a sin in His sight as many others which appeal to us by their flagrant coarseness and transparent immorality, such as drunkenness, adultery, or theft. These are sins which we recognize and can take cognizance of.

But spiritual sins may be just as offensive to Almighty God; and we remember that the one sin which has no forgiveness is a spiritual sin: the sin against the Holy Ghost. But this is not all. Of course the Majesty of God needs no defence from man; but, looking at the other side of the question, could we afford, regarding the needs of *man*, his wants and requirements, could we afford on this ground, to treat the doctrine of the Holy Trinity as an open question? Most assuredly we could not part with the true faith without doing serious injury to the cause of truth and progress in the world. It *does* matter most seriously, whether a man believes or not, that he is responsible to an unseen God for his actions, that he has a great Father in heaven watching him, that he is working a work for Him, and that he looks for the rewards, and dreads the penalties, which He carries in His hands. It is no light matter that we should be asked to admit into our Legislative Chamber men whose actions are not guided and overshadowed by this solemn conviction, who admit of no higher witness than their own to the sanctity of their name, who are bound by no higher ties to their sovereign than mere allegiance, who own no moral code but their own inclination.

Or again, it makes a serious difference to the world, whether or not the loving Saviour is deposed from the throne of His Godhead. Christianity has removed the words "Barbarian" and "Gentile,"[1] it has laid the axe to the root of "caste." It is the bulwark of the

[1] Col. iii. 11.

universal brotherhood of mankind. Take away
Christianity, and something is gone from the progress
and happiness of mankind.

Or again, can the sanctifying Spirit be removed
from the forces of the spiritual world with impunity?
Is conscience to be only a moral sense swayed by the
passing breath of a conventional morality? Would
the world lose nothing if God's Holy Word were to
take the level of Shakespeare? Have the Church
and the Sacraments been such a doubtful blessing
to mankind that they can afford to part with them?
Oh, the great heart of the world throbs with belief
unto righteousness. Its hundred-tongued voice confesses unto salvation, when it proclaims the eternal
truth of the Holy Trinity, which we could never
afford to part with without our distinct and irreparable loss.

III. And, of course, equally true is it of each single
one here, that faith is the secret of righteousness,
that this confession is the seal of their salvation.
The life of a true Christian is a perpetual "Glory
be to the Father, and to the Son, and to the Holy
Ghost."

(1) What could we do in life if we had not the
thought of that loving Father to sustain us? Would
not work overwhelm us, would not trouble crush us,
and sin deceive us? Should we ever have courage
to rise from the food of swine and the dregs of misery,
did we not remember our Father's home, and the
plenty of His house? Now we know what life is, and
what it means; we can see through the chastisement

of sorrow, the tender love which will not withhold it; we can see in temptation the way to escape that we may be able to bear it.[1] Yes, all life, in its chequered course, has a fresh dignity, a fresh responsibility, a fresh awe, as we are conscious of the great Father from Whom it sprang.

(2) And could we do without a Saviour? What has kept us from despair with ourselves and with the world but a Saviour blind and deaf to our miserable imperfections? "Who is blind, but My servant? or deaf, as My messenger that I sent? Who is blind as He that is perfect, and blind as the Lord's servant?"[2] What has kept back the waves of sin from us? Though they toss themselves they have not prevailed, though they roar, yet have they not passed over.[3] What do we look to in sorrow, but to see Jesus crucified at our right hand, in all our sufferings afflicted with us—"acquainted with grief"?[4] What do we look for in the hour of death, but the support and comfort of His rod and staff?[5]

And is the Sanctifying Spirit nothing to us? Is it nothing that we have His voice in our conscience, saying, "This is the way, walk ye in it,"[6] warning us of the approach of danger, cheering us in the paths of good? Is it nothing that we have God's Holy Word breathed into by His life-giving breath, "that we through patience and comfort of the Scriptures might have hope?"[7] Is it nothing that we have the

---

[1] 1 Cor. x. 13. [2] Isa. xlii. 19.
[3] Jer. v. 22.   [4] Isa. liii. 3.
[5] Psa. xxiii. 4. [6] Isa. xxx. 21. [7] Rom xv. 4.

heavenly and Divine Sacraments working mightily to our soul's welfare by the power of His co-operating grace? Is it nothing that we have the Church, hallowed by His blessed indwelling Presence, to be our support and stay as we journey through the world?

Oh, God is working indeed wonderfully for our deliverance and strength; and in our better moments we feel it. If any one of us have overcome the wicked one, have attained to any measure of sanctity, have risen above ourselves, surely out of his grateful heart should rise, " Glory be to the Father, and to the Son, and to the Holy Ghost;" to God the Father Who made me, to God the Son Who redeemed me, to God the Holy Ghost Who sanctifieth me.

And reaching out from this, feeling what God has been *to us*, we ask ourselves, what must He be to others? Can *they* do without Him? can they prosper without His help? can they feel happiness without Him, or attain to deliverance apart from His grace? And this leads us to be bold in the faith, this sends us out as missionaries, this makes us all burn with a holy zeal to spread abroad this glorious truth. Oh, if on Trinity Sunday we feel any glow of gratefulness for all that God has been to us, for all that God has done for us, let us resolve, with an earnestness based on the deep conviction of our hearts, to hand on the doctrine of the Holy Trinity undimmed and unimpaired. Let us say, I will declare Thy name, O Lord, from one generation to another. What our fathers have told us, we have proved to be true, and what we have proved to be true we will hand on to our children. So shall the people give thanks unto Thee, world without end. Amen.[1]

[1] Psa. xlv. 18.

SERMON VII.
Clerical Assumption.

"*And they gathered themselves together against Moses and against Aaron, and said unto them, Ye take too much upon you, seeing all the congregation are holy, every one of them, and the Lord is among them: wherefore then lift ye up yourselves above the congregation of the Lord?*"—NUMB. xvi. 3.

THIS rebellion of the children of Israel you will have noticed is different in character from many others which disfigure the history of God's people. It was not directed against God, but against Moses. Just as a fretful, petulant nature will sometimes change the object of its attack, so this was a variety, based on a real tangible ground of complaint. Whatever might be the cause of their prolonged stay in the wilderness, and of their numerous troubles, the position of *Moses* was certainly intolerable. He was now altogether making himself a prince over them,[1] pretending to be the mouthpiece of God, making promises which he could not fulfil, holding out vain delusive expectations, and deceiving the people. It was not reasonable to suppose that God should be

[1] Numb. xvi. 13.

with him more than with the rest of the people. *All* were God's people. *All* were holy. It was time to rebel, to assert the rights of the national Church. And the rebellion was a very serious one. It was numerous and important. There were two hundred and fifty princes, or, as we should now say, noblemen, with Dathan and Abiram, and two hundred and fifty Levites, or, as we should say, ecclesiastics, with Korah; Levites who had already distinguished themselves in the part which they took when Israel sinned in the matter of the golden calf, and who had been expressly honoured by God.[1]

It was the protest, then, of men of influence and of men who presumably knew what they were about in ecclesiastical cases, who had studied the question all their lives, and who, perhaps, had seen too much of Moses' tyranny. And whatever Moses might feel, there was no doubt on their side. They were confident that they were right. When Moses told all who wished to escape their curse to depart from their tents, Dathan and Abiram came and stood in the doors of their tents, their wives and their sons and their little children; and Korah no less was willing to accept Moses' challenge, to take his censer and stand to minister before the Lord, and to invite the judgment of God. They had a real grievance, and they were confident that they were right on general, or, as it is sometimes called, *a priori* grounds, that is to say, what you would have expected, prior to all experience to the contrary. In the nature of things, was it likely

[1] See Newman's Sermons, vol. iii. p. 270.

that God should choose a man like Moses to be his mouthpiece and agent instead of dealing directly with His people?

And here, of course, was the flaw in their case. God does not act in accordance with those principles which we should have expected in the nature of things; and these men had, and much more now have we, experience to the contrary. God almost always, it would seem, instead of acting *immediately*, acts through means or channels. For instance, in the early chapters of Genesis, life is attached to the eating the fruit of a tree.[1] Later on, restoration to health is given to those who were bitten by serpents on the condition of their gazing at the serpent of brass.[2] The walls of Jericho fell down, not by the Almighty *fiat* of God, but after a sevenfold procession on the seventh of seven days round the walls.[3] Naaman was healed, not by the Almighty word of God, not even by the healing word of the prophet,[4] but by washing in the river Jordan, whose humble stream he despised. And so it is in the Christian Church. The whole principle and spirit which breathes through her Sacraments and ordinances is grace through outward means. And further, the ordinary means which God chooses for distributing his gifts are *men*—poor, weak, fallen, sinful men.

Some accept this, some do not. And so we find the religious world sharply divided into two great sections: those who believe in a Divine Ministry—

[1] Gen. iii. 22.
[2] Numb. xxi. 8.
[3] Josh. vi. 20.
[4] 2 Kings v. 14.

that God appoints men as "stewards of His mysteries," and those who do not, but who say that God always gives directly, without a medium, and that all the congregation are holy, every one of them. The whole question, it will be seen, really turns upon *ordination.* Every one will tolerate up to a certain point clergy, preachers, teachers, moral improvers, in proportion as they have more or less education, or mental endowment.

But, on the other hand, considerable antagonism is raised in many minds directly they see any indications of a claim such as this: God has given me a gift for you, not to be obtained ordinarily in another way, so that for certain things I stand in the relation of steward to God; such a position as appears to be asserted in the words of the ordination commission: "Be thou a faithful dispenser of the Word of God, and of His holy Sacraments, in the Name of the Father, and of the Son, and of the Holy Ghost."[1]

We ask, then, almost instinctively, is there any trace of such a thing in Holy Scripture to warrant this position and assertion? And we recognize at once, as a great fact, that one essential part of Christ's plan was to found a kingdom upon earth—His Church—and that this kingdom at His departure was administered by Apostles, who spoke in this way: "And all things are of God, Who hath reconciled us to Himself by Jesus Christ, and hath given to us the ministry of reconciliation; to wit, that God was in Christ, reconciling the world unto Himself, not

[1] See "Service for Ordination of Priests."

imputing their trespasses unto them; and hath committed unto us the word of reconciliation."[1] We find them baptizing,[2] confirming,[3] breaking the Holy Bread,[4] remitting and retaining sins,[5] acting as stewards between God and man. Then, as the Church expanded, still within the pages of God's Holy Word, we see deacons[6] appointed, and elders,[7] or, as we should say, priests, or, as they are called in the Pastoral Epistles, bishops,[8] and bishops (according to our usual idea of the office) under the name of angels,[9] as we read in the messages to the seven Churches in the Book of Revelation.

And these orders, as we find them in the Bible, exist down to the present time. Certainly all history and all language—if language has any meaning—seem to point to the clergy as believing themselves to be and ordained by God to be, *stewards*,[10] *i.e.* agents, bearing God's gifts to men. And an appeal to Holy Scripture seems certainly to leave us with this result, that there have always been certain accredited ministers to whom God imparts gifts, that they may distribute them to their fellow-men.

And it has been pointed out[11] that we are accustomed to this, as a principle, in other things. God rules this world, but not immediately. His power is distributed through "the powers that be" in all the different departments of political rule, and of social order, from the delegated parental authority of father

[1] 2 Cor. v. 18, 19.   [2] Acts xvi. 33.   [3] Acts xix. 6.
[4] Acts ii. 42.   [5] 2 Cor. ii. 10, 11.   [6] Acts vi 5, 6.
[7] Titus i. 5.   [8] 1 Tim. iii. 1.   [9] Rev. ii. 1.   [10] 1 Cor. iv. 1.
[11] See Dr. Liddon, "University Sermons," 2nd series, p. 104, etc.

over son down to the lowest exercise of His goverance committed by God to man in the divers relations of daily life.

In the same way God gives His support to all. He protects all, and feeds all; but He lodges wealth in the hands of a few, which it is their privilege to use for the good of the world, and their condemnation to misapply. In the same way, again, knowledge is in the hands of the few: there are "priests of science," who minister to the good of their fellow-men; in short, to sum up, "He makes a minority the guardians and trustees of the means of blessing the majority."

But where, then, is the difficulty? For since the days of the Israelites this doctrine has been a difficulty to some. Surely it has come in a good measure, although not entirely, from this—there is the constantly recurring feeling "ye take too much upon you, ye sons of Levi;" "all the congregation are holy."

On the one hand, there is the natural pride of man, and, on the other, it is true, men have forgotten, and will forget, that they are stewards. It is true that "all sorts of inferior minds may parade the doctrines, until men say the doctrine itself is detestable." But now we can see what a safeguard there is in ordination. When a man comes with a commission from God, in the power of the Holy Ghost, in obedience to a call distinct and clear, ordained by the Bishop, set apart for his office, what a safeguard there is in all this against thoughts of pride! How could a man of even ordinary humility venture to set himself up in the congregation to speak to people very often better and wiser than himself, because he simply thought himself clever, or gifted, or with a talent in that direction? Would not his position be intolerable? But let him once feel that he is not speaking of himself, or in himself, or for himself, but as a steward, ordained and commissioned, it at once has a tendency to drive away that self-conceit or self-assertion which more than anything else has produced Korahs among the clergy and Dathans and Abirams among the people of the Lord.[1]

If this is any way a true statement of the case is it not clear that certain duties devolve upon the people with respect to the clergy?

And, first, I venture to say that reverence should be shown to them, not merely personal, for that they may or may not deserve, but official. Their office is a holy one; their call is a high one; their ordination is a special gift of the Holy Ghost conferred upon them. If there have been sons of Aaron who have offered

[1] It will be observed that the rebellion of Korah, Dathan, and Abiram, though having a common object, arose from two different classes. Korah was a Levite, and his revolt would have its exact and literal counterpart in these days in a claim of men without any valid ordination at all, to discharge the functions usually supposed to reside exclusively in the Priesthood, the Diaconate, and Episcopate. Dathan and Abiram, on the other hand, belonged to the tribe of Reuben, and their rising was a lay protest against the claims of any ministerial caste whatsoever, emphasized probably by the fact of their being members of the tribe of the firstborn of the sons of Jacob. It may also have had in it something of a revolutionary spirit, as Moses was a political no less than a spiritual leader.

strange fire, if there have been Balaams who have sold their prophetical gifts to the highest bidder, if there have been sons of Eli who have made the Lord's people to transgress,[1] if there have been shepherds who have fed themselves instead of feeding the flock,[2] yes, if there has been a Judas among the Apostles, still the office is a holy one. We must respect the ambassadors of the Lord, if not for themselves, at least for His sake, in Whose Name they come, and Whose interests they represent.

Then, secondly, we should make allowances for them. The ministerial office is a very difficult one, and a very responsible one. They have to offer their liturgy to the Almighty God on the one hand, and, on the other to minister to man. They have to come very near to holy things, to bring forth out of their treasure things new and old,[3] to stand in the full light of the burning sun, and to concentrate its rays on the heart which God seeks to kindle. Oh, how sad if, while grace is passing through them, they themselves, like the burning glass, are cold all the time,[4] albeit they kindle a flame in the hearts of others! Oh, how piteous if, like Balaam, they are the mouthpieces of Heavenly truth, to which their base hearts give no response! Truly there is no office so dangerous and so responsible as the office of those who are brought very near to God, to whom He entrusts the guardianship of His chosen flock; and does not this danger and responsibility demand at least a fair

---

[1] 1 Sam. ii. 24.   [2] Ezek. xxxiv. 2.   [3] S. Matt. xiii. 52.
[4] This simile is one of Bishop Wilberforce's.

consideration of their acts at the hands of their judges?

And then we ought to pray for them. It is easy to criticise; it is hard to wrestle with God in prayer for the priest who is gone within the Holy Place to offer the incense. Surely it is for you to support him while he offers his petition; it is for you to stay up his hands when he intercedes; it is for you to strengthen him when his spirit faints and fails, by sympathy and encouragement and help; it is for you to elevate his character by showing him how much you expect from him, and the depth of his degradation should he fall from grace.

Oh, if ever the priest of God is tempted to think of himself more highly than he ought to think, if he is puffed up by the dignity and greatness of his office, one look at his position should be sufficient to recall him to himself. As a fellow-sinner he ministers to sinners; his weakness and his sins and infirmities, seem to stand out in a stronger light, as he is brought nearer to Him Who is the truth itself. For the tender Shepherd of the wandering sheep is at the same time a consuming fire,[1] a God very greatly to be feared in the council of the saints, and to be had in reverence of all them that are round about Him.[2] And it is quite possible that many who are first now in the ungrudging respect of their fellow-men, may be last hereafter in the award of unerring judgment, thrust down to hell *because* they were exalted [3] unto Heaven, and misused their opportunity.

[1] Heb. xii. 29.   [2] Psa. lxxxix. 8.   [3] S. Luke x. 15.

SERMON VIII.

Sunday.

"The same day at evening, being the first day of the week, when the doors were shut where the disciples were assembled for fear of the Jews, came Jesus and stood in the midst, and saith unto them, Peace be unto you."—S. JOHN xx. 19.

EASTER has not only left its mark on our faith and hope, transformed our churchyards, and elevated our life, but Easter is also remarkable as leaving a trace behind it in our Church calendar, flashing the good news of Christ's resurrection by the beacon lights of Sunday, from week to week, throughout the Christian year. On Easter day the Church passes from the bondage of the Sabbath into the purer, holier light of Sunday. Week by week, one day shining with borrowed lustre speaks of Christ's resurrection. The Day of light, the Day of peace, the Day of grace, the Day of prayer, the Day of refreshment, the Day of holy work—in one word, "The Lord's Day." Pardon me, therefore, if, on this our last service of the Easter festival, I venture to speak quite practically of that which is the reflection, the outcome, the prolongation of this glad festival; the Christian Sunday.[1]

[1] This sermon was preached on the 1st Sunday after Easter.

I. First of all, then, I would ask you to notice that the Sabbath and Sunday are two entirely distinct and different days. They are different in their origin, different in their observance, different in their time. The Sabbath was a day of solemn obligation imposed upon the Jews for two reasons—the one because God rested from His work of creation on the seventh day,[1] the second reason being to remind them of the time when God brought them out of Egypt with a mighty hand and stretched out arm.[2]

To break the Sabbath in old times was to be punished with death.[3] And in our Blessed Lord's day, when all vital religion had for the most part died out, the Jews still clung to this institution with passionate energy, while they overlaid it with countless restrictions and burdensome rules. This we find our Blessed Lord gradually breaking down, while He prepared the way for better things, until after the resurrection the day was changed altogether; the early Christians keeping holy the first day of the week, at first perhaps together with, then afterwards instead of, the Sabbath, or seventh day.

There are sundry indications of this in the New Testament. For instance, in the passage quoted above, the apostles were gathered together on the first Easter Day, being the first day of the week; again, we find them gathered together once more in the same way, eight days afterwards;[4] again, on the day of Pentecost, which in that year fell on the first day of the week,

[1] Exod. xx. 11.   [2] Deut. v. 15.
[3] Exod. xxxi. 14.   [4] S. John xx. 26.

they were all with one accord in one place;[1] or again, at Troas, many years after, S. Paul and his companions arrived there; and "abode seven days. And upon the first day of the week, when the disciples came together to break bread, Paul preached unto them,"[2] or again in the Epistle to the Corinthians, S. Paul writes "upon the first day of the week let every one of you lay by him in store, as God hath prospered him;[3] and, later still, we find the Christian assembly taking a definite form, "not forsaking the assembling of ourselves together, as the manner of some is;"[4] until, in the Book of Revelation, we find that the Christian Sunday is existing with a name and title of its own—the Jewish Sabbath has given place to "the Lord's Day,"[5] the seventh to the first, the deliverance from Egypt to the deliverance from death, the rest from the old creation to the rest from the new. The Sabbath has become Sunday, changed by the mind and voice of the Church, in order, as we may believe, to commemorate Christ's resurrection, and as a day set apart for the honour and glory of the Lord.

And so we find it in early Christian writers, directly we emerge from Scripture, spoken of in the same way as, and taking its place in the economy of the Church, with Confirmation, Ordination, Infant Baptism, and all such things, as we may believe that our Lord confided to His Church when He spoke to them during forty days of the things pertaining to the kingdom of God.[6] And we must carefully notice these facts connected

[1] Acts ii. 1.   [2] Acts xx. 6, 7.   [3] 1 Cor. xvi. 2.
[4] Heb. x. 25.   [5] Rev. i. 10.   [6] Acts i. 3.

with the Christian Sunday. It was never confounded with the Sabbath, but always distinguished from it. It was not a day of severe Sabbatical observance, but it was a day of solemn meeting for Holy Eucharist, for prayer, for instruction, for almsgiving. And nowhere is the fourth commandment appealed to as a ground for the observance of the Lord's day. Therefore, we can only look upon the Jewish Sabbath as a type or figure of the reality, the true Day of the Lord.

II. Two errors, as it would seem, have sprung up as regards Sunday. The one, which would treat it as a day of worldly festivity, very much like any other day, overlaid with gaiety and pleasure, and with such circumstance as the world gives to its day of rejoicing; the other, which treats it like the Jewish Sabbath, or in accordance with our ideas of the Jewish Sabbath, as a day of gloom, and morose austerity. And in connection with this view it is instructive to notice, that even granted that the observance of Sunday and the Sabbath should be identical, we are probably mistaken in viewing the Jewish Sabbath itself as a day of austere mortification and gloom.[1] It is remarkable to find, that even in our Blessed Lord's time, when the observance of the Sabbath had reached to a pitch of strained fanaticism, that He was invited to the house of one of the chief Pharisees to eat bread with him on

---

[1] "The whole social Rabbinical legislation on the subject (the Sabbath) seems to rest on two sound underlying principles; negatively the avoidance of all that might become work, and positively the doing of all which, in the opinion of the Rabbis, might tend to make 'the Sabbath a delight.'"—Edersheim, "The Temple," p. 117.

the Sabbath day,[1] and that He clothed the details of one of His parables in the imagery suggested by a number of guests, and the eager contest for precedence at the table of their host on that day. A Pharisee, the scrupulous religionist of his time, thinks it compatible with strict religion to give, as we should say, a party on the Sabbath Day.[2]

III. The practical question then remains for us, How shall we keep Sunday—the reflection of Easter throughout the year? Surely the Apostle furnishes us with the key when he calls Sunday the Lord's Day. Monday to Saturday are business days, or pleasure days, Sunday is the Lord's Day—a day that is set apart for the worship, praise, honour, thought of, instruction about, God. And let us note carefully, first of all, how Sunday is *not* kept. Many people think that getting up late, a change of clothes, a walk in the garden, an absolute repose, is keeping Sunday—if so, many people keep a perpetual Sabbath.

Let us be clear on this point. Idleness is not rest. It is not work that is the curse of the fall, but fatigue. Adam worked at tilling and dressing the garden before he fell into sin; afterwards it was hard, dreary, unblessed work—work in the sweat of his brow which was his curse. Work in itself is Godlike and Divine, as our Blessed Lord said, "My Father worketh hitherto, and I work."[3] No; ceasing from labour, as

---

[1] S. Luke xiv. 1.
[2] "It appears to have been the custom to close the Sabbath day with a joyous meal."—Edersheim, "The Temple," p. 163.
[3] S. John v. 17. "Idleness is quite as much contrary to the Sabbath

labour, is not the point in Sunday observance; it is ceasing from the labour of the world, to labour for God, to do His work, which is the highest labour, and the hardest labour; giving God His tithe of the week, the firstfruits of our time, as a mark of the respect and allegiance which we owe to Him. And, therefore, as in the case of the Jew the sacrifice was doubled on the Sabbath, so let us remember that we rest on Sunday from servile labour, that we may work more earnestly for God, and that Sunday rest from the service of the world is Sunday leisure for the service of God.

How, then, shall I keep Sunday? The highest, and best and most primitive way, no doubt, is to attend the service of the Holy Communion, as was their habit of whom we read "upon the first day of the week, when the disciples came together to break bread."[1] This was the universal custom certainly fifty years after the death of Saint John. This is the way in which we comply with our Blessed Lord's command, "This do in remembrance of Me."[2] This is the way in which we "shew the Lord's death till He come;"[3] here is the manna in the wilderness, the rock in the desert, the food of immortality; this is the way in which we can render each Sunday a true Lord's Day. But, short of this, every one can do what is meant by "going to Church;" nothing should hinder us in this

---

law as labour: 'Not doing thine own ways, nor finding thine own pleasure, nor speaking thine own words' (Isa. lviii. 13)."—Edersheim, "The Temple," p. 161.

[1] Acts xx. 7. [2] 1 Cor. xi. 24. [3] 1 Cor. xi. 26.

but absolute ill health, because it is the Lord's right, and the Lord's due, that we should "bring presents and come into His courts." Certainly, when we think what is the sequel to those words, " But Thomas, one of the twelve, called Didymus, was not with them when Jesus came;"[1] when we think of the consequences to him of his absence on one Sunday from the Christian assembly; and when we compare with this the privilege which fell to the lot of Anna, because she was *always* in the temple, constantly serving God with fasting and prayer, night and day;[2] then we are able to see the importance to ourselves of that waiting upon God, that constant attendance in His house, which is one of the privileges of Sunday. Oh, when we lie sick upon our bed and cannot go, then we miss it, and wonder that we should have held it so cheaply before. Yes, and we miss it also, even if we do not recognize the fact, in our daily trials and week-day business. The Gibeonites take us in, we have not asked counsel of God. The enemies of Israel beat us back, the ark of God is not in our midst. The week is unhallowed and unsanctified, "for if the first fruit be holy, the lump is also holy."[3]

And for what remains; it is true that worship and waiting upon God cannot take up the whole of the day. But at the same time, the thought of Sunday, as being the Lord's Day, should colour and tinge all our recreations. Our walks and conversation should be such as was theirs who found a third companion in

[1] S. John xx. 24.   [2] S. Luke ii. 37.   [3] Rom. xi. 16.

Jesus Christ, as they walked into the country in the sad sorrow which overshadowed the morn of the first Sunday.[1] Our books, our amusements, our occupations should all be chosen with this idea. Sunday is the Lord's Day, a day of holy solemnity, if at the same time it is a day of holy joy.

So may Sunday help us all on our journey heavenwards, so may Sunday be a day of resurrection in each week; one stage nearer home, another day of refreshment, another day of grace, another day of rest, another day of the Lord. For the light of our Sundays is to many of us already beginning to pale before the light of that eternal rest which remaineth for the people of God; whose glory is projected even across the dark valley of the shadow of death.[2] Our ears lose the sound of music here, as heaven's harmonies become louder and more clear. Sacraments, and symbols, and signs seem more and more fulfilled with the unveiled light of the presence of God.

Oh, may Sunday indeed lead us on here, step by step, "until the day break, and the shadows flee away;"[3] while the Lord directs our hearts into the love of God, and into the patient waiting for Christ,[4] and so instead of turning Sunday into other days, we shall insensibly turn other days into Sunday, waiting for the eternal Easter of heaven.[5]

[1] S. Luke xxiv. 13.   [2] Heb. iv. 9.
[3] Cant. ii. 17.   [4] 2 Thess. iii. 5.
[5] It was a saying of Mr. Keble's, I believe: "So far as you turn other days into Sunday, so far and no farther have you a right to turn Sunday into other days."

SERMON IX.

The Saviour of them that believe.

"*For therefore we both labour and suffer reproach, because we trust in the Living God, Who is the Saviour of all men, specially of those that believe.*"—1 TIM. iv. 10.

THESE words of S. Paul might give a motive, if motive were necessary; an encouragement, if we needed encouragement; a great object, if you will, for undertaking the duties and responsibilities of a Guild like this,[1] whose anniversary is being held to-day, which in the Name, and under the immediate protection, as we hope, of the Most Blessed Saviour, is endeavouring to perfect, as far as may be, a small portion of the complicated and vast machinery of mission work in that diocese of Natal to which the eyes of the Church, more than once, and now the eyes of the whole nation, have been turned with great anxiety and apprehension.[2]

Labour is more than repaid, reproach is more than wiped away, by the sense of working for such a

[1] This sermon was preached at All Saints', Margaret Street, London, before the members of the Guild of the Most Holy Saviour, Natal, June, 1879.
[2] The Zulu war was then going on.

Master. In all mission work, faithfully undertaken, we are not working for an opinion, or for a principle, or for a policy, however good and laudable in itself, but we are working for the living God, Who holds all the forces of life in His hand—whether, as Creator, He orders all things by the word of His power, as He clothes the grass of the field with beauty, or writes His sermon on the lilies of the field, or His precepts in the life of the fowls of the air; or whether, as Redeemer, He arrests the stream of death, implanting His new law of love in the hearts of men, feeding the soul with heavenly food, or arresting the march of His foes by the all-prevailing intercession before the throne of God; or whether, as the Sanctifier, He fashioneth the hearts of men, and turneth them whither He will, as the Spirit of order broods upon the face of the troubled waters of heathendom, and God says, "Let there be light,"[1] and the light of the Gospel shines through the gloom.

Labour is light, and reproach is glorious, in working for a *living God*, Who is the Saviour of all men, Who has died for all, Who preserves all, sending His rain on the just and on the unjust,[2] " Who will have all men to be saved, and to come unto the knowledge of the truth,"[3] but Who is more especially the Saviour of those that believe: "Unto" us "which believe He is precious;"[4] "Unto the godly there ariseth up light in the darkness."[5] The horrors of war are lightened to us by the vision of God sitting above the

[1] Gen. i. 3. [2] S. Matt. v. 45. [3] 1 Tim. ii. 4.
[4] 1 S. Pet. ii. 7. [5] Psa. cxii. 4.

water-floods, a king for ever.[1] If death comes to us, He slays us in the light, our death is illuminated by the dawn of day. We know we have a Saviour near us in the Sacrament of the altar, a Saviour who can wash our sins in His own most precious Blood, a Saviour Who is able to do more mighty works in our souls because we believe, and Who, although the Saviour of all men, is on this account more especially the Saviour of those that believe. And this Guild is banded together, then, in the power and in the love of the Saviour. By its link of the two or three gathered together in His name, it claims the especial blessing and presence of the Saviour of those that believe. And then, in the force of a corporate life, it reaches out after those heathen who are saved by the Living God, but who do not as yet know what it is to have the special blessings of the Saviour of those that believe. And therefore this society is one of those earthen vessels, which contain something of the fire which Christ came on earth to kindle. If we can break the pitcher of carelessness and worldliness and indifference, which so often stifles the fire entrusted to these Guilds, then our flame may mount up steadily, with heat and warmth and power; and spread, so that "others, too, may catch the living flame" which is burning within.

How, then, are we spreading the influence of the Most Blessed Saviour in Natal? How are we widening the inner circle of believers, and bringing others within the reach of the flame of Christ's love?

[1] Psa. xxix. 9.

1. First of all, we trust to *Intercession*. The first rule of this society provides that all its members shall intercede for the Church in Natal at their daily prayers, and especially when present at the Celebration of the Blessed Sacrament.

Do we realize the greatness of the work which we have undertaken? What is intercession? It is, as its name will tell us, "a coming between," *i.e.* a coming between God and the natural course of certain events. For instance: here is a man, neglecting or insulting God day after day, injuring himself and others. I come between God and that man; I ask God to suspend a law of His kingdom, the law of rewards and punishments, because I ask Him. That is, I imagine, that the claim which I have upon God, the interest which I have with Him, will counterbalance the awful cry of sin and indifference mounting up to the ears of God, and clamouring for vengeance. Is it an impotent impertinence, when I compare my persistency in good with the terrible persistency of the sinner in doing evil, "with both hands earnestly,"[1] to think that I shall prevail?

Or God, in His mercy, is preparing some great national chastisement. He puts us to confusion, He goes not forth with our armies.[2] My intercession means, that I am trying to divert God from His purpose, by a claim which I have upon Him. I believe that the royal decrees will be stayed, the avenging army of Heaven recalled, the counsels of God turned back, because I ask Him.

[1] Micah vii. 3. [2] Psa. xliv. 10.

Or, to take the daily, the frequent work of this Guild, there is the dense ignorance of heathenism; there is the inert sluggish force of a corrupt human nature; there is the worship of devils, the miasma of centuries of false and degraded superstition; which I am trusting to move, to stir, yes, to utterly disperse, by the strength of that petition which forces spiritual help and weapons from God; more unyielding in His goodness and justice, which will not put a constraint upon man's free will,[1] than the unjust judge in the parable, who would not put his justice in motion, but at the lengthened importunity of the persistent widow. If this is intercession, who is sufficient for these things? But yet it can be done. "Elias was a man subject to like passions as we are, and he prayed earnestly that it might not rain: and it rained not on the earth by the space of three years and six months. And he prayed again, and the heaven gave rain, and the earth brought forth her fruit."[2]

Do we not remember also how God had respect to the prayer, the self-denial, and the holiness of S. Paul, more than to the careless heathenism of the two hundred and seventy-six souls sailing with him, in his voyage to Rome, and addressed to him these cheering words: "Fear not, Paul; thou must be brought before Cæsar: and, lo, God hath given thee all them that sail with thee."[3] It can be done. But who is sufficient for these things? It is then, when we feel the magnitude of the work and our own

---

[1] "Non dat nisi petenti, ne det non capienti."—S. AUGUSTINE.
[2] S. James v. 17, 18.　　　　　　　　[3] Acts xxvii. 24.

weakness, that we lift up our eyes and see a ram caught in a thicket by his horns,[1]—a sacrifice ready to hand, when faith, devotion, and obedience have done their part; it is then that we remember the scarlet thread which Rahab bound in her window.[2] It is then that we remember Who it is that said, "Whatsoever ye shall ask the Father in My Name, He will give it you."[3] "This do ye, as oft as ye drink it, in remembrance of Me."[4] "As often as ye eat this bread, and drink this cup, ye do shew the Lord's death till He come."[5] And we recognize in our altars, the mount of intercession; the levers whereby we may lift the world. "Whatsoever." There is no apparent limit, if only we can plead that Holy Name, if only we can put on the priestly vestment of sacrifice, if only we can wave the censer of prayer, if only we can come with clean hands and a pure heart. Here at the altar to-day, we learn the magnitude, the power, the all-prevailing efficacy of intercession through Jesus Christ. And we feel that intercession is not a light repetition of a few stated prayers, but a real "coming between" of our whole being; a coming between God and the great difficulties and obstacles of life; trusting in Him to remove them, through Jesus Christ, the

---

[1] Gen. xxii. 13. "Aries hic cornibus hœrens, et suspensus inter vepres, significat Christum in cruce suspensum."—See Corn. à Lapide, on Gen. xxii. 13, and the authorities there quoted.

[2] Josh. ii. 18. "Quæ timuit Deum, cui dictum est ut per fenestram mitteret coccum, id est, ut in fronte haberet signum sanguinis Christi." —S. AUGUSTINE.

[3] S. John xvi. 23.   [4] 1 Cor. xi. 25   [5] 1 Cor. xi. 26.

Divine Victim of the altar, Who taketh away the sins of the world.

II. And another work which, as I gather, this society has undertaken, is to extend that burning circle of fire in which "the Saviour of those that believe" works, by material means, such as money and other necessaries of practical mission life.

We know, alas! to our cost, that an army, however well equipped, must stay for supports, before it can move from its base of operations. And surely it is a work which may well devolve upon those who stay at home, to relieve those who are contending in the front, from the anxiety, the hindrances, the crippled efforts which result from want of supplies. Of course, we know that with many people their sole mission work has been to contribute so much money, sent out with no idea of what it was going to effect, without prayer, without thought, as a tax, and not as an offering. And therefore there is a natural dislike, very often, when speaking of missions, to introduce at all the question of supplies, lest mission work, to us who stay at home, should again become a question periodically to be bought off with the hush-money of an annual subscription.

But almsgiving, after all, is a religious question. It is a subject which finds a place in that quintessence of Christianity, "the Sermon on the Mount." And as members of this society, all who belong to it surely feel constrained in some way to adjust their theory and practice of almsgiving so as to help in this work.[1]

[1] Preached in the week after 1st Sunday in Trinity.

Are my brothers the heathen but the beggars of to-day's gospel, whom I magnificently patronize with a seat at my gates, and with a few crumbs which I should otherwise throw away? Or am I curtailing my purple and fine linen, and sumptuous living, that I may lift them, beggars as they are, from the dunghill, who are craving after truth with a hunger which God alone can satisfy, that God may set them with the princes, even with the princes of His people? Almsgiving is not a commonplace of a missionary sermon. It is a practical portion of the perfection of Christian life.

III. And then, lastly, I gather that the remaining rules of the society amount to this: that any one who is a member shall try and feel an *interest* in mission work. Oh, how we do all need to rouse ourselves to this. Do we not all need to mount with the Apostle of love in to-day's Epistle, into the higher regions of pure truth, from which to contemplate our fellow-creatures as God sees them. "*If God so loved us, we ought also to love one another.*"[1] Our love for man, not only for our friends, our companions, our nation, but our love for *man*, ought to be of that same character which induced God to send His own Son into the world.

Oh, surely, it would be the sign of a high sanctity to be able to take an interest in mission work, as mission work. It is the disciple who leans on Jesus' breast, the disciple who seeks to penetrate the deep mysteries of the Incarnation and the Sacraments, who

[1] 1 John iv. 11.

speaks to us of the blessing, the sanctity, the necessity of love. And the more we seek to know God, the more we are gathered up into Him, surely the more shall we see men as He sees them—human beings placed in this world with that grand future, those splendid opportunities, that eternal inheritance, that awful gift of life, reflecting in reason and free will the image, if broken and distorted, still the image of God. Precious possession, bought back by the blood of Christ, "the Saviour of all men." So many souls "for whom Christ died," Temples of the Holy Ghost, the sanctifying Spirit, Who puts "no difference between us and them,"[1] the same Lord rich unto all that call upon Him.

Oh, this interest! it cannot be galvanized into life in cold and dead hearts. It grows up where the soul is full of prayer, whose daily petition is, "Thy kingdom come." But still we can try to give a portion of our mind to the interest so near to the heart of all Christians.

"While we were yet sinners, Christ died for us."[2] Am I holding back myself from mission work because it does not interest me? Am I withholding any friend from the mission field because it is full of hardships, with few chances of distinction, much work and little glory? Am I echoing on that foolish cry, "Why do not the missionaries do more?" Surely when we think of Bishop Selwyn, of Bishop Patteson, of Bishop Grey, of Bishop Milman, of Bishop Douglas, of Bishop Venables, and many more, we

[1] Acts xv. 9. [2] Rom. v. 8.

English people must feel that we have already sent the bones of Joseph into our promised land. The kingdoms of the heathen have become the sepulchres of our fathers; and God forbid that we should sell them to Ahab, and to Baal the god of this world.

Oh, may our circle ever be widening. May the Saviour of us who believe be gathering daily more and more sheep into His fold. He has left a great work for us to do—to cut down the boughs of the wood, the wood of the cross, and to lay them on our shoulders as we see Him do;[1] to stay up His hands on the mount of intercession, until the sun of this world sets for ever,[2] that more and more may be gathered up into His heart of love, Who wishes all to be saved, and all to come to the knowledge of the truth. "The Saviour of all men, specially of those that believe."

[1] Judg. ix. 48.   [2] Exod. xvii. 12.

SERMON X.

The Holy Innocents.

"*Suffer the little children to come unto Me, and forbid them not; for of such is the kingdom of God.*"—S. MARK x. 14.

WE can see at a glance that the Church to-day, in the midst of our Christmas joy, bids us contemplate something more than a cruel episode in the early years of the Infant Saviour. The festival of the Holy Innocents is in some sense unique in the Christian year; and has lessons all its own, which demand our most serious attention.

And, first, it will be well to put the facts clearly before us as recorded in the pages of Holy Scripture. Herod, being alarmed at the inquiry of the wise men from the East (whose coming we must probably place *after* the Purification), apprehending danger to his own kingdom from Him that was born King of the Jews, endeavours first to destroy the Holy Child under the pretence of worshipping Him. God warns the Magi, and they return another way to their homes. This disappointment enrages Herod. He "sent forth, and slew all the children that were in

Bethlehem, and in all the coasts thereof, from two years old and under,"[1] hoping thus to involve the young King in the massacre. But in the mean time Christ had fled into Egypt under the care of Saint Joseph and His mother; and the exceeding bitter cry goes up from Bethlehem, which was prophesied by Jeremiah, " Rachel (as if the mother of Joseph and Benjamin, who died and was buried at Bethlehem, represented all the mothers of that grief-stricken city), Rachel weeping for her children, and would not be comforted because they are not."[2]

Now, some may ask, why did God permit this? Why was the young Child spared and these innocent ones destroyed? Why was Bethlehem plunged into grief by the presence of the Holy Child at Whose birth angels sang, " On earth peace, good will toward men?"[3] We can only glance now at the very outskirts of the great question. But does not this murder of innocent children, allowed, yes, even brought about, by the Presence of God, warn us that we have no ground on which to place the balance in which we would weigh the justice of God? We come with our little souls, from our little life, and feeble light, and ask how God could be good, if He, in the full light of His predestinating knowledge, created Adam and Eve knowing that they would fall? Or how it is compatible with the justice and love of God to punish any soul with eternal punishment? or why He places such penalties and restrictions on the intellectual acceptance of truth? In all these things we see that we have

[1] S. Matt. ii. 16.   [2] S. Matt. ii. 18.   [3] S. Luke ii. 14.

obviously no rule by which to measure the actions of God. We can but guess at the truth, and feel that in the end we may be wrong. Therefore the thought suggests itself at once—

I. Was God inflicting an injury on these infants?

Ponder well those beautiful words of the book of Wisdom, " Honourable age is not that which standeth in length of time, nor that is measured by number of years. But wisdom is the grey hair unto men, and an unspotted life is old age. He pleased God, and was beloved of Him; so that living amongst sinners he was translated. Yea, speedily was he taken away, lest that wickedness should alter his understanding, or deceit beguile his soul. . . . He, being made perfect in a short time, fulfilled a long time. For his soul pleased the Lord: therefore hasted He to take him away from among the wicked."[1] Even the heathen had their saying, that "those whom the gods love die young." If life were all *here*, if there was no immortality, no hope beyond the grave, if there were no crowns and cities *there*, no rewards of victory, then it might be that these children were robbed, deprived, mulcted of a natural right to live, by the jealous caprice of a tyrant who might have been restrained. But the broken hearts of parents, and ruined homes and blighted hopes, the vacant seat of the prodigal at the fireside, the haunting shadow of a dear one in want in a far country feeding swine; yes, even those examples which lie open in the book of experience under our eyes—all these tell the same tale. Life

[1] Wisd. iv. 8-14.

here is not always a blessing to those who use it; there are so many turns, and so many to turn aside; so many briars, so many thorns, so much trouble, so much sin. We can conceive it possible—nay, we can see that it is even probable—that God may give early death in special cases as a special favour; and deliver the righteous from the evil to come. God was not injuring these children; He was calling them home. But more than this, the Church does not hesitate to call them martyrs. Martyrs in deed, although not in will; accepting unconsciously the baptism of blood, and meriting in the mercy of God the glory and the decorations and the renown of the tried soldier of the Cross. No, He was not injuring the children. It was a calling of slaves to the adoption of sons; it was the crowning of those who had not yet learnt to fight the battle; it was a largesse of royal bounty on the birth of the King's Son.

II. But suffering there certainly was, of some kind. For what can we say of the mothers bereaved of their children, and of the pain and anguish and bloodshedding which made this day so terrible? But here again, taking man's life as a whole, is suffering an evil? Christ Jesus distributed suffering almost as a privilege. "All who came near Him, more or less, suffered by approaching Him, just as if earthly pain and trouble went out of Him, as some precious virtue for the good of their souls."[1] His blessed mother, as she clasped Him to her heart, clasped with Him a sword which pierced her soul. S. John Baptist, His

[1] Dr. Newman, "Plain and Parochial Sermons," vol. ii. p. 62.

forerunner and friend, passed away to meet Him in His triumph from out of a loathsome prison. The twelve apostles gained the steps to their twelve thrones in twelve martyrdoms.[1] The great apostle of the Gentiles was shown how great things he must *suffer* for Christ's name's sake.[2] This Child was set for the fall and rising again of many in Israel.[3] Pontius Pilate, who was appointed unwillingly to try Him, ended his days in exile. Jerusalem, which He came to save, within forty years was in ruins, after unspeakable anguish. Run through the list of your friends and acquaintances; take those who seem to follow Christ nearest; what does He seem to give them most often? Suffering of body, anguish of spirit, or trouble of mind.

> "If I find Him, if I follow,
> What His guerdon here?
> 'Many a sorrow, many a labour,
> Many a tear.'"

Therefore, suffering cannot be unmixed evil. May it not be that it is pure good? The suffering which Christ sends is *remedial*. For there are three sorts of suffering which *man* inflicts in punishment of offenders. First, there is vengeance, which the law takes on criminals to satisfy justice for the advantage of the offended; then, there is punishment which is inflicted as a deterrent to others for the advantage of the community; and then, thirdly, there is punishment which is inflicted for the good of the offender,

---

[1] S. John being a martyr in will but not in deed.
[2] Acts ix. 16.   [3] S. Luke ii. 34.

which is called correction, and this is the suffering which Christ sends to those whom He loves—correction for the good of their souls.

Such suffering a poor wounded soldier longs for on the field of battle—the sharp knife of the doctor, which alone can save his life. Such suffering the poor patient in the hospital sends for, pays for—the sharp suffering which is to restore health. And so suffering is the only way in which, sometimes, the Good Physician can save our souls. Something has to be cut away, something to be driven out. And hence it comes to pass, that "Whom the Lord loveth He chasteneth, and scourgeth every son whom he receiveth."[1] And therefore in the agony of Bethlehem, we see something of the curse culminating, "In sorrow thou shalt bring forth children."[2] The great Man Child is born into the world, and is surrounded at His birth by the sorrow of mothers. But, also, we see suffering approaching Him, that suffering which He carried in His hand, and carries still, to cut and to burn, to purge and to renew the fallen nature of man.

III. And almost the first suffering falls upon children; God loves little children, and says, "Suffer the little children to come unto Me."

It is a day for us to remember the pattern which He gave us for our example, "Verily I say unto you, except ye be converted, and become as little children, ye shall not enter into the kingdom of heaven. Whosoever therefore shall humble himself as this little

[1] Heb. xii. 6.   [2] Gen. iii. 16.

child, the same is greatest in the kingdom of heaven."[1] And the life of a little child presents an ideal, which it is difficult to analyze, yet which we ought to understand. These are they whom the King delighteth to honour. There is a freshness, a power of being impressed, a docility about little children—so many paths all beginning, and as yet only reaching out into a dim future—which makes the companionship of a child a refreshment to us who have grown older in this world.

"A child, more than all other gifts,
Brings hope with it, and forward-looking thoughts."[2]

What makes us so jaded, so hard, so finished off; moulded to some shape or another, growing to the things of this world and taking their form? It is that we are spoiled children. We have done what we were told not to do; we have wearied ourselves out with play, and a satiety of lower things; we have lost "the guidance of His eye," and now bit and bridle can scarcely hold us.[3]

Can we make ourselves young again? Can we shut up the book of knowledge of good and evil? Can we throw aside the playthings of this world, and begin life's work? Ah, yes, we can go straight to our Father's knees, and ask Him to teach us, instead of this weary world, whose gospel is ever altering, where the mistakes of one generation are the sport of the next, and whose reed-like support goes through the hand and pierces it. We can go straight to God,

[1] S. Matt. xviii. 3, 4.　　[2] Wordsworth.
[3] Psa. xxxii. 9, 10.

and ask Him, "Lord, what wouldest *Thou* have me to do?" Not what the world says I may do, or what other people do; not what my circumstances, or position, or tradition permit; but, looking in my Father's face, waiting for His look, for the indication of His Providence: "Lord, what wouldest *Thou?*"

Yes, and we can shut up that book of evil. If we dream of it, if a sinful memory haunts us, still we can read no more. We can satisfy our mind with right and proper food, and close the door to evil. And we can try to please; we can anticipate His wishes, we can obey His commandments, we can follow His advice. We call Him "Father;" He calls us "Sons," and He wishes His sons to be, not mere men of this world, but dutiful children, who will learn from Him.

Christ, then, on this festival honours infants, consecrates suffering, holds up to us the minds of little children; and it is another radiance and beauty added to the manger throne of Bethlehem, that from it streams the gospel of the poor, the gospel of the lonely, the gospel of the sick, the lost, the afflicted, the gospel of little children. The wisdom of Greece and Rome could only spare at this time a push, or a threat, or a curse, which said to the little, the poor, the weak, Depart; get you out of the way;[1] it was left for the glorious gospel of the Blessed Lord to say, "Suffer the little children to come unto Me and forbid them not, for of such is the kingdom of God."

[1] See Dupanloup, "Life of Christ," introduction.

We are reminded to-day of the great company standing upon Mount Sion, before the throne, worshipping the Lamb with praise and honour and blessing, and the harpers are there, harping with their harps.[1] Men whose lives have been strung, and drawn, by the tension of suffering, until they have emitted in the blows of martyrdom, the song of praise acceptable before God.[2] And, to-day, they sing a new song. It is the song of infant wailing; an inarticulate cry; the voice of those whose only language is a cry. The new song of Christianity, which Stoic and Epicurean had failed to learn; the dignity, the force, the power of simple suffering. Oh, that great blessing of Christianity! Suffering is all useful, part of the world's expiation, part of the soul's purification; a work to do, a binding to the cross. This was indeed a new song to the world; yes, a new song to heaven; because before the cross there was no one to elevate suffering.

There they stand, these harpers, singing the new song, the songs, indeed, which have no words, no achievements, no great actions to commemorate; a song mixed up with no imperfection, and no sin. Think of the words of the songs of the greatest saint! of a S. Peter, a S. Paul, a S. James, or a S. John, or a S. Thomas—something is amiss, something is wrong —but these are without fault before the throne of God.[3]

Let us try, then, and learn this new song, which can only be learnt by children: "Except ye be

[1] Rev. xiv. 1.   [2] Dr. Neale.   [3] Rev. xiv. 5.

converted and become as little children, ye cannot enter into the kingdom of heaven." While we learn to forget—forgetting those things which are behind, let us have the child's faith, to reach forward to those things which are before,[1] and in the child's loving, earnest trust, patiently wait for Christ.

[1] Phil. iii. 13.

SERMON XI.

Religious Indolence.

"*Not every one that saith unto Me, Lord, Lord, shall enter into the kingdom of heaven; but he that doeth the will of My Father Which is in heaven.*"—S. MATT. vii. 21.

THERE is nothing, I suppose, in which the natural indolence of corrupt human nature betrays itself so much as in *religion*. Wherever we turn, we meet with indications that religion is a hard and difficult matter; and yet almost everywhere, also, we find devices and shifts to throw off its burden, and lessen its responsibilities. For proof of this statement, take, first, the two revealed religions of the Bible, which yet are only one, Judaism and Christianity (for these are not really distinct religions, but Christianity is the completion, the development, the full growth of Judaism, differing only as the fruit from the flower out of which it grew), and you will see that in both these systems of religion the obligations imposed are immense.

We can see at a glance, the time, the trouble, and the expense which his religion must have cost the

Jew, in all its solemnity as a religion coming straight from God. And one glance at the Sermon on the Mount, on the other hand, with the law of the Beatitudes, the spiritualized law of the Ten Commandments, and the three great Christian duties of fasting, almsgiving, and prayer, will equally serve to show that our Christian obligations are no less severe; rather a great deal heavier, entering into the inmost recesses of the mind and spirit. If we look outside the actual religious precepts of revelation, we see just the same thing. A Roman general, ignorant of all art, is said to have discovered the extreme value of some work of art which the fortune of war had brought into his possession, only by the great price offered for it, when he wished to part with it. And so, as it seems to me, if any think religion to be a light matter, he should look at the price paid for our Redemption; he should weigh well the lowliness of the Incarnation, the bitterness of the Passion, the humiliation of the Cross, the loneliness of the Grave. He should contemplate, bring within the field of his vision, all that is meant by the Atonement; and at the same time, growing out of this, consider the minute care, and provident love, which distinguishes the foundation of the Church on earth. On every ordinance and every rite is stamped God's care and man's need. Yes, one glance at the cross, and the Kingdom of God must show us again that we live and move under a law of great obligations.

And there is only one other place, where we should turn our eyes, and that is *within*, as we open the door of our heart, and are conscious of that mighty rush and roar going on *there*. What is to curb those passions, and control those appetites, and subdue those impulses? Is a whim, or a wish, or a sentiment, or a feeling, strong enough to check that mighty flow which dashes itself against the barriers which restrain it, and which threaten every moment to sweep away and overmaster the will, and to obliterate the whole being in a ruinous overthrow? It is the same story everywhere. God proclaims, the Cross postulates, our weakness demands, that religion should be a strong and weighty matter, adequate to the work which it has to perform, commensurate with the vigour and energy which has called it into being. And yet, as I said, side by side with this, human indolence is ever seeking to slip out of the strain. The Jew compounded with minute ritual observance and shifted to the tithing of mint, anise and cummin, the responsibility to perform judgment, mercy, and faith, and the weightier matters of the law.[1] And with Christians, also, there has been a tendency at all times, to rest upon some religious formula, or religious rite, and to slip out of the strong responsibilities and obligations that religion imposes.

And one of the most common forms which this tendency has taken, and one most disastrous in its effect, is alluded to here by our Blessed Lord, when He says, "Not every one that saith unto Me, Lord, Lord, shall enter into the kingdom of heaven, but he that doeth the will of My Father, Which is in heaven,"

[1] S. Matt. xxiii. 23.

—that spirit which lingers in the phraseology and forms of religion, while neglecting to do the will of God, which is the basis of all religion. It saves trouble, it is soothing, it lulls to sleep, to live in the gentle murmur of "Lord, Lord," and to forget the stern necessity of doing something for our religion, of working out our own salvation with fear and trembling,[1] of pushing beyond the mere idle formula of assent to the stedfast doing of the will of God.

II. Now religion is the force which has to grapple with the motions of death within us. If we had grown up in the ways of God, all would have been easy; as temptations grew, strength would have grown to resist them, grace would have added to our spiritual stature inch by inch and step by step,[2] until we came to the perfect man, "the measure of the stature of the fulness of Christ."[3] But as it is now, with most of us, religion has to divide itself into three forces. One has to deal with the past; another with the present; a third with the possibilities of the future; and in each and in all of these there is need of vigorous energy and effort. And human indolence is ever resisting the effort, and trying to slip out of the obligation and lessen the task.

(1) It is a serious question with all of us, what are we to do with the arrears? What are we to do with the past? Are we to hide our head in the sand and forget it?—all those wasted "years that the locust hath eaten,"[4] all those open and notorious sins, all

[1] Phil. ii. 12.
[2] See Dr. Newman, "Plain and Parochial Sermons," vol. i. p. 97.
[3] Eph. iv. 13.   ·   [4] Joel ii. 25.

those secret and hidden sins, that waste of grace and opportunity, those rebellious wanderings from God's love? Can we imagine that God, Who has entrusted us with the few pounds of life, will be contented with a buried pound, or a lost pound, or a terrible diminution of that which He entrusted to us?

Here man in his indolence looks to a "Lord, Lord." He will go on, as it appears, even to the last day, when men shall stand without, with their "Lord, Lord, open unto us," and shall begin to say, "we have eaten and drunk in Thy presence, and Thou hast taught in our streets."[1] It is to be with them as it was with the penitent thief,—one convulsive "Lord, remember me,"[2] is to open for them the gate of Paradise; it is to be with them, as with the great Saint Paul,—one mighty burst of light and glorious vision, and overwhelming voice, is to separate them from the past in the throes of a conversion.

But religion does not reserve these ways to the many, nor promise that they will lead to the kingdom of heaven. The Bible says little about conversion, with its impassioned "Lord, Lord." It says much about repentance. And this is hard; this is difficult; this is, if you will, prosaic; this implies the diligent searching of the heart, the long and weary investigation of past sins, past negligences, past ignorances; this implies the broken and contrite heart, broken up, pulverized with sorrow, into a soil once more receptive of good; it means the driving away of the birds, the diverting of the hard mule-path, the pulling

[1] S. Luke xiii. 26.   [2] S. Luke xxiii. 42.

up of the briars, the upheaving of the rocks, a heart bruised and broken up, or, as it is said, a *contrite heart*.[1] It implies that humble loving confession, "Father, I have sinned,"[2] not merely in that general acknowledgment which does but "bless with faint blame," but in the conscious shame of individual shortcomings and failure, leading us to a painful, weary, laborious amendment. How different to the easy "Lord, Lord," with which the soul thinks it can rush into God's presence with hands yet foul with black deeds, with feet yet weighted with a life's sin, before Him, Who washed away the sin of the world only with His own Blood. Repentance is troublesome, but it is the will of God. The "Lord, Lord," is easy, but it has no promise of rolling back the gate which bars the access to the kingdom of heaven.

(2) And if we look at life as it stretches out around us, turning our back upon the storm clouds which sweep across the past, and gaze only at the smiling landscape at our feet, still there is the same difficulty. Life is armed with a thousand troubles; it bristles with dangers; we carry about with us those forces which a spark may explode and scatter in fury.

And so religion is ever urging watchfulness, earnestness, care, diligence. We must not drift into temptation, and trust to a "Lord, Lord," to get us out. Alas! if we pass a day without sin, we owe it too often to absence of temptation rather than to victory over sin. Religion says, "Watch," "be on

---

[1] Psa. li. 17.   [2] S. Luke xv. 18.

your guard against the besetting sin." Indolence says, "Every one has his weak points, and I have mine." There are privileged sins, temptations which we go into knowing that we shall fall, because we are not striving against them.

Well, it is easy thus to allow ourselves a certain number of faults. It is easy to assert that God allows every one a few mistakes. But it is not religion. Doubtless it is harder, day by day, to battle with a besetting sin, which men call a fault, than just to give way, and call upon the Lord to pardon it. But does it stop here? Is it not just at the weak point that the whole strength gives way? The strength of a chain is the strength of its weakest link. Did it avail Moses that he was good, devoted, generous, pure, faithful, brave, religious? His hasty temper, once subdued, so that he became noted for meekness, broke down again, and with it went the earthly crown of his life. Did it avail Judas that he was an earnest, self-denying apostle? He broke down in covetousness. S. Peter again, strong in other points, broke down in self-confidence. No, if religion is the force within us which seeks to restrain the powers of death, it is not in the easy acquiescence in a low standard, but in the vigorous determination to overcome *all* evil, that she pursues her toilsome and hard task. It is hard and difficult to regulate our rebellious life according to the will of God; it is easy to say, "Lord, Lord," from a life of no effort and no ambition. But "Lord, Lord," is no watchword when the gate is closed; "Lord, Lord, open unto us," will not fill the empty lamp, nor kindle the flame which heralds the bridegroom's approach.[1]

(3) But there is also *the future*, with its menacing storm-clouds, which threaten to burst and overwhelm the soul. Here, too, there is a religion which is the will of God, and there is a religion which hopes to meet all difficulties with a feeble cry, "Lord, Lord." The way of the Church is "prepare;" the way of the world is "drift." Certainly the obligations of religion may seem severe, when the means of grace are apparently so free, but whose effects are neutralized by a want of earnest preparation and carefulness.

The will of God seems to be that we should meet our spiritual foes with spiritual weapons, with prayer, and Sacraments, and holy life. Is it any use to cry "Lord, Lord," asking for extraordinary help, when the ordinary help lies wasted and unused? It is certainly a serious responsibility to neglect the will of God, as manifested towards us when we see men shattered and shivered by the force of their passions, crushed and bruised under the weight of affliction, tossed and distracted by the strange contrarieties of life. As we are conscious to ourselves of the same working, the same principle, as we move through the same infected plain, what is to save us? The issues are immense, and the conflict is immense too. But it must be something more than the cry of "Lord, Lord," which does little to touch the greatness of our need.

Everything, then, points to a religion which is strict, vigorous, and strong, if it is to be of any avail.

[1] S. Matt. xxv. 11.

Human indolence prefers to stand outside it, and to trust to its own weak cry. But if we once approach our lives, as those who wish to be good and true, then we shall find what a vortex of wild inclinations, passions, and temptations we have stepped into, and we shall find the only refuge is to throw ourselves into the will of God, which in the end will carry us to salvation, where to cry "Lord, Lord," serves only to mock our despair.

SERMON XII.

Now![1]

"Behold, now is the accepted time; behold, now is the day of salvation."—2 Cor. vi. 2.

"Now" is a little word with a great moral history. Adam and Eve fall from their high estate while they grasp after the "now" of a momentary gratification. David unsheathed the sword which never again leaves his house, he overshadowed the past and blackened the bright future by a "now" of successful sin. While Pharaoh parries a "now," Egypt is destroyed. By a "now" of sincere repentance, Nineveh turns to God at the preaching of Jonah, and is saved. It is the warcry of many a battle in the Christian soul. The earnest soldier meets his enemy with the triumphant "now," while he is assaulted by that foe whose watchword is "then." Sinners hope for it; penitents watch for it; wise men use it as it is brought before them; that *now* of the accepted time, that *now* of the day of salvation.

And the Church has her "now;" year by year, as

[1] Preached in Worcester Cathedral, Lent, 1878.

the seasons go round, when there is so much to make us careless, so much to make us linger in the cities of the plain, so much to make us delay, she gets her up into the high mountain, she lifts up her voice, and calls all her children together. "Bring in what you have done, and note its shortcomings." "Come with fasting, come with penitence, come with sorrow, come while it is called to-day, and repair in a time of sorrow the harm and the loss which your life has experienced in its rough contact with the world." The Church calls to us with no uncertain voice. In this season of Lent, in every church throughout the land, Joel has published his warning, "Turn ye even to Me" (saith the Lord) "with all your heart, and with fasting, and with weeping, and with mourning: and rend your heart, and not your garments, and turn unto the Lord your God."[1]

Yes, every town, every village, every congregation, every man who attends his church, knows that this is Lent—a time for repentance, a time for sorrow, a time for preparation, the great spring fast of the Church.

But here, of course, there is a divergence. The message falls on different ears. The sower soweth the Word, the fruit depends on the soil; not all welcome it, not all obey it. Some scoff at the whole thing; Lent is the same as any other time to them, Lot "seemed as one that mocked unto his sons-in-law,"[2] because "they did eat, they drank, they bought, they sold, they planted, they builded,"[3] while

---

[1] Joel ii. 12, 13.   [2] Gen. xix. 14
[3] S. Luke xvii. 28.

judgment was gathering up over the doomed city. And so Lent appeals very often to deaf ears, when men are too absorbed in the glare and dazzle of this worldly life to see the dark clouds mounting up behind them, soon to eclipse the sun on which their very life depends. No, if a man is not sorry for sin, he is so far honest in saying so. Lent is nothing to him, and he declines to profess a sorrow which he is unable to bring himself to feel.

Others, again, throw out that dark obscuring controversy, when hard pressed by the half-convinced conscience; when the net of the Church is just about to enclose them. The waters are darkened by this inky fluid, and the soul escapes from the good influences. We have an instance of this in the woman of Samaria. Jesus Christ, the Great Physician, who knows the heart of man, He probed the very depth of her heart by that searching command, "Go, call thy husband."[1] He had laid His finger on the deep festering sore of her life; that was the crack in the cistern of grace through which all the living waters would eddy away. Although at first put off her guard, as soon as she recovered herself, controversy is thrown out to cover her retreat: "Our fathers worshipped in this mountain; and ye say, that in Jerusalem is the place where men ought to worship;"[2] and controversy was to mask conviction. And so, alas, now. Many, when half convinced that Lent ought not to slip by unobserved, unnoticed, uncared for, content themselves with saying, "It is superstitious," "It is foolish,"

[1] S. John iv. 16.   [2] S. John iv. 20.

"It is hypocritical," "It is Pharisaical," "It is wrong," and so escape from the obligation which has forced itself upon them. Dear friends, surely it is not necessary here to enter except on the very borders of this question. You will all agree that we cannot do wrong in imitating our Blessed Lord. If He fasted for forty days and forty nights, fasting in itself cannot be wrong. If He said, "When ye fast," ye shall not do so and so,[1] He did not mean to say you must never fast. When He said, "then shall they fast in those days,"[2] He clearly looked forward to those settled days of Church order when the expectant bride should await with eager longing the return of her Lord and Bridegroom. If He said of some kind of devil, that it goeth not out but by prayer and fasting,[3] He implied more than that fasting was not wrong, but that further in some cases it was a necessity. Now, Lent may speak to us all in these three ways, out of its retirement—its fasting, its self-denial, its prayer. Is there anything which I ought to do? Is there anything which I ought to give up? Is there any defect which I ought to make good? But here the angel, God's messenger, who would warn Lot— the preacher to whom God intrusts the message—is met by, "The man lingers;" "It is to be some day;" or else the resolution is made in Church, "It shall be done;" "Yes, that evil habit *shall* be rooted out;" "That good habit *shall* be formed;" "I will be a Christian, not in word only, but in deed and in truth."

[1] S. Matt. vi. 16. [2] S. Luke v. 35.
[3] S. Matt. xvii. 21.

The seed falls on the heart, the good seed, the good word of God.

But the fowls of the air are waiting outside the Church. The resolution lies on the surface; through that heart runs a hard roadway, worldly thoughts course up and down it, everything is admitted, everything tramples it down; there is no deep thought, no deep resolution, no retirement, no prayer, no fasting; religion falls on the road with the rest, and the birds soon take off the good seed, which nothing has protected, and the good resolution is carried off almost as soon as it is made. But, if I might be permitted, I would venture to urge upon all with a persistency not impertinent, because it is real—"Now." That is my text, and that is my sermon—"Now."

"Behold, *now* is the accepted time; behold, now is the day of salvation." As time is slipping from us we ought all to look to the Lenten call. Even while we speak, time is slipping, passing, going away, and what am I doing with it? Life to the Christian is one great "now," that little word whose derivation carries us back to a point[1] in time, "that which has no part, no magnitude," which we cannot fix, which flies from us as we grasp it; which is being ever absorbed into the past. This "now," which is such a real point to the earnest practical Christian, is put before us. To delay is dangerous, is destruction, is a dead loss.

And this is a consideration which needs our most

---

[1] "Now," said to be derived through the Greek νῦν-νυς, νυσσειν, to prick or pierce = a point.

earnest thought. We neglect to turn to God, we neglect to occupy our true position, we neglect to give up that wrong thing, we neglect to do that good action at a distinct loss.

In old days we read of the Sibyl who came to the king with the nine books of oracles in her hands, and asked her great price for the volumes. While the king hesitates, three books are burned, and lost for ever; but she still asks the same price for six which she before asked for nine. While he still hesitates, she burns three more, and then asks the same price for three, although the six are burned and lost. And then the king, who buys three at the price of nine, finds what he has lost in the priceless contents of the volumes he has received.

Time is that Sibyl. Every time she comes, she asks the same price for turning; every time she comes she brings less in her hand.

I. Let us examine this a little closer. Let us take an extreme case:—everything shall go as we wish; Balaam shall go with the princes of Moab; God shall give him his desire; he shall have his house full of silver and gold; he shall curse God's people; he shall turn to God; he shall be sorry; he shall repent; he shall "die the death of the righteous, his last end shall be like his."

Has Balaam lost nothing? has he craftily made the most of both worlds? Oh, no! he has lost happiness out of this life. If you want to make a man thoroughly miserable, give him his own way in everything. "He gave them their desire and sent leanness withal into their soul."[1] He has lost God's discipline. Oh, it is hard to bear. When life is covered with the cold snow, or biting frost, or the sharp wind blows upon it, or the driving rain beats upon it, or scorching sun dries it up, it is hard not to interfere, to leave it all in God's hands; but when we see "the peaceable fruit of righteousness,"[2] we remember no more the discipline of the time of sorrow. God grant that He may never give us a king in his anger, and take him away in his wrath.[3] God's chastisements, God's discipline withdrawn, is Balaam's distinct loss. And then again, is sin a pleasure—that heavy burden pressing down the soul? Is it a pleasure to be haunted with that sinful memory? to have scenes of past sin coming between us and everything else, "as obstinately as when we look through the window in a lighted room, the objects we turn our backs upon are still before us, instead of the grass and trees?"[4] Is it nothing to bear that schism in the body, to find all our slaves armed against us, our senses revolting in a civil war, to feel that craving after something, that thirst of sin, which makes men swallow the salt water of this world's sea in a thirst which God Himself would fain have satisfied?

And then, again, is it nothing to lose all the pleasures of religion, that satisfaction of the spirit, the highest part of our being? If there is a certain pleasure in satisfying the hungry appetite, if there is a real pleasure in satisfying the hungry mind, what must

[1] Psa. cvi. 15. [2] Heb. xii. 11.
[3] Hos. xiii. 11. [4] George Eliot.

be the pleasure of satisfying the spirit! Think what Holy Communion is to us! The sinner dare not come; Sunday after Sunday, day by day, he shrinks from it, to his distinct loss. "He that eateth me, even he shall live by me."[1] There is no growth, because there is no food. Think again what a blessing prayer is; but how can a man pray whose heart is not turned to the Lord? When he puts the incense into the censer there is no warm coal of devotion to kindle it; there is no sweet savour mounting up before the throne of God. Think what a blessing public prayer is, as we meet here in this beautiful house of God. Does a man lose nothing when, as he hears the bells ring out, he says, "Not to-day, I have bought the field, or go to prove the oxen, or have married the wife, and therefore I cannot come?" Oh, how often you have felt what a blessing it is to find here a sacrifice ready to your hand, to have come here in joy and in grief, in penitence and in thanksgiving! The sinner has lost all this; he has thrown it away. And we, if we hesitate, while we hesitate are losing the priceless gifts of God. They are going, fading away, while we hesitate; things which we should wish that we had brought with us at the last; they are going from us for ever.

Therefore, I say once more, is there anything which I ought to do? is there anything which I ought to give up? is there anything which I ought to make good? because, "Now is the accepted time," because, "now is the day of salvation."

[1] S. John vi. 57.

II. But I venture to say "now" once again, because if we delay we are not only losers in this world, but it is quite possible that we may be also losers in the next. If we put off the Lenten blessing, we are driving God's bounties from our very door; but are we also preparing for ourselves a lower place in heaven? Many of our divines tell us very seriously that from an examination of Holy Scripture it seems quite clear that all places are not equal in heaven. "In My Father's house are many mansions;"[1] the Apostles are to sit on thrones "judging the twelve tribes of Israel;"[2] there is a right hand and a left hand of the throne to be given to them for whom it is prepared of the Father;[3] some are rulers of five, some of ten cities.[4] In the resurrection of the dead, "one star differeth from another star in glory."[5]

And there is a great and terrible passage of Holy Scripture which fits in with these other indications. S. Paul speaks in the Epistle to the Corinthians in this way: "According to the grace of God which is given unto me, as a wise masterbuilder, I have laid the foundation, and another buildeth thereon. But let every man take heed how he buildeth thereupon. For other foundation can no man lay than that is laid, which is Jesus Christ. Now if any man build upon this foundation gold, silver, precious stones, wood, hay, stubble; every man's work shall be made manifest: for the day shall declare it, because it

---

[1] S. John xiv. 2.   [2] S. Matt. xix. 28.   [3] S. Matt. xx. 23.
[4] S. Luke xix. 17, 19.   [5] 1 Cor. xv. 41.

shall be revealed by fire; and the fire shall try every man's work of what sort it is. If any man's work abide which he hath built thereupon, he shall receive a reward. If any man's work shall be burned, he shall suffer loss: but he himself shall be saved; yet so as by fire;"[1]—the meaning being this: There is one foundation, Jesus Christ; many may build upon it. Some may put upon it gold, silver, precious stones, a good superstructure; some may put upon it wood, hay, stubble, a rotten superstructure; and that a fire is coming to test these buildings at the last day. And then, mark the words, "If any man's work shall be burned, he shall suffer loss: but he himself shall be saved; yet so as by fire." Even if we are saved, still if it should be that our work for God here is worthless, mere "wood, hay, stubble," we are saved at a fearful loss. Oh, think of "the losses of the saved!"[2] Think when we come before God with a wasted life. Think of the shame of seeing what we might have been, and then to know what we are! The grand foundation, the Church, our Baptism! our privileges! our education! And then to see some poor ignorant savage, whom we thought to be lost, preferred to us, and put first; all our life swept away as a gigantic failure! To see that ease, that enjoyment, that comfortable religion, and the labour of a lifetime turn out so much hay, and we ourselves saved, but so as by fire!

Then think of the reproach of Christ! Such a

---

[1] 1 Cor. iii. 10-15.
[2] Dr. Pusey, Lenten Sermons, between 1850 and 1874: "Losses of the Saved;" and Bishop Bull, Sermon vii.

foundation, and such results! Think what He has done! how He has tried to help our ignorance by the light of His truth! how He has strengthened our weakness! how He has wrestled with that deadly love of Egypt which stays our heavenly path! How He has prepared a table before us against them that trouble us, how He has anointed our head with oil, and our cup is full.[1] But for all that "saved so as by fire," our work burnt, and we ourselves suffering loss.

And further, this means, perhaps, actual pain and suffering which we are laying up in store for ourselves hereafter. Oh, not only because we are losers in this world, but because we may lose also in the next, we must, we who profess to be God's children, make our prayer unto Him in a time when He may be found, for in the great waterfloods they shall not come nigh Him.[2]

III. But I have said nothing as to the urgency[3] of these thoughts, which is brought home to us when we think that "now" is the only point that we can call our own. It often happens that the wheel of God's providence revolving round brings at one point, and at one only, the great opportunity within our reach which never comes again. It was so with Pontius Pilate; at one supreme moment in his life, he was brought face to face with truth. Then, or never! He hesitated; the wave which had carried him up to heaven, carried him down again to the deep; he lost his opportunity, and perished. It was

[1] Psa. xxiii. 5.   [2] Psa. xxxii. 7.
[3] Incertis de salute, de gloriâ minime certandum.

so with the penitent thief. The rough waves of trouble brought him close to mercy itself. He laid hold of the tree of salvation, as it was wafted by him, and was saved. Alas, it was so with the young nobleman. A grand opportunity came to him. Would he make the plunge? would he leave land and riches and position? would he trust himself to the unknown future of the cross? His lands, his wealth, his position sunk him. He stands in history as the instance of the great opportunity lost, the great refusal.

We cannot count on another Lent, on another week, on another Sunday. It was not long ago, in the London mission, that a woman was found dead with this resolution written on her table: "I will turn to God this day month." This was erased, and in its place was written, "I will turn to God this day week." But too late; that night her soul was required of her. "Now is the accepted time. Now is the day of salvation." Oh, let us not be losers by delay. While we linger, opportunities, blessings, rewards, dignities are slipping by. "Death approaches, time flies. O Christian, why dost thou loiter?"

SERMON XIII.

The Religion of the Body.

"*I beseech you therefore, brethren, by the mercies of God, that ye present your bodies a living sacrifice, holy, acceptable unto God, which is your reasonable service.*"—ROM. xii. 1.

IN this chapter of the Epistle to the Romans, the Apostle enters upon the second half of his treatise, which contains his precepts on Christian morality, its obligations and its difficulties. And he commences in this verse by showing the Christian's duty as regards his body. And note, that it is evidently an important subject, both from the way in which it is introduced, "I beseech you, brethren, by the mercies of God," and also from the terms in which he clothes his precept, the Christian must consecrate his body, it must be a sacrifice to God, not a slain sacrifice, like those offered under the Old Testament, but living; not an offering offensive to God, such as those of which we read, "Thinkest thou that I will eat bull's flesh, or drink the blood of goats?" but a sacrifice well-pleasing, acceptable unto Him; and this not a mere external, mechanical asceticism, but a reasonable service, that is offered willingly, intelligently, and religiously to God, by the soul, the spirit, and the will. Let us think, then, a little to-day, if you will, about the body.

I. The Christian's relation to his body is a great, a stupendous, nay, in some ways, an inexplicable question. But in attempting to arrive at a right estimate of the subject, there is one thing which we should notice most carefully, as a great and important fact, and that is, that Christianity takes the body into its most serious and earnest consideration. It uses the body, it dignifies the body, it preserves the body, yes, in one sense, it immortalizes the body. And therefore, it is most necessary that we should guard ourselves against a false spirituality, which finds favour in some quarters. Christianity is not entirely a spiritual religion; Christianity is not entirely an intellectual religion, like a philosophy. It is the religion of man, and so makes proper provision in its Divine economy for the body of man.

And this is remarkable, because when Christ came on earth to found His kingdom, we might call the prevailing religion of the day the worship of the body, whether under the guise of beauty of form, as in the splendid monuments of Greek art; or of material power, as manifested in the iron Roman empire; or of sensuality, dominant all through the world. But when He came to deliver man, He passed by the nature of angels,[1] He came not as an angel, a phantom, or a spirit, but took upon Him our flesh, "and

[1] Heb. ii. 16.

was made man;" and somewhere now in glory is His body. And further, although seeing all around him the love of what was coarse, and material, and sensual, He did not say to His followers, " Crush your body," "ignore it," "neglect it," "trample on it;" "the spiritual part of man is all in all, his body is a prison, a burden, a defilement." No, in Christianity the body is treated with honour, with reverence, with respect, if at the same time with anxiety and repression. It forms far too important an element of our composite life, it is far too subtly bound up with the mind and spirit, far too great a help or hindrance, as the case may be, to be neglected; therefore it would seem to be almost a summary of the Christian's attitude towards the body, when the Apostle says, Glorify God in your body, as well as in the spirit, which are God's.

II. Let us look at this a little closer. Apart from its corruptions and defects, if there was no pain, and no sin, and no disfigurement, we should all agree that what we call the human body, is one of the most beautiful works of God. Yes, let us gratefully go with the Greek sculptor in his splendid art, and see in the human form, in its strength, its features, its play, the stamp of God, the image and likeness of the Creator. Let us go with the anatomist; and in bone and muscle and fibre, in sense and organ, trace the marvellous adaptation of means to end. Let us go with the philosopher and learn our lesson from the symbolism of the body, let us see the many members working out the good of the whole being. Let us trace with him the educational powers of the body as it conveys to the mind, at the lips of its five messengers, the senses, the materials which go to form the great book of experience. Let us trace with him its moral usefulness in developing the will, while the temptation, nay, the inclination to brutality is constantly checked by the governing power within, so leading to temperance, fortitude, prudence, justice, to what we call in one word, strength of character, while we see the very passions in their violent force, thrown, checked and regulated, into the great motive energy of life. Just as the mighty powers of fire and steam, water and air, are curbed and harnessed to the service of man, forgetting their fury under the regulating, guiding hand of science.

But let us go with Christ even further still. Let us recognize in the body "the temple of the Holy Ghost," "our members as instruments of righteousness unto God." A body alive with His life; a body fed by that Divine Sacrament which is to "preserve both body and soul unto everlasting life;" a body which through touch and taste, and sight and smell, is ever bringing in gold, frankincense, and myrrh to Him, Who sits within, receiving the adoration of each day's experience.

Ah, we know how body and soul are knit together; we know how the character from within shines through the body. We all know the dull, stupid, besotted look on the face of the sensualist, where the soul is overmastered by the body; we all know the sharp, quick, intelligent glow which lights up the countenance of a man of intellect, where the mind illuminates the face, and perhaps we know the bright and heavenly expression such as the old masters loved to paint, where the soul breaks through the earthen vessel, and shines with a light which Christ Himself has kindled. Yes, most assuredly, the body "within which I make a shadow" is a faithful reflector of the life within, acting and reacting upon it, and as Christians we will not part with our bodies, while we are moving here in the discipline of life.

III. And this subject has a very important bearing on what we may call, perhaps, the great lesson of the Epiphany[1]—worship. It was for this that the wise men tracked the star through the desert, braving ignominy, scorn, and difficulty—it was simply to worship. No mere satisfaction of an idle curiosity, no mere solution of a curious problem, no petition for themselves or for others brought them to Jesus—they came to worship.

And this is a subject which we ought to consider carefully in all its bearings. What part does the body play in worship? For when we come to church, or when we kneel down at home to say our prayers, we do not divest ourselves of our feelings or of our senses; we cannot make ourselves pure intelligences or simple spirits; but we come, as God expects us to come, with our bodies, as One Who bade us, through His Apostle, present our bodies a living sacrifice, holy, acceptable unto Him. We cannot divest ourselves of them, even if we would. See, for instance, how bodily

[1] Preached on the first Sunday after the Epiphany.

weariness will make itself felt, and soon dim the intelligence, while it vainly struggles against it. See how bodily distraction, much more bodily pain, will altogether drive away the higher faculties from their work. See how dependent men sometimes become on the surroundings of religious worship, so as to be distracted by the presence or absence of certain outward accessories of Divine service.

And, knowing this, who can doubt the wisdom of the Church in appealing to the bodily senses to help the flagging soul? we know the power of association; how certain scenes seem to carry with them appeals which affect us as deeply as if they were visibly stamped and impressed upon them. Certain places, views, and landscapes seem eloquent with voices which cannot be stilled. And so the Church surrounds us with associations of worship, to remind us insensibly of God; we learn to worship where everything reminds us of religion. Or you have felt the power of music, such as is shadowed forth in the fable of Orpheus; the Church has enlisted music to draw our hearts to God. Or you have felt the ennobling power of art; in painting, sculpture, architecture, and beautiful forms; the Church has enlisted art to make the place of God's feet glorious; accessories, if you will, dumb accessories, misleading accessories, if we stop there; but all recognizing the power of the senses to assist the soul. And why, if I find them a help in life; why, if I find them a help to banish care, or to elevate the mind or the soul; why, if I look upon them as great and Divine products of human genius—

why should I be called upon to lay aside all this beautiful side of my earthly nature, so elevating and so helpful, when I come before the God of beauty to perform that most difficult of all tasks—to worship?

But there is a lower and more practical estimate still than this. The body, from its subtle intertwining with the soul, has the most marvellous effect upon it. We all know how the mind affects the body; in a similar way the body affects the mind. For instance, when I kneel down, I thereby place myself in a posture of humble adoration before God. Is it an indifferent thing, then, whether I kneel or not? Let doctors and philosophers answer, not theologians only. They will tell you "that between the postures of the body and the successive emotions of the soul there is an intimate correspondence; that you cannot as a matter of fact feel in your inward soul a sinner's self-abasement before the sanctity of God, while you lounge back in a chair, with your arms across, and with eyes gazing unthinkingly on any object that may meet them."[1] Kneeling, standing, bowing, as we do in different parts of our service, are all outward helps to inward devotion, helps which the poor body gives to the soul to recognize the presence of the King of kings.

IV. But there is one aspect of this subject which still needs to be considered, and that is, the dignity of the body, arising from that great truth embodied in the last clauses of the creed: "I believe in the resurrection of the body and the life everlasting."

[1] See "The Guidance of the Star." Christmastide Sermon by Dr. Liddon, p. 366.

We must not stop to speculate now, how, why, or in what way, this shall be, or try to understand something of the marvellous revelations of S. Paul as to the resurrection body, or attempt to follow him when he says our Lord Jesus Christ shall change our vile body, that it may be fashioned like unto His glorious body, according to the working whereby He is able even to subdue all things unto Himself.[1] We will assume, as surely we may do, in the presence of those who heartily accept the Creed, that the body will be joined to the soul again at the great resurrection. If this be so, oh, what a call to us to reverence that everlasting companion! to reverence the body with all its hopes! Oh, we know the awful nature of sins of the body; awful in their prevalence, awful in their nature, awful in their punishment! If this body of beauty, of adapted design, of spiritual indwelling, is not to suffer, not to be punished, here and hereafter, it must be reverenced, cherished, kept holy.

Here, in its acute susceptibilities, it is a terrible witness to sin original and actual; *there* we read of the worm that dieth not, and the fire that never shall be quenched.[2]

And if we reverence it in life, let us also reverence it in death. The Christian funeral should be ever a solemn and a holy act; and men must not be surprised if we think of something else beside sanitary requirements in the disposal of our dead. Cremation was the common pagan custom, and a custom which was viewed by the early Christians with abhorrence, for

[1] Phil. iii. 20, 21.   [2] S. Mark ix. 43, 44.

this very reason, that they reverenced the body. Cremation is twice mentioned in the Bible; the bodies of Saul and his sons were burned after their savage mutilation; but only apparently as a sad necessity, to save further indignities. And in the book of Amos it is said, "And a man's uncle shall take him up, and he that burneth him,"[1] this being viewed as part of the melancholy curse predicted by him, that a man should not have a decent burial, but be burned. Certainly, if only we would view the body as God would lead us to view it in His Holy Word, if we would remember that He has for ever dignified it by His glorious Incarnation, we should in life and in death treat it with reverence and respect. In this body, in its powers and senses, there are helps or hindrances to the soul; in this body I may recognize the shrine and temple of the Holy Ghost; in its lusts and passions a discipline of the will. I would present it therefore a living sacrifice, holy, acceptable unto God. For if He has saved my soul, and quickened my life, and trained my will; He is the Saviour also of the body.[2] And in the same Creed wherein I own my belief in His glory and power and might, in the power of the Holy Father, in the love of the Blessed Son, in the sanctity of the Holy Spirit, I add to my faith in Him a glorious and a solemn faith about myself—I believe in the resurrection of the body.

[1] See Dr. Pusey, "Minor Prophets," Amos vi. 10.
[2] Eph. v. 23.

SERMON XIV.

The Creature.

"*For the earnest expectation of the creature waiteth for the manifestation of the sons of God. For the creature was made subject to vanity, not willingly, but by reason of Him Who hath subjected the same in hope.*"—Rom. viii. 19, 20.

IT is impossible to read this passage in S. Paul's epistle without feeling that we are touching on most deep and mysterious ground, a ground where human understanding can but grope in the dark, and feel its way by an indication here and an indication there, and at last only lose its track and stop short. S. Paul is speaking of the surroundings in which we live, which he calls "the *creature*," or more literally "the creation," namely this material visible world. He tells us—what is indeed not hard to see— that there is a doom of *failure*[1] hanging over the world; or, as we here translate the word, *vanity*— great possibilities destined never to be realized, great fruitfulness choked with weeds, pain fastening with corroding tooth on life and vigour, earthquakes and storms and volcanoes desolating the earth; a great

[1] ματαιότης.

wail of pain and incompleteness and aimless effort going on all around us. We see it in the waste of life, in the pain which animals suffer, in the degeneracy of earth's fruitfulness without tillage, and in what we are accustomed to call "fallen nature." S. Paul says this is the result of the fall. These are the lines of pain and care furrowed on the brow of the material world; these are the chains which Adam's sin imposed upon an unwilling creation; these are the groanings and pangs of the creature which interpenetrate with the sorrow and sin of man.

But he would point out here, or rather guide our eyes into the region of a mysterious possibility, that, if the lower creation shares thus in man's fall, if the ground has been cursed for the sin of man, yet that the creature has its mysterious longing and expectation of better things, that, "while faith in the form of belief to the Christian, and dim intuitions to the heathen, is the prerogative of the rational creature, *hope* is the gift that has not been denied to the irrational creation. Hope is common to all."[1] Hope binds nature and mankind in a close and enduring union; and therefore man, with his great longings, his implanted certainty of immortality, is supported by a hoping world, which, having shared not willingly in man's fall, may share too somewhat in the new heaven and new earth, wherein dwelleth righteousness,[2] when those mysterious times of restitution shall have come—in the days of the regeneration.

[1] "Destiny of the Creature." Sermons by the Lord Bishop of Gloucester, 1865, pp. 15, 16.   [2] S. Pet. iii. 13.

I. If we shrink from drawing out S. Paul's words to their full conclusion, if we see in their depth and indefiniteness an indication and a warning not to follow him any further, yet the hope stamped on the waiting world all around us is not without its influence on our Christian life. For, I suppose, that just as he who goes about doing good, who ministers to the sick, who relieves the poor, who teaches the ignorant, who guides the blind, who rescues the sinner, recovers the fallen, restores the penitent, is carrying out the blessings which God conferred upon the world when He sent His dear Son to teach men to love one another and to do good, so he who does anything to help progress, who does anything to alleviate pain, who draws out the powers of this earth, who grapples with diseases and death, who strikes out new beauties of form and combinations of colour, fresh charms of sound and melody, who does anything to develop this earth and its resources, is really carrying out His will, Who came to restore the world from its fallen state and stamped anew on creation the hope which animates it, until there comes the complete freedom from the bondage of corruption in the glorious liberty of the children of God.

The Church of Christ can never be at war with progress; she views with no jealous eye the discoveries of science. If electricity can be captured and trained to our service, if the sun is to paint our portraits, if steam is to supplement and almost supersede labour, if history can be found and deciphered, which is written on the rocks, if the possibilities and hopes of material progress are well-nigh inexhaustible, this does but add to the Christian joy; part of the failure, part of the vanity, is being removed from the earth; something of that wailing is being hushed, something of that sweet longing is being gratified. Only—man must retain his supremacy. As the free will of man was conquered in the garden by the fruit of a tree—as earthly possessions and earthly possibilities have over and over again driven out the heavenly hopes—so, if God's testimony in the rocks is to be quoted against His testimony in the written word, this is a hindrance; if earthly prosperity and material advance are to keep us down to this earth, instead of lifting us up to Heaven, this is a snare. People who take a superficial view, say, "You are giving man too much education, you are forcing him to develop his powers at too great a speed." But man will not find God by stinting his intellect. God does not want mutilated slaves to enjoy His creation, but those who have full power to speak, only with the will to restrain themselves. We cannot find God by looking downwards, but by ever pressing upwards. If God has given you a mind, develop it; if God has given you earthly prosperity, cultivate it, make the most of it. But as God has given you a soul, let that ever have the mastery—free, emancipated, unencumbered with the burden of corruption, which weighs down the travailing creation, even under the ennobling aspiration of hope.

II. But if S. Paul hints at the glorious destiny of the creature, at the beauty of even a fallen world, yet at the same time he paints in strong colours the depths of its misery, when he speaks of failure, and bondage, and corruption, suggesting aimless suffering, which is its lot. It is the great privilege and blessing of man that he can utilize suffering. S. Paul is, in fact, answering here a tacit objection on the part of the Jews. "If you Christians were right, you would not suffer so much as you do; the Jews are God's favoured people; did He not say of them, 'All people of the earth shall see that thou art called by the name of the Lord;'[1] whereas you Christians are the offscouring of the earth, hated by God and man." And S. Paul is saying that this is not a fair estimate, that suffering is not a thing to be ashamed of, but rather that it plays an important part in the Christian life, that it is part of our fall, which the lower creation shares with us; the difference being, that man can suffer with Christ, that to him suffering can be made remedial, helpful, useful, while it is but a "blow without a word" to the creature. And indeed it is very important that we should give suffering its proper place. Ours is not the aimless agony of the creature, not the vanity, not the bondage of corruption; but it is suffering with Christ—a filling up that which is behind of His afflictions,[2] a contribution to a world's expiation. And I suppose that every one of us is prepared for suffering in some way or another— whether it be the sharp pain which racks our sensitive bodies, or the sudden accident which paralyses our self-reliance, and opens our eyes to the immense forces which are whirling and revolving around our lives, or

[1] Deut. xxviii. 10. [2] Col. i. 24.

rejection at the hands of our fellow-men, or the failure of our cherished schemes, or the manifold disappointments of life. These are common to us all. But have we learnt to utilize them? Do we remember that we have more than hope for the future; that we have faith in the present? As we see how persistently God is working at the formation of our character, how He wrestles with us, crushing Balaam's rebellious foot against the wall, dashing down David's cup of successful vice, violently wrenching round the fanaticism of Saul into the groove of Christian zeal, let us ask what is suffering doing for us? The daily knocking of fatigue, with its warning voice, we, "as soon as we were born, began to draw to our end;"[1] the *warnings* of suffering—the daily crossing of the will, which forces into play the latent virtue, which makes us use with painfulness and difficulty that weak and broken limb of our character which we should shrink from exercising; the *discipline* of suffering—the consolations of the Church, the voice of the beloved, the form of the Crucified hanging at our side, as we suffer justly the due reward of our sins;[2] the *Divine comfort* of suffering—what are we doing with all this, the loving chastisement of God? Oh, if it is sent as a curse upon the creature from which hope delivers it, it is a blessing to us, which faith intensifies—"Joint heirs with Christ; if so be that we suffer with Him, that we may be also glorified together."[3]

III. And there is just one thought more. Are we taking our proper place at the head of creation?

[1] Wisd. v. 13. [2] S. Luke xxiii. 41. [3] Rom. viii. 17.

Hope should play its part with us, just as it does with the lower creation? We all recognize the power of hope. We trace its energy in the enterprise and speculation of the commercial world; we see fresh powers and latent capabilities bursting into life under its magic touch. As emulation opens up the horizon which has bounded hitherto the field of vision, obstacles melt away, difficulties vanish, before a hope which refuses to understand the meaning of the word "impossible." But there is also a spiritual vigour in hope, which invests it with a power and value of its own. How many sit down before the royal gates, and think that its bounty and riches and blessing is not for them. How many give in beaten and vanquished in the long battle of life, and think that, because the Philistine has insulted the host of God for forty days, defeat and misery must be always their portion. Oh, there is an energy in the mere hope of victory. The fresh dawn, the new day, the recurring seasons of the year, by the very breaks which they bring in the monotony of life, come to us charged with this energy of hope.[1] Things may be better. "He will not alway be chiding, neither keepeth He His anger for ever."[2] Hope lifts up our head out of the prison house. Hope refuses to bind our soul down to the earth. Hope remains to us a glorious gift, when trouble and sorrow and misery fly with desolating grief across our soul.

Yes, if the creature looks out of his bondage in hope, much more should man, who to hope can add

---

[1] See Dr. Pusey, "Nine Addresses," Ser. 1, p. 5.
[2] Psa. ciii. 9.

faith, be able to face life, with all its difficulties, however dark it may seem to be.

Oh, if we did but put forth all our powers! If we did but move once more, like Adam, erect and free amidst the creation around us! But one thing is certain—we live in the midst of mysteries; the Fall has laid its hand on us, and on the lower creation also; but while faith lights up our path and shows us whither it tends, we are saved by hope,[1] a hope which in some sense is shared by the lower creation as well.

[1] Rom. viii. 24.

SERMON XV.

Church Restoration.

"*The glory of this latter house shall be greater than of the former, saith the Lord of Hosts: and in this place will I give peace, saith the Lord of Hosts.*"—HAGG. ii. 9.

THAT was a wondrous rebuilding, of which Haggai was the prophet! The heathen king, Cyrus, moved by the power of God, had given an order for the rebuilding of Jerusalem. Everything seemed working round in its ordered course to the consummation of this object, until difficulties arose which seemed well nigh insurmountable. First, those who should have been most forward in accepting the invitation hung back; some despaired; everything was laid waste—the walls, the temple, the altar—what could they do? Others preferred their ease and comfort, their ceiled houses, their prosperity and their sin. Of the twenty-four orders of priests, only four returned, and of the Levites, only seventy-four men. It was but a remnant who returned, and some of them timid and half-hearted.[1]

[1] See Dr. Pusey on Hagg. ii., and Introduction to the book.

And besides all these difficulties from within, there was misrepresentation and hostility from without, at the hand of the Samaritans. Further still, God was angry with His people; they laboured without His blessing, the crops failed, His wrath was abroad, on every side there was gloom and despair.

But in the midst of this an earnest preacher of repentance was raised up, the prophet Haggai, and he, by warning, by encouragement, and by blessing, urged them on to their great undertaking. The work was begun, the foundations were laid, and the temple began to rise with this blessing upon it, "The latter glory of the house shall be greater than the former, saith the Lord of hosts."

I. And you will see that many of these difficulties, which threatened to hinder the rising of the temple, were sentimental ones. Sentiment was at the bottom of most of the obstacles. The people could not face the thought of what the rebuilding meant, the trouble, the self-denial, the opposition. The baser natures preferred, as of old, the inglorious fleshpots to a self-sacrificing patriotism. Prejudice and jealousy and wild suspicion stirred up their old enemies, the Samaritans; and when the work was now fairly commenced, and so many difficulties had been overcome, the voice of weeping mingles with the shouts of praise, as the foundation of the new structure was laid. Impotent regret "folded the wings of hope." They wept for a material glory, for the gold, the silver, the precious stones, which had once made their temple magnificent, for lost opportunities and forfeited blessings. But braver was the courage and joy of men like Haggai, who, having seen the first temple and entered into its true glories, yet stifled the sighs of grief for a glory which sin had cast away, and threw themselves with the ever-reviving energy of hope into the rejuvenescence of God's covenanted blessing. For God had told him, speaking to his heart, "The silver is mine, and the gold is mine, saith the Lord of Hosts;"[1] for the glory of His house, He needed not silver or gold; "If I be hungry I will not tell thee, for the whole world is Mine, and all that is therein."[2] Think not the temple inglorious because it lacks silver and gold; Mine is the silver, and Mine is the gold, saith the Lord of Hosts; I seek rather true worshippers; with these I will gild the temple, and the latter glory of this house shall be greater than the former. It was the same temple in the eyes of God, but the Desire of all nations Himself should come to it, in these latter days; "and in this place will I give peace, saith the Lord of Hosts."

II. And sentiment, dear friends, is a dangerous thing. It does so little good, it may do so much harm. We must not despise it, in its proper province, and in its own place. I know it breathes through patriotism, and gives us the hero, who dies content if he can save the honour of his country, if it be but to rescue a piece of silk, the colours of a regiment, upon which a public sentiment has fastened a nation's reputation. I know it softens the rough blows of opposition, the chilling scorn of indifference, the lower

[1] Hagg. ii. 8.   [2] Psa. l. 12.

materialism of a practical worldliness; an enthusiasm lifts the zealot up to that commanding position, from which he carries all before him. I know the intense force with which certain surroundings of life seem, as nothing else can, to draw out the deep vibrating chords of our nature, in the marvellous power of association. I know, I value, dear friends, the heartiness and the joy, which has carried us along through the anxieties, the fatigues and the labour of this rebuilding.[1] But let us remember that, if we are elevated, lifted up from the earth by a great bound of thankfulness, something else will be needed to keep us poised in devotion before the unapproachable God. It was not the absence of material glory in the new temple which should have made the old men weep, it was not the rising walls which should have made the young men shout; the house of God consisted not really in the former magnificence, nor in the latter revival. The temple of God was one, through all the apparent changes of outer accidents. God needed neither silver nor gold to perfect His worship; and in His eyes, and with His blessing, the latter glory of the house would be greater than the former, inasmuch as it would be blessed even more by the immediate presence of the Divine glory.

Ah, yes, there is a real danger of losing ourselves in sentiment nowadays. Sentiment says of God's temples, they are architectural studies, and nothing more; not a stone shall be touched, lest you impair

[1] Preached on the Sunday in the festival of the reopening of S. Matthias Church, Malvern Link, 1881.

the history of the development of architecture. Sentiment says the churches of our land are historical shrines, records written in stones; not a timber must be moved, not a defect repaired. You are disturbing history; you are rooting up associations; you are disturbing those ties which link us to the past. Ah, perhaps some are weeping to-day in their inmost hearts, at the severance of those bonds of old associations, which gathered round the former church, familiar to them and dear. And from my heart I should sympathize with you, did I not hear through it all that echo which lingers on, even as affection, or interest, or sacred ties, or past offerings, seem to have claimed the temple. "*Mine, Mine,*" saith the Lord of Hosts. It is God's house after all. If architecture, or historical associations, or gold, or silver, or old memories, overshadow and dwarf the first purpose of a temple, which is *worship,* then God is preparing to leave it. Just as He said of old, "The silver is Mine, and the gold is Mine," so now He will say, "The association is Mine, the architecture is Mine, the history is Mine." "The latter glory of this house shall be greater than the former."

But on what conditions?

III. The better Jews knew that this house lacked yet its true glory; they built, and they waited, but the prophesied blessing came not. There were five things wanting now,[1] which they had gloried in before. There was the Ark, the mysterious dwelling-place of God; the Urim and Thummim, by which

[1] See Dr. Edersheim, "The Temple," p. 39.

God revealed Himself to the High Priest; the Sacred Fire, kindled by God Himself in the tabernacle, kept ever burning while the tabernacle stood, and rekindled in Solomon's temple; the Shechinah, manifesting forth the visible presence of God; and the abiding power of the Holy Ghost in the spirit of prophecy. This was the true magnificence of the temple of old,—the presence of God; this is its true magnificence now, this was its value to you before,—the presence of God. These ornaments are nothing without the five treasures—the Altar of God, the revealed Will, the fire of His Grace, the veil of His sacramental Presence, the quickening power of the Holy Ghost. For this the feebler natures wept, the stronger natures waited, to see the breaking in of the light, which heralded the approach of the latter glory, promised to the temple of God, as yet chill and bare without it.

And when it came, when that holy Mother entered the temple to purify herself and to present the great First-born to the Lord, where were the Jews? An old man, worn out with waiting; an old woman who lingered in the courts of the Lord; these, as far as we know, represented the multitude whose shouts then rent the air; these were alone ready to receive the glory so long promised, when the Lord Whom they sought so suddenly came to His temple. Or, again, in the holy procession down the slopes of Olivet; in the ass's colt; in the hymning children; in the humble Apostles, who recognized the returning fire? The King, Whose throne should be the altar; the King, Whose wisdom should again speak through the Church;

the King, Whose atoning blood should be the fire of the sacrifice; the King, Who should again dwell between the cherubim; the King, Who should reveal to us His mysteries through the power of the Holy Ghost?

Ah! dear friends, you know now how He comes, in quiet and in peace; you know if your heart is elevated by the outer magnificence of the Church how it soon droops; you know if you are lifted up in worship how you need some support; you know that Christ comes still in the hidden mysteries of His Sacraments; in the quiet of your own devotions; in the fire of His Holy Spirit coursing through your hearts. This is the latter glory of His house, the Church; this will be the glory of this renewed Church, if we use it aright,—the abiding presence and power of Jesus Christ.

IV. "And in this place will I give peace, saith the Lord of Hosts." Oh, blessed words! As we see the world tossing around us, the nations furiously raging, the people imagining a vain thing,[1] to be able to rest our eyes on God's Word, firm and strong, unmoved amidst the tumult, to see God at rest, fashioning the hearts of kings, and turning them whither He will. As we see the Church rent and torn and tempest-driven, to find underneath it all the calm still waters of the Creed, to be able to say, "Lord, Thou hast been our refuge from one generation to another."[2] As we find our hearts racked and convulsed with pain and weariness, to be able to find

[1] Psa. ii. 1.   [2] Psa. xc. 1.

within these very walls rest unto our souls. Oh, what a blessing if this house can be a house of peace; if the Son of Peace be here; if His peace be resting on it; if in the fulness of its meaning, in this place He vouchsafes to give peace, Who is the Lord of Hosts.

Oh, dear friends, it is time for us to give up sentiment; to push by our first enthusiasm and joy; to brush past the praise of friends and the criticism of enemies; to put on one side our rejoicings in the new and our regrets for the old, and see what is the glory of this house; to seek for the presence of God until we find it, and to seek for this alone: His presence in these buildings; His presence in the Sacraments; His presence in the Bible; His presence in the services. Rest not until you find Him; rest not until you can say, "O God, Thou art my God." Ah, many of us who remember the former house may perhaps be weeping—weeping for the old days of childhood, when we first came hither; weeping for friends now no longer with us whose tender care brought us here; weeping for the ardour of our first Communion; weeping for those "days of the Son of Man;"[1] weeping for the days of innocence, when the Good Shepherd carried us in His arms. But braver and truer is it to shout, if it be with a broken heart, for God's new mercies, as we see the Shoulders bent down and the Good Shepherd leaning over us, His brow scarred, His hands bleeding with thorns and briars; if the glory of innocence was great, the glory of penitence

[1] S. Luke xvii. 22.

shall be greater. If the Good Shepherd carries the lambs in His arms, He also carries the lost sheep upon His shoulders. "And in this house will I give peace"—peace amid doubt and difficulty and sorrow. This house shall indeed be Jacob's ladder; its foot shall rest here, at our weary head, its top shall reach beyond the clouds, where He dwells Who is our Peace. And there indeed the Lord will wait that He may be gracious unto us,[1] and God, even our own God, shall give us His blessing.[2]

[1] Isa. xxx. 18. [2] Psa. lxvii. 6.

SERMON XVI.

Care.

"*Casting all your care upon Him; for He careth for you.*"—
1 S. PETER v. 7.

WHAT is care? Something, I suppose, which gets its name from lying very near to the *heart*;[1] the heart which fears, the heart which feels, the heart which plans. And there is a good care and a bad care; a distinction which you will have noticed already. There is a care which, as here, is man's natural tendency; which we know better under the name of *anxiety*; a torturing, disabling, agonizing care. And there is a care which is one of the great attributes of God, of Whom men speak sometimes as care personified, when they speak of Him as *Providence,* Who in calm and certain omnipotence deliberates and plans and has a care for us. And following the words of S. Peter as they were written, we find this distinction in the very passage before us, which might be rendered, " casting all your *anxiety* upon Him, for He has a care for you."[2]

[1] Care is derived probably from the Greek τῆρ, the heart.
[2] πᾶσαν τὴν μέριμναν ὑμῶν ἐπιρρίψαντες ἐπ᾽ αὐτὸν ὅτι αὐτῷ μέλει περὶ ὑμῶν.

And now another thought arises. Where does *anxiety* come from? Does God send it? Is it one of His chastisements, like sickness, sorrow or bereavement? "A life of constant anxiety"—we often hear of this. Where does it come from, from God or from man? Must we not answer, from man himself? God sends trouble, sorrow, sickness, difficulty, doubt; man converts them into anxiety; that is, he lets these different burdens settle upon his mind, until they divide it, cut it into pieces (such is the meaning of the word),[1] so that the poor sufferer cannot bring his whole being to bear on anything. He cannot face to-morrow; he is too anxious. He cannot pray; he is too anxious. He cannot enjoy the present; he is too anxious.

Oh, it is a terrible scourge which men lay upon themselves, so common, so persistent, as it is! The gray hairs, the furrowed brow, the listless eyes, all tell the tale of the dissecting knife of anxiety, which is cutting the heart in two. But it need not be there; that is the sad part, or, perhaps, the happy part. Man is born to trouble, but not to anxiety. For has not our Blessed Lord Himself said, "Be not therefore anxious for the morrow,"[2] "Come unto Me all ye that labour and are heavy laden, and I will give you rest"?[3] Are we not told again, "Be careful for nothing"?[4] So that perhaps, as in Holy Scripture there is a cure for so many ills, there is a cure for this too. Perhaps these very words contain the secret which many a sore heart and throbbing brow is

---

[1] μερίμνη, from μερίζω, to divide into different parts.
[2] S. Matt. vi. 34.   [3] S. Matt. xi. 28.   [4] Phil. iv. 6.

seeking for. Certainly one who could charm men out of anxiety would draw the world after him, entranced with the sweetness of his song.

I. The advice given us here, then, is "cast it out," rather "transfer it," rather "throw it down upon God."[1] Day by day the business of a world is being administered from the council of Heaven. Day by day the invitation goes out for more work. Bring your care and throw it down upon the other business which is being transacted there, and leave it. For your necessities are at this moment occupying the attention of Heaven.

What, then, is our anxiety?

(1) In the first place, whether consciously or unconsciously, every man is anxious about himself, his true self, his soul. What of the past, that mysterious and awful region of the past, which cannot be forgotten? "The hours waste away and are reckoned to our account."[2] The past—where has it gone to? Those wasted hours, those evil deeds, those sins with others. "God requireth that which is past."[3]

Or the present again. Am I doing what I ought? Is my life preparing me for heaven? Is my soul receiving its proper nourishment? Will this temptation overwhelm me? How shall I escape from it? Or the future. What is to become of me when I die? What about that great eternity, the state beyond the grave? These are all questions which beat down upon a man and frighten him, while they demand an

---

[1] This is the meaning of the word used here, ἐπιρρίπτειν.
[2] "Pereunt horæ et imputantur."   [3] Eccles. iii. 15.

answer. And, of course, there are different remedies. Indifference will shut out the past; unbelief will push aside the present; and recklessness will hide the future. But this is only for a time. Repentance will cast the burden of the past upon God, and rise with a lightened burden. Faith will seek God in present trouble, and return with help and peace. Hope will face the future, moving step by step, one day at a time; one day's cares, one day's victories, one day's grace, leading on to the next; and so going from strength to strength will reach forth unto the God of gods in Sion.[1] Do not stifle conscience in this respect, dear friends; do not stop its cries. But let it bring you to God, Who will turn anxiety into holy fear.

(2) But of late years, at all events, these harvest thanksgiving services[2] have been of a very mixed character. Perhaps no life is made up of such constant anxiety (as the world counts anxiety) as the lives of those who depend almost entirely upon the influence of climate and season, and other things so utterly beyond their control, for the welfare of their bodily estate, for their subsistence and earthly comfort. The worries of life—how to live, how to get on, how to face what is called misfortune; life, with its terrible uncertainties, its strange contradictions, its awful separations, its pains and aches, and accidents and losses; it is the anxiety of life which weighs people down. You must have known some, perhaps several,

[1] Psa. lxxxiv. 7.
[2] This sermon was preached on the occasion of a harvest thanksgiving during a bad season.

to whom these last seasons have meant simple ruin.
All classes have felt it; even now a better harvest
will scarcely serve to extricate many. Is there any
remedy for this? Can I bring my empty purse, my long
arrears, my impending liabilities, my losses, and cast
them down upon God? My brethren, one thing is
quite clear. In these things He does care; He is
caring for you. For, think, we must have some
trouble; and the tree out of which your cross is cut
is most often grown on your own estate. The rich
man's cross comes in the way of his wealth; the poor
man's in his poverty; the farmer's in his trade.
Here is his cross; and is it not to be taken up?

If any man will come after Christ, there must be
the cross; and to those who walk with Him, and who
follow in His footsteps, God gives freedom, calm, and
peace. For, first of all, He gives experience. Those
memories of outlived sorrows in ourselves, and in the
book of experience unfolded in the life of others.
And then He gives "toil and sympathy,"[1] the two
best earthly comforts to mourners—we can still
work, and we are conscious of hearts that beat with
our heart in joy and sorrow—and then He gives
strength with which to meet our difficulties. Just as
we read in the book of Esther, when the massacre of
the Jews had been determined upon,[2] Esther obtained
favour from the king to avert it. But what was to be
done? "The law of the Medes and Persians, altereth
not." Although the attack on the Jews could not be

---

[1] Schiller, quoted in the Memoir of Catherine Tait.
[2] Esther iii. 7.

counter-ordered, yet the Jews were allowed to *defend* themselves, and a massacre was turned into a victory. So it is with us. God will not drive away our enemies altogether; but He will give us strength with which to defend ourselves, so that in the vigour and honour and peace which comes from the victory, we can, with the apostle, count it all joy when we fall into divers temptations.[1] And so some have felt this blessing; some have called out in the fulness of their consolation, "What a cross to have no cross!" because they found that, having cast all their care upon God, He was caring for them all the time in the fulness of heavenly love.

Yes, He means us to go travelling on. What if His steps lead up the Mount of Sacrifice! What if we look anxiously at the fire and the knife, and say, "Where is the lamb for a burnt offering?"[2] And the thought forces itself upon us that we are the sacrifice! Still we must keep step with God our Father. "They went both of them together."[3] Step by step, day by day, walking with God. The future is hidden; the gloomy to-day may be sunshine to-morrow. We must go on step by step. There is a ram caught by his horns in the thicket somewhere. God can do anything. God loves me more than I love myself. God cannot wish, or allow anything really to hurt me. For He has commanded with His own mouth, "Have no anxiety for the morrow." He has bid me pray, "Give us *this day* our daily bread,"[4]

---

[1] S. James i. 2.
[2] Gen. xxii. 7.
[3] Gen. xxii. 6.
[4] S. Matt. vi. 11.

without looking forward to the morrow. And if there be anyone here who on this day of glad thanksgiving has come with a heavy heart because times are bad, and troubles are thick, and cares are many; if anxiety is clouding the brow, and crippling the hand, and clogging the brain, and injuring life, dismiss it at once; rather cast it down upon Him by drawing close to God, by a life hidden in God. "Thou shalt hide them privily by Thine own presence from the provoking of all men; Thou shalt keep them secretly in Thy tabernacle from the strife of tongues."[1] Trouble He sends us, but not anxiety; and trouble faithfully borne brings us nearer to God; anxiety does but drive Him away.

II. "*He careth for you.*" Oh, that we daily more and more learnt this secret. It is written on this beautiful world. The grass of the field, the fowls of the air, the stars in their courses, the sun in its splendour, the moon in her beauty, the songs of the birds, and the sweetness of the flowers, and the richness of the earth, they all proclaim the same story— "*He careth for you.*" It is written in God's Holy Word. The "patience and comfort of the Scriptures"[2] preach to us, deep answering to deep, speaking to our inmost heart; the revelation of His will, the preaching of the Cross, the record of His love, all say the same thing—"*He careth for you.*" It is written in the Sacraments, where the bright leaves and luxuriant growth of holiness mark the course of the channels of grace, as they trickle through the sandy plain of

[1] Psa. xxxi. 22.   [2] Rom. xv. 4.

this vale of woe—The wells of the Lord bless the Lord,[1] and say, "*He careth for you.*" It is written on our own experience. Look back and see. Did ever any trust in the Lord, and was confounded? or did any abide in His fear, and was forsaken? or whom did He ever despise, that called upon Him?[2] As we cast our eye over our life, we see it still, "*He careth for you.*"

It is written in the mission of those angels, of whom we have lately been thinking, offering their liturgy before God and coming down to minister to man.[3] As they wing their flight to us, they, too, say, "He careth for you." Yes; it is written on this very harvest thanksgiving; you know that "it is of the Lord's mercies that we are not consumed."[4] And the harvest as it has come round, out of gloom and sorrow, has yet come to us; to give us this message—*God still careth for you.*

Yes; the world is full of anxiety; only God has not sent it; man puts it there. Surely S. Peter calls upon us all to walk more closely with our God. Prudence, faith, interest, all demand it; for however much I may think to care for myself, there is One who cares for me more; and if I cast all my care upon Him, it will be better for me in the end. For which of us by taking anxious thought can add as much as one cubit to his stature.[5]

[1] Benedicite. Cf. Isa. xii. 3.   [2] Ecclus. ii. 10, 11.
[3] Heb. i. 14. Οὐχὶ πάντες εἰσι λειτουργικὰ πνεύματα, εἰς διακονίαν ἀποστελλόμενα;
[4] Lam. iii. 22.   [5] S. Matt. vi. 27.

SERMON XVII.

The Broken Net.

" *And when they had this done, they inclosed a great multitude of fishes; and their net brake.*—S. LUKE v. 6.

THIS miracle, as you will have already seen, is one of those which was twice worked by our Blessed Lord; once at the beginning of His ministry, as here, and once at the end, after His resurrection. And, further, both these miracles belong to that class which is symbolical; that is, in both there are many minute incidents recorded, insignificant incidents apparently, but incidents which have been fastened upon, in both ancient and modern times, as conveying instruction and mystical truth, both to those who first witnessed the miracles, and to us who read the inspired record of them in the pages of Holy Writ.

The two miracles, then, have been compared together,[1] and in the first, recorded by S. Luke, we would seem to have a figure of the Church *as it now is*, gathering in members from the world. In the second, the figure of the Church *as it shall be*, after the resurrection, with the great gathering in of the

[1] See Archbishop Trench on the Miracles, pp. 459, 460.

souls of the righteous which shall then take place; and the details of the miracles lend themselves to this parabolic interpretation.

In the first miracle, the future fishers of men are directed neither to the right hand nor to the left hand of the ship, but simply to let down their nets in the broad sea, gathering fish, bad and good. In the second, the direction is, "Cast the net on the *right* side of the ship;"[1] prefiguring the final gathering in of the righteous only. In the first, "the net was broken," all were not secured; in the second, "For all there were so many, yet was not the net broken;" all the elect, that is, are safely gathered in. In the first, the fish were brought into the ship, which was still tossing on the sea; typifying the Church militant, riding on the stormy waves of this world; in the second, the nets are brought to the shore—the safe and quiet shore of eternity. In the first, a large multitude is enclosed; in the second, a fixed number of *great* fishes; typifying the fixed number and greatness of the elect. And so on with other and deeper significations.

Enough, however, has been said to show that there is good and sufficient authority for regarding the miracle, in a symbolical light, as containing deep lessons beneath its simple and graphic incidents. And I am asking you to confine your attention to-day to one main feature in this miracle; namely, *the broken net*. Just as every one recognizes in the fish living in the water the ancient and appropriate symbol

[1] S. John xxi. 6.

of the Christian living by the water of baptism, so in the net, and in the Greek word used by our Lord when speaking to S. Peter after the miracle, "thou shalt catch men for *life*,"[1] we can discern quite clearly the system, work, and energies of the Church, in her great mission of gathering in souls for Christ. And this net, under the eye and in the presence of Christ, *breaks*, causing, as we may suppose, several fish which had been enclosed to swim away and escape.

I. Now we hear people, who may or may not know much about the matter, talking airily about the Church not retaining her hold over the masses. They point to the state of our large towns, the great schisms, the wild religious fanaticism, the careless unbelieving Christians, and say the Church is obsolete, she frightens, she repels, she cannot hold her own. All that can be said, dear friends, is, that as a general fact nothing can be more conspicuously beside the truth. Of course there is, as there always will be, the broad road, which is the road of the many, and the narrow road, which is the road of the few; but there never was a time, from the days of early British Christianity until now, when the Church of England had a more real, a more genuine, a more vital hold upon the affections of the people, than she has at the present day.[2] You will not find it in the columns of newspapers, in amateur census-taking, or in any purely

[1] ζωγρεύειν.
[2] The *Times*, certainly an unprejudiced witness, thus speaks: "No one can doubt that the Church of England is at the present moment more powerful for good, and more popular, in the best sense of the term, than it has been for many a generation."—*Times*, April 11, 1883.

numerical test. There are certain signs of vitality, of great vitality, of intellectual, moral, and spiritual vitality, which cannot be mistaken. The net encloses at this moment a great multitude of fishes, and yet for all that every candid person must admit that both now and at other times of her history, *the net breaks*, and some, nay, many, escape.

And why is it? Surely the answer is plain: it is the price of prosperity. It is the glory of the Church that she encloses so many and such various kinds of fish in her net. And mark, to net means to contract liberty, and to draw on to a definite point; on all whom the Church nets, she puts this gentle force, a contracted liberty, and a drawing in, and a drawing on, and if you like to press the metaphor further, " a *death* unto life."

And, first of all, think of the numbers on whom the net of the Church is cast; think of our towns, our villages, our colonies, our dependencies! think of the fishermen taking their bark into the dark seas of savagedom and heathendom, and casting their net over those great masses of souls, who have to be drawn on with no weak hand when their wild liberty and immorality has been checked and restrained by the teaching of the Gospel! A good many escape, because there is not strength enough to bring them in. The populations in our large towns outgrow the Church schools, or the old church built in quieter times; the heathen who ask for instruction, or the churches which need consolidating and administering, outnumber and overpower the strength of the struggling fishermen, and many break away into heathenism and infidelity, because there is not strength enough to deal with these large numbers.

Or if we look at the variety of the fish, it is just the same. The Church casts the same net over the rich, the poor, the intellectual, the ignorant, the morally weak and the morally strong, the sceptical mind and the believing mind, the eccentricities of perverted intellect, and the calm deliberations of genius; fish good and bad, great and small, are enclosed in her net. The Church has settled down over the field of literature, science, morals, art—wherever we turn. There are great varieties in characters and pursuits, and great varieties in the members of the Church; and this variety, as well as her numbers, is sometimes a cause of weakness, as she endeavours to draw them in. And this is not unfrequently objected to the Church of England by those who regard her with no friendly eye. "You are like the builders of Babel, you all speak different languages; it is confusion." If one man works for souls in one direction, somebody calls after him and says he is a Methodist; if another works in another direction, one shouts after him that he is a Papist; another is roughly reminded that he is an infidel. Certainly it were possible to reduce these discordant cries, but it would be at a great sacrifice of vitality. A dead uniformity is not always life; there was a time, it has been pointed out, when the builders of Babel all spoke the same language, but they were then all fatally in the wrong.

Subjective religion, "God's dealing with the soul;

objective religion, God's dealing with the Church; intellectual religion, or religion in reference to scientific truth; these, to return to the original metaphor, are all sides of the gospel net; and some fish are pressed against one side, some against another. Variety within the limits of the net is not an evil; but at the same time it strains it to its utmost capacity, and sometimes the net breaks. For the gospel does, as I have said, put on us a restriction and a constraint. It puts a restriction upon our understanding and upon our life, not only upon what is gross and bad, but on thoughts and tendencies and even on things lawful. Yes, the gospel does draw us in, more and more within the recesses of that ship in which we are to be landed, dead to the world, that we may live only unto Him on the shores of eternity.

II. Now, you are reminded to-day, dear friends, by the appeal which is being made to you,[1] that the resources of the Church, both here and elsewhere, are being taxed to the uttermost, by the number and variety of the souls which she is trying to bring in to her Lord and Master, Jesus Christ. In some quarters the very number and extent of the works for good which gather round the Church, are a serious claim upon her strength and resources. Here in this town, the expense of maintaining the schools in proper efficiency is very great; and the school is only one, out of many agencies for good, which make demands upon the energies, the good will and the charity of

[1] Preached on behalf of the Malvern National Schools in The Priory Church, 1883.

Church people. There is the public worship of the Church to be conducted in a way becoming the service of Almighty God. There are clergy to be provided, who shall bring means of grace home to us, while they rouse the careless, recover the fallen, and restore the penitent. There are the sick and afflicted appealing to us in His name who is the friend of the poor. The heathen are stretching out their hands to us, and saying, "Come over and help us." The heathen at home in our large towns are a subject of anxiety and care. And over all these the Church manfully casts her net. But sometimes the net breaks, the strain is too great, it is beyond her strength.

And what a gigantic work is the work of education alone, which falls upon the Church; the training of the young in the faith and fear of God. The drawing them *in* from the evil world, the drawing them *on* to the ship of safety. I am sure that you must regard with sorrow and apprehension any signs of breaking or giving on this side of the net; for there is no work to which the Church ought more devotedly to cling than this education of the young. If she loses her children, she loses her hope. For we know that Christian education is conferring a blessing on us who give it, on those who receive it, and on ages yet unborn, who shall profit by it.

You will have noticed that ever since God undertook to restore fallen man, this is a solemn duty which He has left to His Church—*to teach.* It was laid upon Moses, He "gave Israel a law, which He commanded our forefathers to teach their children; that their posterity might know it, and the children which were yet unborn; to the intent that when they came up, they might shew their children the same."[1] That is, God speaks once, He gives the deposit of faith to this man, or to that family or tribe, with the solemn obligation to teach it, to hand it on.

So it is with the Christian Church. The message is, "Go ye therefore, and *teach* all nations."[2] To teach, to train, to hand on the faith; to throughly furnish the man of God unto every good work,[3] is part of the office of the Church, and a very important part too. And it is for this that she casts her net over her young to bring them in *alive* unto God. And you know the difficulties. Some would try to frighten the fish away, and preach of freedom, and nature, and liberty, and life. Besides this, other fishermen are netting the waters. The devil draws a strong net through, and is desperately anxious to exclude religion from useful knowledge; the world is drawing along its net, and is trying to entrap, by a worldly education the children, whom it would make like itself, worldly—speaking of the world, living for the world, dying for the world—successful materialists; the flesh is drawing its net; indolence, vice, indifference, in children and parents, are drawing many away.

And the Church has to hold her own over all these, and multitudes come to her net. It is not that the Church is failing, or unpopular, or neglected; it is

[1] Psa. lxxviii. 5, 6. [2] S. Matt. xxviii. 19.
[3] 2 Tim. iii. 17.

that she can hardly deal with the multitudes that come to her.

Ah, dear friends, you would not like to see the gospel net break, so as to lose our young. You would not wish, where a little money would repair it, to see these precious hopes lost and thrown away. You know what that net is to you. Yes, you welcome it, amid the wild unbelief of the present day, in its gentle loving restraint. You love to feel the word of God speaking to you with authority, sufficient to satisfy doubt, but not sufficient to take away the merit of faith; to feel the gentle pressure of the net, as the wild sea of speculation surges by you; a restriction, but a support at the same time; to see, when luxury or sinful desire presses upon you, the dark side of the net, sharply severing you from sin or from a careless life. It is this restraint, this support severing them from what is bad and gently drawing them in to what is good, that we want for the children; and the net is a little strained by the pressure. Will you help? Surely there must be many who are anxious to show some kindness to others, some return to the Lord for spiritual blessing here or restored health; who have found God amid these beautiful scenes, and who, loving Him, love their fellow men. Here there is a work of no doubtful utility, of no slight importance; which He will prosper Who loved little children, and blessed them when He was on earth. In helping the schools, you will be doing something to further the great mission of the Church, and Jesus Christ is watching you from the everlasting shore.

Oh, what a blessing to be allowed to help in the great fishing of the Church! Oh, what a privilege—"I will make you fishers of men." Ah, yes, all who are working for Christ and His Church, cleric or layman, male or female, man or child, may expect at the last great gathering in, when Christ stands on the shore, to hear His voice saying, "Bring of the fish which ye have now caught. . . . Come and dine."[1] And they shall sit down at the great gospel feast with Abraham, Isaac, and Jacob, in the kingdom of heaven.[2]

[1] S. John xxi. 10-12. [2] S. Matt. viii. 11.

SERMON XVIII.

The Joy of the Holy Ghost in the Saints.[1]

"*The Lord thy God in the midst of thee is mighty; He will save, He will rejoice over thee with joy; He will rest in His love, He will joy over thee with singing.*"—ZEPH. iii. 17.

WE reach this evening a subject surely of more than usual mystery and awe; a subject which can only be approached with the greatest reverence, caution, and even fear. For "the wind bloweth where it listeth, and thou hearest the sound thereof, but canst not tell whence it cometh, and whither it goeth."[2] Here there are no familiar words, no recognized starting-points, such as "Father," and "Son," from which to plunge into the contemplation of the infinite love of God. But here we commence at once with the unknown and the unknowable, warned at the same time by the Truth itself, that "He that shall blaspheme against the Holy Ghost hath never forgiveness, but is in danger of eternal damnation."[3]

[1] This sermon was preached, as part of a course of sermons, at All Saints', Clifton, November, 1880.
[2] S. John iii. 8.   [3] S. Mark iii. 29.

We can but guess, we can but speculate, we can but proceed with cautious inference, from the manifestations vouchsafed to us in Revelation and experience, when we speak of the joy of that indwelling Spirit in His saints. That there is such a joy we cannot doubt; we are bidden to pray that God's loving Spirit may lead us forth into the land of righteousness;[1] we are told that the Spirit also helpeth our infirmities, making intercession for us in the unutterable groanings of the soul;[2] we are warned not to grieve the Holy Spirit of God, whereby we are sealed unto the day of redemption.[3] And experience tells us the same; we know and feel in the power of grace, in the voice of conscience, in the life illuminated by God, that the Lord our God is in the midst of us, mighty in power; that He saves us by His great strength, that He rejoices over us with joy, that He is silent in His love, held in silence by the very depth of his love, whose meaning as He prays and intercedes within us no words can convey, silent as to our waywardness and many faults. Yes, He is silent in His love, while He joys over us, with singing, in the unuttered, unutterable jubilee of the heart.

I. What, then, is our conception—our common conception—of joy? What is joy to us? As on the answer to this question may perhaps depend our guesses, our speculations, as to the joy of the Holy Spirit. Joy seems to be, in some sense, an outward expression of a happiness which is alike absorbing and

[1] Psa. cxliii. 10.   [2] See Romans viii. 26.
[3] Eph. iv. 30.

real. We see the genuine joy of little children, shouting in their games; absorbed, and wrapped up in the pursuit of the moment. We see the deeper joy penetrating even to the face of an intellectual man, as he is enjoying, as we say, some scientific pursuit or some study in literature. And there is a joy we may believe all its own, which is the peculiar property of the soul, such as we find breathing through the pages of our Prayer-book, and many other books of devotion, showing them to be the outpourings of the hearts of men, who have found a satisfaction more real and more exultant than earth can give. So that joy would be the radiant atmosphere which plays around pleasure; and pleasure is the consciousness of an exact correspondence between a faculty and its object;[1] as, for instance, in the body meeting with its proper exercise, the mind with its proper use, the soul with its true object; so that, speaking quite roughly, we may call pleasure satisfaction, and the highest pleasure, the highest satisfaction—that is, the satisfaction of the highest part of our being; and joy the illumination, half conscious, half unconscious, which plays about and around the life of pleasure.

If this, or something like this, is what we mean by joy, may we take this as a scale of measurement, whereby to mark off distances and spaces in that joy of the Holy Spirit, which is immeasurable, incomprehensible, unknowable? May we say that the Holy Spirit joys in His saints in so far as He is satisfied?

[1] See "Ar: Eth: Nich:" vii. 12. Dr. Liddon, "Bampton Lectures," p. 311. First edition.

In so far as there is no resisting of that Holy influence in so far as the temple is ready for Him; in so far as there is a correspondence between the soul, and His own Divine Personality; in so far as that hunger is satisfied by a correspondence on the part of man— where there is no longer that painful striving[1] of the Holy Spirit with man, but where men are the true sons of God, and His Spirit remaineth in them.

II. If this be so, how shall a man correspond with the Holy Spirit? What is there in man, which shall satisfy with a holy joy that loving, gentle Guest? And here we are reminded that there are certain symbols of the Holy Spirit—condescensions to the understanding of man—to help him to realize the action of that Holy Being. And one of them, with which perhaps we are most familiar, is the symbol of the Dove.

(1) The Holy Ghost, we read, "descended in a bodily shape like a dove upon Him."[2] The Holy Spirit, then, is a Spirit of gentleness and tenderness in the world—Gentleness and Tenderness personified. The Holy Spirit, winging His way from the ark of heaven, flies over the flood-covered surface of our heart. Is there any rest for the sole of His foot there? Is there any correspondence *there?* Any gentleness to meet Gentleness? Any tenderness to meet Tenderness? For we may believe that if we could meet the Gentleness of God with the gentleness of our life, there would be satisfaction, and if satisfaction, then that joy of the Holy Spirit abiding in the heart, where

[1] See Gen. vi. 3.   [2] S. Luke iii. 22.

the green trees of grace are slowly appearing, and the flood of sin subsiding.

Can we meet, dear friends, this Holy Spirit of Gentleness, the Holy Dove, with any gentleness which shall satisfy His holy longing? Gentleness, I suppose, is a sort of feeling of reverent tenderness, self-restraint, respect, which comes from living in the presence of God. "Such as are gentle, them shall He learn His way."[1] "Thy gentleness hath made me great."[2]

Oh, surely we ought to move with gentleness always, amidst the handiwork of God; with reverence, with uncovered head, as we walk beneath the overarching beauty, life, order, and vigour of creation. We should move with a feeling of responsibility. The lilies, the ravens, the sower, "the signs of the times," are all preaching to us; they are telling God—"*they are without excuse.*"[3] Yes, with a feeling of awe, as we think of the destiny of the creature, and the mysteries all around us, more especially when we look at man, or look at ourselves, who are the work, the purchase, and the temple of God.

Alas, it is only too possible to look God in the face day by day, and to forget Him; to talk in a confident, boastful way about the laws of nature—to move in the world, making a perpetual jar and discord in the harmony of created order—as we thrust ourselves out of our place.

Yes, it is true now, as always, "such as are gentle, them shall He learn His way."—"Thy gentleness hath made me great." Gentleness is that which teaches

[1] Psa. xxv. 8.   [2] Psa. xviii. 35.   [3] Rom. i. 20.

us the way of God; and therefore the Holy Spirit of order, the creative Spirit of God, loves gentleness. Are we doing anything for God? Oh, let us do it in His way. *Creative* work requires a gentle hand. If we would build up any work for God, it must be the gentle hand that builds it, the hand which leaves the impress of reverence, responsibility, and awe. This work is work done for God, before God, with His materials, whether it be work in the Church, or work in the circle of home, or work in the hearts of others. Let us throw away all that offends the Spirit of Gentleness—that self-will, that want of consideration, that air of superiority, provoking the natural retort, "who made thee a ruler and a judge over us?"[1] The Holy Spirit, we may believe, loves gentleness. And gentleness alone will help us in God's way, as our work rises bearing the true marks of gentleness— growth, progress, development—so many steps whereby we reach God.

And it is the same with *Redemptive* work. There must be no breaking of the bruised reed, no quenching of the smoking flax; work among the fallen, work among sinners, must breathe the spirit of Him Who prayed for His murderers, Who was merciful to the penitent, Who welcomed the dying thief. It must be gentle, as coming from those who owe themselves ten thousand talents while they are dealing with one who owes a hundred pence. It must be gentle as dealing with souls for whom Christ died;[2] with those who are specially the objects of His love, Who carries

[1] Acts vii. 27. [2] Rom. xiv. 15.

penitents as well as innocents, the lost sheep as well as the lambs.

And *sanctifying* work, too, must be gentle. We need to be gentle, even with ourselves. "The wind bloweth where it listeth." Grace comes to us in manifold ways. We must not be perplexed, or vexed, and annoyed, if we fail in one course and have to try another. We must measure our own strength, recognizing cheerfully that we cannot all do the same things, and that we must not neglect plain duties for others less plain; and so learn to work quietly, as with God's gifts.

And then the Holy Spirit will joy in the gentleness of our work, as beneath the fire of enthusiasm, and the earthquake of effort, there sounds the still small voice within, which tells that the Spirit of the Lord is there, in the joy and peace and love which breathes through gentleness.

(2) And so we pass to another manifestation of the Holy Spirit. Beside the Dove of gentleness, the Holy Spirit is shadowed forth to us as *the Wind*, or *the Breath*. "Suddenly there came a sound from heaven as of a rushing mighty wind, and it filled all the house where they were sitting."[1] "He breathed on them, and saith unto them, Receive ye the Holy Ghost."[2] The Holy Spirit is a great and mighty influence filling all the world, penetrating into the inmost corners of the heart. It is the air which the saints breathe; it is the great moving force in grace, strong, subtle, irresistible, blowing upon the king's garden, that the spices thereof may flow out.[3]

[1] Acts ii. 2.   [2] S. John xx. 22.   [3] Cant. iv. 16.

Is there any correspondence here? Does deep answer deep here? Is there any subtle influence emanating from our heart, which may mingle with that breath from heaven, and so give joy to that Holy Spirit? In short, are our lives, lives of spiritual influence? Of course, in this we touch on a subject of great and vital importance. We may be sure that, whether we know it or not, from our lives streams forth a breath of influence, either for good or for evil. From each nation, from each town, from each family, there ascends that mysterious vapour-like influence which forms the moral atmosphere in which men live, and which we know under the name of public opinion.

So, our Blessed Lord wept over Jerusalem, as if Jerusalem had a corporate life; as if the different vices and sins, obstinances and rebellions of the individual men and women in that city, had made one great perishing soul, the soul of Jerusalem. So Sodom is punished as *a city;* so Amalek and the Canaanites as *nations.* So Nineveh, again, as a *city* is threatened, and repents as a *city.* And, bad or good, we all do something towards forming that public opinion, in some sense we are responsible for it. Just as Lot might have saved Sodom; just as S. Paul influenced by little units the Prætorian guard, so that his bonds in Christ were manifested in all the palace;[1] so, for good or evil, we are influencing the place or community where we live. Is that influence a good one? for how much depends upon it!

[1] Phil. i. 13. See Dr. Lightfoot *in loc.*; ἐν ὕλῳ τῷ πραιτορίῳ.

Think of the great corridors of life down which school influence reaches, as boys and girls start out to their manifold work in life. Think of that mysterious way in which minds act and react on each other through the literature of the day. Yes, think of those great windows which are open in our life, through which we can influence those whom we have never seen or known, as the spices flow out of prayer and blessing, wafted by the Holy Spirit at our intercession. Oh, Christ's kingdom waits for you ; the ships which are to carry "the unsearchable riches of Christ" to the heathen are waiting for our prayers to fill their sails. The dark and fetid murky atmosphere, which pollutes those dens of infamy in Christian England, is waiting for the strong clearing wind of holy prayer, the cleansing influence of holy love. "For their sakes I sanctify Myself."[1] Not only does the Holy Spirit rejoice in the temple ready for His presence, but he rejoices in the influence, the soft, clear, health-giving air, which rises to meet Him from the windows of our life. Those windows open toward Jerusalem,[2] which give and receive back again, which receive and give out, the fragrance of a holy life.

(3) And there is a third manifestation, a third symbol of the Holy Spirit still. Not only is He the Dove, and the mighty wind, but also He is the Fire. "There appeared unto them cloven tongues like as of fire, and it sat upon each of them."[3] Beside the spirit of gentleness, and of holy influence, there is further in the Church that mighty flame burning

[1] S. John xvii. 19.   [2] Dan. vi. 10.   [3] Acts. ii. 3.

steadily upwards, and enkindling all who come within its reach. Is there a correspondence here? Does any flame leap out of the soul to meet the light and warmth which the Holy Spirit sheds abroad? Is there any of that zeal for God's glory, that zeal which burns up lower, baser, and more sordid motives, and is on fire with the love of God?—zeal, that jealousy for God, that warm, earnest rivalry of heart, which becomes a virtue, when it is pressed into God's service, which proclaims God everywhere, God only, God always, God above all; the zeal of a Phineas, an Eleazar or a S. Paul; the zeal of Boanerges the sons of thunder. Oh, zeal is a virtue which we sadly need; not intolerance, there is plenty of that; not enthusiasm, which evaporates in feeling, but zeal; "an earnest desire for God's glory leading to strenuous and bold deeds on His behalf."[1] Zeal is the flame which burns up indifference—indifference, which is the greatest foe to man's spiritual life. Indifference has been compared to a moth called forth by the very costliness of the material which it feeds upon.[2] And indeed it requires nothing short of Christianity to produce indifference.

God claims the world, its forces, its produce, its population. He directs it, orders it, governs it. But take up any newspaper of the day. Where is God? Is He blasphemed? No, He is ignored. God claims each one of us. He made us, He redeemed us, He sanctifies us. What occupies the thoughts of the majority of mankind? Ah, we ourselves must feel

[1] Dr. Newman. [2] Dr. Liddon.

that there is not that zeal which should correspond
with all our privileges, that we hold truth loosely and
lightly, that the flame of our love does not burn
steadily and clearly. But the fire of God is waiting.
If we have any sacrificial fire ready, if we have prepared the sacrifice, if our hearts are set in order, the
fire of God will descend, and then there will be joy
in the mingling of these two holy flames.

III. And there only remains this solemn question:
Does the Holy Spirit joy in *me*? Is there this correspondence, this spiritual life to meet spiritual gifts?
We can tell. Where the Spirit of God dwells, the
flood has subsided, there are green patches of peace
and love and liberty. Where the Spirit of God dwells
there is power and eloquence and progress. Where
the Spirit of God dwells, there is a growth, there is
fruit. He brings with Him the tokens of His
presence, "Love, joy, peace, long-suffering, gentleness,
goodness, faith, meekness, temperance."[1] If the Spirit
is to joy in us, we on our part must walk in the
Spirit, and aim at that correspondence which produces joy in satisfaction.

[1] Gal. v. 22, 23.

SERMON XIX.

The Following Rock.

"They drank of that spiritual Rock that followed them: and that Rock was Christ."—1 Cor. x. 4.

S. PAUL is here following apparently a Jewish tradition, which in some hands became fanciful and strange, that not only was the rock stricken in Horeb, but that also, wheresoever the children of Israel journeyed, there was water from the rock to refresh them; some of the Jewish rabbis interpreting this to mean that the rock itself accompanied them in their journeys, going with them as they went; others, that the streams of water which gushed from Horeb, flowed out after them, following their journeyings in a perpetual stream. But the Apostle, instead of these strange fancies, would seem here to say, that just as clouds followed their course from which the manna fell, so, that there never failed a rock out of which gushed living water at Moses' command, typical of the life-giving grace of Christ, which accompanied them in their journeys. "He clave the hard rocks in the wilderness, and gave them drink thereof, as it had been out of the great depth. He brought water out of the stony rock, so that it gushed out like the rivers."[1]

And so we have here described a presence of life, typical of and foreshadowing that other great Presence which is the comfort of the pilgrim Church: "Lo, I am with you alway, even unto the end of the world. Amen."[2] We, too, drink of that Rock which follows us, and that Rock is Christ; to us, too, the promise is true and abiding—"he shall dwell on high: his place of defence shall be the munitions of rocks: bread shall be given him; his waters shall be sure."[3]

I. And see how the following Rock, charged with living water, has never failed the Church. When, in her infancy, she was yet hiding in the catacombs, dragged forth only to be "a spectacle to angels and to men," the sport of loathsome emperors, the plaything of imperial Rome, whose sports were suffering, and whose games were torture; still after those weary days and nights, in the dark gloom of the subterranean city, over the grave of some sainted martyr, by the dim light of the flickering candles, the hunted, stricken hinds, faint in the chase, "athirst for God, yea, even for the living God," found here the following Rock, smitten and broken for them, from which they might quench their thirst. And even now the stranger can trace in the rude painting on the wall, in the fish, roughly portrayed over the altar, or the loaves of bread, the grateful traces of souls refreshed by the

[1] Psa. lxxviii. 16, 17.   [2] S. Matt. xxviii. 20.
[3] Isa. xxxiii. 16.

water from the Rock. Or in the calm words, "In peace," which mark the resting-place of some Christian martyr, may still be seen how, amidst the rage and fury and hate which hurled their souls out of this world, still there was a Rock which was higher than they, a strong tower and defence against the wiles of the enemy; how a rock had followed them through it all, and that Rock was Christ.

And so again, when the Church emerged into the more dangerous toleration, or the even more dangerous patronage of the State, still amidst the splendour of churches, the gold, the silver, and the incense, there was the hard rock—the one Body sacrificed for all the stream from the stricken Rock which followed them. So through all the ages of heresy and corruption, through those great upheavings when the Church seemed deserted by God, still there has always been the following Rock. It was only the other day, that we saw that it had reached that God-forsaken spot, the slave-market of Zanzibar. There is the Rock, overshadowing that weary place. There is the stream of water flowing now, where men and women before, huddled together, without hope, without friends, "without God in the world." There now is a Saviour to befriend them, a God to help them, Grace to refresh them.[1] Yes, we see it everywhere, in towns as well as villages, in parts frequented and in parts remote, there is the overshadowing Rock, with its living Water. And as trees and verdure in the desert

[1] A Christian Church has been consecrated on the site of the old slave-market in Zanzibar.

proclaim from afar the little spot where water is, so round each church there gather the beauties of architecture, and the signs of progress. The refreshing water laps over, and in its path arise the schools for the young, the refuge for the fallen, and the many Christian homes, all dwelling within the sound of its soft ripple, all so many trees planted by the waterside, which shall bring forth their fruit in due season.[1] Lo, I am with you alway, even unto the end of the world. Amen. Yes, when there is that great forsaking, when the remnant is but a Joshua and Caleb, still while the desert lasts, the rock will last. Whoso eateth and drinketh of the food of immortality shall never die. For He Himself, the Fountain of life, has said it, "If any man thirst, let him come unto Me, and drink."[2] And "the water that I shall give him shall be in him a well of water springing up into everlasting life."[3]

II. But as it has been with the Church, so it is with each individual, with each Christian Israel, who as a Prince has power with God and with men, and has prevailed.[4] With each Christian soul, who as a pilgrim goes through the wilderness, at each stage of his pilgrimage, there is water from the rock. He drinks of a Rock that follows him, and that Rock is Christ.

(1) And, first of all, the Red Sea is passed, the waters of Baptism have closed over him, and he enters on his journey; and he has not gone many days into

[1] Psa. i. 3.
[2] S. John vii. 37.
[3] S. John iv. 14.
[4] Gen. xxxii. 28.

the wilderness before he feels his need of water, in the hot, weary land. Although infant Communion has ceased in most parts of the Church, yet still for him the Rock is smitten, still he partakes unconsciously of the Fountains which flow from that stricken Side. For him the Body is broken, for him the Blood is shed, for him the great intercession is pleaded before the Father. When he was baptized he was baptized into Christ's death; he was buried with Him by baptism into death;[1] he was baptized into Christ to die to sin, as Christ died to sin, to live in Him unto God, as He lived. So that Baptism is the immersion into the full flood of the new life; and bathed in this he travels on, until the hot sun of the world dries up the Baptismal dew, and the scorching wind plays upon his life.

If the poet's dream be true, that there are memories of another state in infancy, much more might we think that there are *Baptismal* memories—memories of the Rock stricken in Horeb.

> "Heaven lies about us in our infancy!
> Shades of the prison house begin to close
>   Upon the growing boy,
> But he beholds the light, and whence it flows,
>   He sees it in his joy;
> The youth, who daily further from the east
> Must travel, still is Nature's Priest,
>   And by the vision splendid
>   Is on his way attended;
> At length the man perceives it die away,
> And fade into the light of common day."[2]

---

[1] Rom. vi. 3, 4.
[2] Wordsworth, "Intimations of Immortality," etc.

He drinks of the Rock that follows him, "and that Rock is Christ." The unquenched dew of Baptismal grace is the refreshing water of the pilgrim's first stage.

(2) But God leads on deeper and deeper into the wilderness. Amalek strives with Israel; the rocks are higher, the sand deeper, the heart fainter, foes fiercer; but once more there is the following Rock, waiting with its treasure of living Water. And Christ says to the opening life of youth, "If any man thirst, let him come unto Me, and drink."[1] The union with God must be closer, deeper, more real yet. The world has to be shunned, the flesh subdued, the devil vanquished, in order that Christ may dwell in our hearts by faith.[2]

Oh, what grace there is in the deliberate choice of Christ in the first Communion. It is not only that strength is there, that grace is there, and refreshment there, but it is the *preventing* grace. If Christ gets possession of that soul *first!* before the dust of life, and the sand of disappointment, and the heat of lust, and the persistence of foes have filled the heart with bitterness—to have Christ there *first!* "when the unclean spirit is gone out of a man, he walketh through dry places, seeking rest, and findeth none. Then he saith, I will return into my house from whence I came out; and when he is come, he findeth it *empty*."[3]

Oh, this Rock follows close on the steps of opening

---
[1] S. John vii. 37.
[2] Eph. iii. 17.   [3] S. Matt. xii. 43, 44.

youth, that the devil, once cast out, may not find the heart from whence he came out, empty. Oh, think of those who are now coming to Confirmation; pray for them that no unworthy thoughts, no false shame, may keep them from the Fountain of living Waters, from the blessing of Communion with Christ. Oh, may they drink of that Rock which follows them— close upon them at their Confirmation—that Rock which is Christ.

(3) And then comes the age of the mirage. The dazzling sun, playing on the hot sand, displays its tempting lakes and verdant patches and cool grottoes. In vain the true guide points onward and onward; men are rushing hither and thither, in pursuit of riches, in pursuit of fame, in pursuit of worldly ease, in pursuit of pleasure; further and further they are lured on; the water comes not, the streams ever further and further flee from their grasp. Happy they who at this time are recalled to the Rock that follows them, whose waters fail not, which are never salt, bitter, or sandy, which are never dried up! Happy they who, when the heart is ready to turn back again into Egypt, or would urge them to lie down and die in the wilderness, when the multitude ask for flesh and the luxuries of bondage, still keep close to that Rock of Salvation; who in that long dull stretch of life, when the first enthusiasm is passed, when object after object separates them more and more from the past, and there is no novelty but the dull stretch of desert, day by day; happy they who, going through the vale of misery, use it for a

well, and the pools are filled with water,[1] who hew cisterns out of life's sorrows, and tanks out of life's troubles, into which the water from the Rock can flow!

Oh, if there be any weary with life's journey, with its very dulness and monotony, still for you there is the following Rock. Do not be led astray by the heedless crowd, who rush madly after that which satisfieth not, but drink deep of those Waters of Life, and let that Rock follow you.

(4) But the sun sinks in the heavens. The forty years' wandering is almost past. Friends have failed and friends have gone. Joshua and Caleb wander alone, among a new generation, amid doomed companions and doubting hearts. "Where is the promise of His coming?"[2] "How can this man give us His Flesh to eat?"[3] "Our soul loatheth this light bread."[4] But still, for those who wait, there is the stricken Rock, the flowing Stream, "The God which fed me all my life long unto this day"[5]—He washes over with the oblivion of forgiveness, the regrets of aged penitence. Yes, even over the entrance to that dark valley, there hangs the overshadowing Rock. Even at that last hour, in the concentrated temptations of that dread moment, there is no fear, for He is with us. In that last food "for the journey," which passes the trembling lips, there is the stream from the overhanging Rock, which reaches up to death, and through death, until God shall be all in all.[6] So all

---

[1] Psa. lxxxiv. 6. [2] 2 S. Pet. iii. 4. [3] S. John vi. 52.
[4] Num. xxi. 5. [5] Gen. xlviii. 15. [6] 1 Cor. xv. 28.

through life, the Rock follows us, higher and higher —from infancy to youth, from youth to manhood, from manhood to old age.

> "Prayer shall not fail, but higher He would lead thee:
> His bosom-friend ate of that awful Bread;
> So will He wait all day to bless and feed thee—
> Come, thou adoring, to be blest and fed.
> 'Tis meet and right, and mine own bounden duty.
> Good Angels guide me with pure heart to fall
> Before His Altar step, and see His Beauty,
> And taste of Him, my first, my last, my all."[1]

---

[1] "Lyra Innocentium."

SERMON XX.

The Saints.[1]

"Grace and mercy is to His saints, and He hath care for His elect."—
WISDOM iii. 9.

ALL Saints' day stands almost alone in the festivals of the Church, in its significance and peculiar tenderness. If we have worshipped God with thankful hearts, overwhelmed with His Graciousness and Love, in the different festivals which gather round the Incarnation; if we have wept with shame at the degradation of man, who on Good Friday, mocked their Saviour and crucified their King; if we have thanked God now only a few weeks ago, for the Angels who leave their liturgy in Heaven, to minister to the needs of men; in all these, it has been Heaven which has been pouring its grace in fruitful streams down upon this earth. But to-day, with deep humility, yet with honest pride, we venture to think of some return which earth has made to Heaven.

The burning sun of God's love has penetrated here and there in corners and crevices of the earth, and

[1] Preached at All Saints, Boyne Hill, November, 1882.

has drawn up out of the cold earthiness of our natures the vapour-like spirit, which the flesh could not restrain. These are the clouds which form His chariot, reflecting the ever changing rays of His Godhead, moved by the wind of His Spirit, charged with refreshing streams, mindful of that earth from which they were drawn.[1] Yes, the saints are the best which earth has to offer to God. They are the return, poor and unworthy, but still a return, which earth makes to Heaven. And if in crowning their merits He crowns but His own priceless gifts, still we are glad for that blessed communion and fellowship which is one more link between earth and Heaven.

I. And we have already heard to-day, that the saints are a great multitude, which no man can number.[2] When, like Elijah,[3] our heart fails, and we wish to die because the faithful are so few, and the ungodly are so many, All Saints' day points to the waving lilies and the clustering palms, and the mingling emblems of martyrdom.

"Multitudes—multitudes—stood up in bliss,
Made equal to the Angels, glorious, fair;
With harps, palms, wedding-garments, kiss of peace,
And crowned and haloed hair.

"As though one pulse stirred all, one rush of blood
Fed all, one breath swept through myriad-voiced;
They struck their harps, cast down their crowns, they stood
And worshipped and rejoiced.

---

[1] See "Dr. Neale Psalms," vol. i. p. 229.
[2] Epistle for All Saints' day, Rev. vii. 9.
[3] 1 Kings xix. 4, 10.

> "Each face looked one way like a moon new lit,
> Each face looked one way towards its Sun of love;
> Drank love and bathed in love and mirrored it,
> And knew no end thereof.
>
> "Glory touched glory on each blessèd head:
> Hands locked dear hands, never to sunder more:
> These were the new-begotten from the dead,
> Whom the great birthday bore."[1]

Saints everywhere; saints from everywhere; saints from Cæsar's household; saints from the Prætorian guard;[2] saints from Corinth; saints from Babylon; saints from the seething mass of corruption rolling along our crowded alleys; saints from among the haggard brows and clutching fingers of those who sit at the receipt of custom; saints from among those who minister to our wants, shut out from the blessed sun, in the bowels of the earth; saints here; saints around me; saints in the blessed memories of home; saintliness, may it be? can it be? in my own heart— And why not?

II. What is a saint? The meaning is clear, and not hard to understand. A saint is a holy person;[3] and a holy person is one who, as in a mirror, with a distorted image and in an imperfect way, reflects that great attribute of God, Who is *the Holy One*. Separate, Sinless, Undefiled, "dwelling in the light which no man can approach unto; Whom no man hath seen, nor can see;"[4] to Whom we offer the worship which alone can express the greatness of His Majesty; "Holy, Holy, Holy," separated off from

[1] Christina Rosetti.   [2] Phil. i. 13.
[3] See Dr. Lightfoot on Phil. i. 1.   [4] 1 Tim. vi. 16.

all else, by the barrier of His awful Majesty, the All Holy, the Almighty God. And this, therefore, is the meaning of "a saint;" it is one who in his measure, as God will permit, is separate, hallowed holy, removed from all that defileth, or "maketh a lie."[1]

And in this sense, we shall understand the frequent use of the word in the New Testament, as applied to the *whole Church;* as, for instance, we read of "all that be in Rome, beloved of God, called to be saints;"[2] or again, "all the saints salute you,"[3] or again, "to the saints and faithful brethren in Christ which are at Colosse."[4] According to this use of the term, every baptized person is a saint. At our Baptism God separated us off from our old nature, and gave us a new nature in which it might be possible to serve Him acceptably. "He saved us, by the washing of regeneration."[5] Baptism is the separation of Israel out of Egypt, through the Red Sea, into the Church in the wilderness.

And then there is a further separation; "with many of them God was not well pleased: for they were overthrown in the wilderness."[6] It most often comes at Confirmation, when the half-hearted Christians die away, dwindle and fall off, and there is the further separating off of God's servants, from the careless unbelieving world. Fresh promises are made, the old vows are renewed, and a new generation enters the promised land. And here again there is a further

---

[1] Rev. xxi. 27. [2] Rom. i. 7. [3] Phil. iv. 22.
[4] Col. i. 2. [5] Titus iii. 5. [6] 1 Cor. x. 5.

separation; alas that it should be so! The enemies who dwell in the promised land are many; they are mighty and seductive, and not all come out to taste of the fruit of the land, the milk and honey of the Heavenly Feast; the Body and Blood of our Saviour Christ, whose Flesh is meat indeed, and whose Blood is drink indeed.[1] Here, again, there is a further separation. Some wish to build an altar on the other side of Jordan, some enter into the fulness of the blessing; and in a life more and more separated off from what is base and vile, from the devil, the world, and the flesh, are perfecting themselves in holiness, by the help and grace of God.

III. And with these God works. With these who fear the Lord and seek Him with their whole heart, God deals wondrously; and shows to them the secret of His power and goodness.

My brethren, you have come so far; you have wrestled with a weak flesh, a corrupt heart, a fiery world, and a hating devil. You have welcomed the separation which your Communions bring, as a time for self-examination, confession and amendment. Day by day you hope that the fierce temptations which rage and swell around the city of God, have less power over you. But have you strength yet to bear what God has to put upon you; that He may separate you not only from what is bad, but separate you also, *to* or *for* what is good? It is written, "Woe unto you that have lost patience (the power of *bearing*); and what will ye do when the Lord shall visit you?"[2] Or

[1] S. John vi. 55.
[2] Ecclus. ii. 14. Væ his qui perdiderunt *sustinentium*.

again, "Whom the Lord loveth He chasteneth, and scourgeth every son whom He receiveth."[1] Have you learnt this, that God has a separation, a refining of trial, for His saints? Ah, we know it, we who have sinned. We have wondered how God will allow us to enter that perfect place, maimed, bruised, and soiled as we are. We have wondered, as the pardon came to us full and free, and the rankling wound and the awful weakness still remained, we have wondered what was to be done, and it dawned upon us that all was not finished with the pardon. The poor soldier lying wounded on the field of battle, as his conquering friends sweep by him, and the enemy, the plunderer, the murderer, are hurled away from his throat, yet knows that the broken limb, the shattered arm, the burning wound, have to come under the surgeon's hand; he learns to welcome that pain which is to heal him. Oh, perhaps already you have entered into the meaning of that Psalm, when David clasping the sword to his soul, which never more was to leave his house, cried, "Wash me more and more from my wickedness and cleanse me from my sin."[2] Yes, God's chastisement is part of His separation, part of His healing love for His saints; He which began a good work in us at our Baptism goes on performing it until the day of Jesus Christ.[3]

And even more so is it with those whom God is calling higher still. They must learn to bear, if they are to receive God's gifts—His best gifts. We are not naturally humble, loving, gentle, meek. Humility is

[1] Heb. xii. 6. [2] Psa. li. 2. [3] Phil. i. 6.

not a natural virtue, meekness is not a natural virtue. God will send you some trial, some little one, or some great one, if He wishes to develop in you this saintliness. Can you bear it? "Woe unto you that have lost patience; and what will ye do when the Lord shall visit you"? Are you "the man of His right hand, the son of man whom He made so strong for His own self"?[1] Or, like S. Christopher in the legend, do you sink beneath the exceeding weight of the Holy Child? It was noticed some time ago, that a man had discovered an invention for making a form of crystallized carbon, which, to all intents and purposes, was a diamond; but his invention was useless, because of the difficulty and expense in getting any vessel strong enough to bear the intense heat to which it must be subjected during the process. And so with some of God's saints, they faint beneath the trial, and the saintly virtue is not formed within their characters, because they have lost the power of endurance.

And so the separation goes on : and we know there will be a final separation between the saint and the sinner; between the sheep and the goats; between the men of the right and the men of the left hand; between the wheat and the tares; between the good fish and the bad; between the good grain and the chaff; and that separation will endure for ever.

Surely this day should quicken our lagging footsteps. A glimpse of that glorious fringe in the train of the most High, Whose glory fills the temple of the world, should make us press on,[2] if not for His sake,

[1] Psa. lxxx. 17.   [2] Isa. vi. 1.

if not for fear of hell, at least that we may meet those whom on earth we have learnt to love. Let us with an intensity of earnestness, as we have never prayed before, pray to-day—separated as I have been in Baptism, separated in Confirmation, separated in Holy Communion, separated in Thy tender and merciful dealings with me—make me, O Lord, at the last, the great, the awful separation—"Make me to be numbered with Thy saints in glory everlasting."[1]

[1] Te Deum.

SERMON XXI.

The Angels.

"For this cause ought the woman to have power on her head because of the Angels."—1 Cor. xi. 10.

MICHAELMAS day is one of those festivals of the Church which carries our thoughts right away from this visible scene to the great unseen world beyond. And therefore, in an age of material progress, and great pride of life, the thoughts which it suggests are more than ever valuable, and not lightly to be passed by, as if the Angels were the fairies of our childhood, and their ministry an ecclesiastical sentiment. Our religion, as we have received it, is the religion of the unseen God. His working is unseen; His dwelling-place is unseen; the home he promises to us is unseen; and therefore, as we might expect, revealed religion from end to end tells us that with our feet we press this earth, but with our head we touch the Heavens; that man is surrounded by two sets of influences—on one side there is the earth, with all that appeals to sense; on the other there is Heaven, with all its mysterious forces and agencies ministering to his eternal welfare.

And so we find the belief in the unseen world is to be the comfort of the Christian. In temptation he is reminded that he must look to Jesus, the author and finisher of his faith;[1] in the presence of sin he is to remind himself that " the eyes of the Lord are in every place, beholding the evil and the good,"[2] that His body is the temple of the living God;"[3] in persecution he is invited with the first martyr, S. Stephen, to look up to Heaven, and by faith behold the glory that shall be revealed;[4] if weary in well-doing, he is to consider the great company of the saints, who surround the arena of life, as a great cloud of witnesses.[5] Yes, again and again we are urged to pierce the veil which hangs between us and the Holy of Holies, where God dwells, that we may see our King and His followers standing on high to help us.

And S. Paul here, while discussing a point of ecclesiastical discipline in the church at Corinth, on a matter which we might be tempted to think almost trivial and unimportant, furnishes another spiritual motive to decency and order—the invisible presence of Angels. "For this cause ought the woman to have power on her head" (that is, a covering in sign that she is under the power of her husband) " because of the Angels."

And this is the thought which the Church puts before us to-day; we ought to quit ourselves like men and be strong, because of God the Father, Who made us, the Son, Who redeemed us, the Holy Ghost, Who

---

[1] Heb. xii. 2.   [2] Prov. xv. 3.   [3] 2 Cor. vi. 16.
[4] Collect for S. Stephen's day.   [5] Heb. xii. 1.

sanctifies us; but also in a far lower, but still in a real sense, "because of the Angels," because of these bright beings who see God and see us, and wing their way between God and man. And you will notice the important part which Angels have played in the history of the world. The Bible begins in almost its first page with Cherubims at the gate of Paradise,[1] and closes with the Angel who tells S. John not to seal up the Revelation.[2] They are Angels who wield the wrath of God, in the destruction of the cities of the plain;[3] in the plague sent upon Jerusalem;[4] in the destruction of the hosts of Sennacherib.[5] Angels lead and guide God's chosen people;[6] the Angel of the Covenant goes before them.[7] They release S. Peter from prison;[8] they are the guardians of little children.[9] Angels trouble the healing pool, to give it its efficacy;[10] Angels wait closely on the Incarnation. Gabriel heralds the approach of the King;[11] the Angels rush out of heaven on Christmas night to supply man's lack of service to the new-born King;[12] Angels minister to the tempted and wearied Lord in the desert;[13] an Angel strengthens Him in His agony;[14] an Angel is privileged to strike the first blow for his risen Lord,[15] which was denied before to twelve legions of the heavenly hosts;[16] Angels wait on the

[1] Gen. iii. 24.   [2] Rev. xxii. 10.   [3] Gen. xix. 15.
[4] 2 Sam. xxiv. 16.   [5] Isa. xxxvii. 36.
[6] Exod. xxiii. 20.   [7] Josh. v. 14.   [8] Acts xii. 7.
[9] S. Matt. xviii. 10.   [10] S. John v. 4.
[11] S. Luke i. 11, 26.   [12] S. Luke ii. 13.   [13] S. Matt. iv. 11.
[14] S. Luke xxii. 43.   [15] S. Matt. xxviii. 2.
[16] S. Matt. xxvi. 53.

Ascension; "The chariots of God are twenty thousand, even thousands of Angels, and the Lord is among them, as in the holy place of Sinai."[1] And Angels will come with Him to judgment at the last;[2] so that if any say they wish to think of the King, and not of His servants, Michaelmas Day will show us that He at least did not disdain their presence and aid, and that they are still "ministering spirits, sent forth to minister for them who shall be heirs of salvation."[3]

And perhaps we should do well to follow S. Paul in this respect, and think of the presence of Angels in the world, as he considered it, as a corrective thought, a thought to restrain and check what is wrong, to develop and improve what is good within us.

(1) "Because of the angels." What a corrective we have here against pride! It is not the thought of the war in heaven, and Satan cast out, and falling through pride;[4] it is not the example of S. Michael, who, when contending with the devil, he disputed about the body of Moses, durst not bring against him a railing accusation, but said, "The Lord rebuke thee;"[5] it is not the significance of his glorious name proclaiming to all ages, "Who is like God?" It is rather the thought of the Angels as the guardians of symmetry and order in this glorious universe, which man disturbs and mars through pride; of that heavenly harmony, whereby the Angels would have all things

---

[1] Psa. lxviii. 17. [2] S. Matt. xxv. 31.
[3] Heb. i. 14. [4] Rev. xii. 6. [5] S. Jude 9.

praise the Lord, and of mortals injuring that harmony by discordant action!

And this is the meaning of S. Paul's warning here —at Corinth women were thrust out of their place in a way which threatened their modesty, and the order of God's creation; and so he says, "For this cause ought the woman to have power on her head because of the Angels,"—for the Angels, being the guardians of decency and order, must view any violation of them with pain and distress. It is such a thought as this which should be a constant help to recall us to ourselves. Man is ever trying to push himself out of his place in creation. There are those who in a rebellious spirit would climb Heaven, and thrust God down; who have tasted of the tree of knowledge, and now would claim to be as gods. They should think of the Angels who see God, and are contented to do His will, as in Heaven so in earth—and be humble. Or there are those who are the slaves of their bodies, who degrade "the high calling of God in Christ Jesus;" they, too, should think of those bright Spirits whom Jesus passed by when He was incarnate (for He took not up in that glorious elevation the nature of Angels)[1]—of those Angels who see God, and those pleasures which are at His right hand for evermore, and wonder how men can forfeit these for the vain and evil pleasures of a sensual life. Or if there be any one who is in any sense unreal, who thrusts himself out of his place—let him feel that in affecting to be something which he is not, he is

---
[1] Heb. ii. 16. ἐπιλαμβάνεται, takes up to help.

destroying the order of God's appointment; let him too remind himself that he must keep in his place, because of those bright Beings who tend the universe with anxious care, who are made by their Creator to be winds, and ministers in the flame of fire.[1]

(2) But S. Paul, no doubt, in his strictures on the Corinthian Church, had also in his mind that strong belief, so common to Jews and Christians alike, that Angels assist more especially in the public services of the Church. Any impropriety unseemly in itself becomes doubly hateful in the public assembly, because of the presence of the Heavenly Host; any immodesty, or want of respect, becomes doubly wrong in view of the Angelic worship with which our worship is linked. For we know that the Angels veil their faces in adoring respect for the presence of God, and worship Him with fear, upon Whom they are allowed to gaze with love. And most assuredly it is a belief which may well act as a wholesome corrective and check to the coldness, indifference, and want of respect which too often mars our service of God. As we think of the stately movements of the Angelic Host around the throne of God, let the thought waken our listless, wayward devotion into reverence and awe. As we hear the faint notes of their hymn coming through the veil, let it quicken our faltering langour, and attune our discordant voices, which have presumed to join "with Angels and Archangels[2] and with all

---

[1] Heb. i. 7. ὁ ποιῶν τοὺς ἀγγέλους αὐτοῦ πνεύματα καὶ τοὺς λειτουργοὺς αὐτοῦ πυρὸς φλόγα.

[2] Service of Holy Communion.

the company of Heaven," in the hymn of the thrice Holy, whose thunder is ever breaking on the shores of the glassy sea. As we catch a glimpse of those veiled faces, wrapt in devotion, let the sight of it raise in us more of that spirit of holy fear, and check our wandering eyes and thoughts. As we see those tossing censers, fragrant with sweet odours, let the sight rouse us to kindle once more the warm coal of devotion in our hearts, and to raise our censers, which hang idly on the ground, and put on the sweet incense of prayer, which may be offered upon the golden Altar. Ah, they must wonder at our coldness and dulness—those Angels who see God. Just as in some concert of music we may sometimes see those on whose ear the splendid harmonies, and the stately rhythm, and the melodious sounds, fall unnoticed, unappreciated, uncared for; or in a gallery of works of art, we may sometimes see those who move untouched, unheeding, and unsympathizing amidst the glories of form and colour and beauty—blind to art: so must we move before the Angels deaf to heaven's harmonies, blind to heaven's loveliness; near to God, yet seeing Him not; within the sound of His voice, yet heeding Him not. What is ugly in itself becomes hideous in contact with beauty; therefore let this thought quicken our devotions. We will adore the Almighty God because we love Him, because He made us, because He comes to us in the Sacrament of His love, because He is the Sanctifier of our souls; but also we will worship Him with a worship more worthy of His presence, "because of the Angels," our fellow-servants in the service of perfect beauty.

(3) But also the Church has ever believed that we have a silent companion, a silent witness of all the secret movements, the secret as well as open sins, and the secret triumphs of our inner life; the guardian Angel, whom Christ has allotted to us at our baptism, such as painters have loved to depict, guarding the steps of the pilgrim as he walks by the side of precipices and pitfalls; an Angel who is ever at our side, who watches over us, and will render up our soul at death into its Master's hand. This, as it is a comforting, soothing, and most blessed thought, so it is also a great corrective to us if tempted to yield to evil. You remember, perhaps, those words in which the poet has tried to express some of the awe and reverence which a belief in the presence of the holy dead should inspire within us if we really felt it—

> "Do we indeed desire the dead
> Should still be near us at our side?
> Is there no baseness we would hide—
> No inner vileness that we dread?
>
> "Shall he for whose applause I strove—
> I had such reverence for his blame—
> See with clear eye some hidden shame,
> And I be lessened in his love?"[1]

Should not some such feeling as this be ours when we once fully realize the great truth of the presence of our guardian Angel, ever beside us, watching each action, sharing each joy and sorrow? When we go into the midst of bad surroundings we must drag him with us as an unwilling companion; he must correct us and

[1] Tennyson, "In Memoriam."

punish us; perhaps it is from his hands that the sickness or sorrow with which God Almighty sees fit to afflict us, is brought upon us. What must be the anxiety, what the fear, of these holy Beings, as they see us tottering like wilful children along our dangerous path, armed with the awful gift of free-will, by which we can not only resist them, but even God Almighty Himself!

Oh! dear friends, on this feast of S. Michael and all Holy Angels, think of that holy company, not "as a mere feeling and a sort of luxury of the imagination,"[1] but as a real help in our heavenly course, a real corrective to our diseased life. Am I playing my part in that vast order over which the Angels watch? Am I in tune in the celestial harmony? Is my worship in the courts of the Lord's house worthy to be joined with theirs, who see God as He is? Do I vex and weary my guardian Angel with all the waywardness and frowardness of a spoiled child; or do I walk soberly and honestly along the paths of life, under his guidance and protection? If our eyes were opened, we should see ourselves, as did the servant of Elisha, surrounded with the armies of Heaven;[2] we should see our daily life, with all its cares and troubles and anxieties, stretching away, like a great ladder, into heaven, and Angels ascending and descending on it.[3] We should be reverent, pure, holy, and good, because we love God; because we fear His terrors and look for His glorious appearing, but also "because of the Angels." We should count it among the restraints,

[1] Dr. Newman.   [2] 2 Kings vi. 17   [3] Gen. xxviii. 12.

as it is undoubtedly among the consolations, of our spiritual life, that we are come "to an innumerable company of Angels."[1] And while the world, in its practical Sadducceism, says that there is no Resurrection, neither Angel, nor Spirit, we shall in this point at least agree with the stricter religion of the ancient Pharisee, and in faith, life, and precept, to our intense comfort, yet wholesome restraint, confess both.[2]

[1] Heb. xii. 22.   [2] Acts xxiii. 8.

SERMON XXII.

Fasting.

"*Whosoever doth not bear his cross, and come after Me, cannot be My disciple.*"—S. LUKE xiv. 27.

THE subject which I have undertaken this morning is a difficult one. Not because it is difficult to understand, not because it rests on any uncertain warrant of Holy Scripture, not because the Church is indefinite on the point. The subject is easy to understand; Holy Scripture is unambiguous, and the Church is precise. But fasting is one of those subjects which men in general have agreed to ignore; to look upon with a kind of complacent pity, or to regard as a kind of rhetorical finish, when they hear of it, as we mention it in the services of the Church, coupled with prayer and repentance. And, therefore, perhaps, I shall not have the sympathy of many of you; the sermon will seem unreal and unpractical, the waste of a Sunday morning in Lent, when I address myself to the subject of fasting. And yet, for many reasons, it is a subject which cannot be neglected or put on one side. In the first place, it occupies an important position in the teaching and practice of our Blessed

Lord. It is put in a very prominent place among the precepts of the Sermon on the Mount; and our Lord's example in this respect is one of the very reasons why we observe Lent. In the second place, its practical utility would seem to be immense, and perhaps indeed fasting offers the true solution of some of the great moral difficulties of the day. Thirdly, it is the consecration, as I shall hope to show you, of vast masses of suffering, trouble, and anguish: forces, as they are, which by many are unutilized, but which, if offered up to God, might form part of the very scheme of Redemption, and hasten Christ's kingdom.

I. Following, therefore, the very simple rule of first investigating clearly *what* a thing is, before you proceed to examine it further, I venture to ask, apart from any preconceived opinion, what is fasting? And the *word* does not help us much; it means something observed or kept fast, or close, a strict rule. It is some rule of the Church, then. What rule? A rule, I find on investigation, which first in its strictest sense enjoins abstinence from food, on certain occasions, and for certain objects; then, abstinence from strong or pleasant food; then, abstinence from luxuries; then, generally, self-denial; then, more generally still, patience under trial.

And there are certain times, when this is put forward as a godly exercise, as we see from the notice in the beginning of the Prayer Book. Such are, the forty days of Lent; the Ember days as they come round, four times a year; the three Rogation days; every Friday in the year except Christmas day: and the eves or vigils of certain holy days. And besides this, many of us can remember that it has been a custom, which, however, has rather fallen into disuse of late, to appoint days of national fasting and humiliation in the presence of some great calamity. Such as, for instance, during the visitations of cholera in past years; and later still during the calamities and distresses of the Crimean War. Now the Church observes these days, first of all as a matter of obedience, and secondly, as a matter of principle. As to the duty of obedience, by which the Church feels herself bound to fast, it is so abundantly clear that I think I may assume it without proof or demonstration. No one looking at the facts of the case can hesitate for one moment to say, that not only did our Lord sanction and·follow the universal custom of the Jewish Church in His day as to fasting, but also He left behind Him positive precepts on the subject, one of which you will remember in the Sermon on the Mount,[1] and another in the answer given to the captious question as to the difference between His disciples and those of S. John Baptist, when He said that His disciples were not yet taught, disciplined, formed, but that the days were coming, when fasting would be one of the direct precepts which they would be called upon to follow.[2]

If I may be allowed, then, to pass this by, as abundantly capable of proof, I would rather address myself to the principle underlying the ordinance, more especially as any doctrine or practice formally adopted

[1] S. Matt. vi. 16.   [2] S. Matt. ix. 15.

by the Church is, by the very hypothesis, scriptural, because it is claimed for the Church over and over again that all her ordinances rest upon and are sanctioned by the warrant of Holy Scripture. What is the principle, then, which underlies the precept of fasting? On what ground does it rest in the wisdom of God's Providence and in the needs of man's weakness? Fasting, we find, in one shape or another, comes before us in all the pages of the world's history, sacred and profane. In the first place, it seems to have been in old times an almost universal way of expressing mourning and grief. And secondly, it seems to have been, and is now, the discipline which, either inside or outside the Church, either with religion or without it, men put upon their bodies. As instances of the first, beside the stated periodical fasts of the Jews, such as was the great Day of Atonement, we have certain fasts occurring on occasions of public or private calamity. We have David spending the time in fasting while the life of his son hung trembling in the balance;[1] Ahab fasted as an evident token of his penitence;[2] the heathen city of Nineveh fasted, from the king on his throne, even to the irrational animals, who were compelled to join in the universal sorrow.[3] Fasting in this aspect would seem to be an attempt to reproduce the involuntary result of sorrow in a voluntary way, to try and make one's self feel what sorrow, if it were real, would in itself produce; for who can eat, drink, and be merry under the weight of some very pressing sorrow? As to the

[1] 2 Sam. xii. 16.   [2] 1 Kings xxi. 27-29.   [3] Jonah iii. 7.

second use of fasting as a corrective and a discipline, we can trace many examples and many forms of this in the ancient world. Perhaps the continued abstinence of the children of Israel during their wanderings in the desert[1] was a discipline, a corrective before they entered upon the luxuries of the land flowing with milk and honey. The vows of the Nazarites embraced much of abstinence from God's creatures, and self-denial; as in men consecrated to God, whose bodies must therefore be in subordination to the soul.[2] Or the prophets, again, in their rough garments and spare diet, were they not perpetual witnesses to the spirit of self-denial and living protests to a careless world ? Or in profane history, are we not familiar with this spirit in the Spartan, who trusted to vigorous asceticism, hardness, and discipline, to develop the feeling of warlike patriotism which is ever ready to sacrifice ease to the welfare and honour of the state ? Or in Stoicism again, is there not a noble, but alas, futile effort to put forward the impassive spirit, untrammelled by the fetters of the body, disciplined by hardness, as a shield and protection against the troubles of life ? Pleasure could not elate, pain could not depress, the body which they despised. Until in Christianity we have this principle which men had approached from various sides engrafted into the religion which is to meet man's inmost needs—man is a complex being, body, soul, and spirit; he must not neglect his body; it is useful, it is blessed, it is holy ; but the body, if a good servant, is a terrible

---

[1] Deut. viii. 3.   [2] Numb. vi.

master. Within every man the will must reign supreme, and therefore the will must show its supremacy. Where Satan is leading hundreds upon hundreds of his victims captive in gluttony and drunkenness all around us, the will of the Christian must be able to show his body temperate, curbed, restrained. He must be able to say, so far from being allured into excess, I can voluntarily cut off those things which men think pleasant or necessary, and forego their very use. When the world is following pleasure and ease, and neglecting the eternal interest of the soul, the Christian ought to be able to say, instead of being entrapped by pleasure, I can of my own free will lay it aside if need be. Where the world shrinks from pain and unpleasant duties, the Christian ought to be able to say, "I welcome pain, I welcome suffering as something which God sends me. The whole principle of fasting is *self-denial.* The flesh is a spoilt child, it cries out for everything which it sees or wants. The will is the disciplinarian who thwarts it, curbs it, controls it, and does not mind in what way, if in any way it can make it obedient. What is an army without discipline? What are the great forces of nature, unless we can regulate them? What is man without self-control?

II. Granted, then, that this is a true account of fasting; what shall we do? You say, "I cannot fast, and if I could, I should be laughed at. And further, I do not yet believe in its efficacy or necessity."

Dear friends, before deciding hastily, I would ask you to look around you first, and see. Is it not a fact, that men are deliberately now inculcating abstinence for life from one of God's creatures, because some have lost control over its proper use? Besides this, there are mutterings already in some quarters, of something like vegetarianism. And the luxury of wealth and the misery of poverty are being brought uncomfortably close together in our large cities, and the extravagance of a refined sensuality is being watched with tiger eyes by squalid penury. Or think, again, how many people there are who have to spend their middle life and old age in all the restraint of a spare diet and strict medical rule, because they have impaired their health by want of self-control when they were young. There is plenty of fasting abroad, only under another name. And which is best, the stern repression of an enforced abstinence, which the will allows to be put upon it, in terror, or the confiscation of property under revolutionary disorder, or the wild dictates of a revived Manichæanism, or the vengeance of an abstinence which self-indulgence has hurried on—these stern, repressive, unloving measures—or the calm, deliberate, self-contained superiority, which, by the grace of God, is able to take or not to take, to eat or not to eat, to drink or not to drink, to use this world as not abusing it—" temperate in all things," because self-disciplined? Do not let us say, we can do nothing. *Anything* which will make us feel, *anything* which will make our rebellious body obedient, *anything* in which we have to sacrifice inclination, however trifling it may be—this will be a contribution to this great principle.

Here, in a measure, will be fasting. And surely everybody can do something, whether they be poor, or invalids, or weak, or little children; everybody can do something in the way, if not of fasting, at least of self-denial.

Alas! how selfish we are! Think if God had dealt with many of us as He has dealt with the poor and afflicted. What should we say if we knew not sometimes where to turn for a meal? What should we do, if when sickness, or want of work, or trouble came, we were told that we were grossly improvident, and had better go to the Union? What should we do, if we had not a home to shelter us, or a place to lay our head, like the Saviour of the world? Blessed be ye poor! Ye are like your Saviour in His lowliness and suffering. Like Simon, ye bear the cross after Him, and share His load. Is there no single pleasure, no selfish luxury we can give up? Is there no pleasure which we can buy by a self-denying action? If God has given us the perilous blessings of the rich, cannot we taste some of the holy sorrow of the poor?

And as we think of many who are racked with suffering, tossing on a bed of pain, whose whole life is one sharp discipline—born apparently to suffer—cannot we lay aside some luxury, or some enjoyment, to show that we really are serving God for nought,[1] that we love Him, and trust Him, and follow Him, not only because He is good, but because He is what He is—the Holy, true, and all-loving God?

[1] Job i. 9.

III. But, day by day, the cross is throwing its shadow over the world. Who is there among us who does not know that cold grey shadow falling upon the soul? Think, if each one of us could narrate now our heart-sorrows, what a record it would be! Some would dart aside out of its shadow; some would let it fall on a front cold and impassive as steel; but the Christian welcomes it, he bows his head to feel that blessed shadow of the cross, as it comes upon him with its icy chill. To take up the cross with the will, not to wish it otherwise, to rejoice in it—this is the highest form of self-discipline; this is that great power, which, as I said, is too often wasted in this world, the power of suffering.

God sees your imperfections, He sees the encroaching disease, He sends the suffering exactly adapted to your need. You send Him impatiently away, in fretful rebellion. God sees your need of discipline. Life with its cares, its business, its pleasures, is weaving a web around your soul; it cannot burst it asunder and be free. God lays His hand upon it; will you call it "misfortune," "ill-luck," and struggle to drive him away?

Oh, there is more done in the world by suffering even than by action. And there is more done in our souls by patient suffering than in any other way. Only take up the cross, in some way or another; ye cannot be Christ's disciples without. The flesh within, the world without, and the devil at their back, are busy with their work to keep down the soul; but they will vanish if they see the cross, not the mere plaything hung round the neck, of a religion without obligation or care, but the hard cross, laid on the back, which bore our Saviour to the ground, without some trial of which we cannot be His disciples.

SERMON XXIII.
Almsgiving.

" *Lay up thy treasure according to the commandments of the Most High, and it shall bring thee more profit than gold. Shut up alms in thy storehouses: and it shall deliver thee from all affliction.*"—
ECCLUS. xxix. 11, 12.

WHAT is almsgiving? It is the giving away of our substance, our goods, more particularly our money, in acts of pity, mercy, and usefulness to our neighbour. Almsgiving in its simple meaning is an act of mercy or pity. It would not be amiss, then, to examine the principle of almsgiving, if it be but in outline, to see what position it has held, and does hold, and ought to hold, in the religious life of men.

I. First of all, then, to give to one another, to help another's need out of our greater abundance, to be kind, compassionate, helpful, to do good, would seem to be, thank God, a law of nature. There is within every man, who is in a healthy moral state, a feeling of compassion, which, if it is not crushed out by selfishness, will lead him to minister to the wants of others and to give help. I need only instance the universal abhorrence in which *the miser*, the pre-eminently *miserable* man, is held, among all nations, and at all times.

Again, mutual help is a great political principle as well; no state has succeeded in maintaining itself without some system of taxation whereby all who have a certain degree of wealth are compelled to contribute to the good of the community, to sacrifice private to public wealth.

Passing within the pages of Revelation, the Old Testament is full of precept and example, as to the need, the blessing, the Divine duty of distributing to the need of others. What touching words these are in Ecclesiasticus! "Lay up thy treasure according to the commandments of the Most High, and it shall bring thee more profit than gold." We know what those commandments are, "Is not this the fast that I have chosen? ... Is it not to deal thy bread to the hungry, and that thou bring the poor that are cast out to thy house? when thou seest the naked, that thou cover him; and that thou hide not thyself from thine own flesh?"[1] Or again, "When thou cuttest down thine harvest in thy field, and hast forgot a sheaf in the field, thou shalt not go again to fetch it: it shall be for the stranger, for the fatherless, and for the widow: that the Lord thy God may bless thee in all the work of thine hands. When thou beatest thine olive tree, thou shalt not go over the boughs again: it shall be for the stranger, for the fatherless, and for the widow. ... And thou shalt remember that thou wast a bondman in the land of Egypt: therefore I command

[1] Isa. lviii. 6, 7.

thee to do this thing."[1] And this, not only for the sake of the poor. The Almighty God says that he stands as it were behind them, that He needs alms and money, that He pleads in their person: "He that hath pity upon the poor lendeth unto the Lord; and that which he hath given will He pay him again."[2] And not only does God ask alms in the person of His poor, but for His service also. "When thou takest the sum of the children of Israel after their number, then shall they give every man a ransom for his soul unto the Lord, when thou numberest them; that there be no plague among them, when thou numberest them."[3] It is in these storehouses that we are to shut up our alms; in the hearts of the poor, in the chambers of the Most High, in works of mercy, goodness, and love, and it shall deliver us from affliction. We are to make friends with the mammon of unrighteousness, as our Lord Himself tells us, that in the time of failure they may receive us into everlasting habitations.[4] These are only a few among the very numerous precepts in the Old Testament, bearing upon this duty; a few among many instances of the blessing promised by God to alms offered to Himself, in His poor and in His Church.

In the New Testament this duty is made plainer still. Our Blessed Lord had to deal with no new precept, but with one already existing, when He mentioned almsgiving; and in the Sermon on the Mount, He purifies it, removes it into the region of

[1] Deut. xxiv. 19-22.
[2] Prov. xix. 17.
[3] Exod. xxx. 12.
[4] S. Luke xvi. 9.

pure spirituality, puts it on its true and proper basis. He says the alms of the Christian must be given without ostentation or vainglory, but as a religious act. The left hand must not know what the right hand doeth.[1] The alms must be given in secret, as to the Father Who seeth in secret, waiting for the great day to reward the giver openly. Indeed, there are some statements which He makes on the subject, almost startling in their force and energy. He tells the young ruler, "If thou wilt be perfect, go and sell that thou hast, and give to the poor, and thou shalt have treasure in Heaven."[2] He tells the Pharisees, when He had been denouncing their hypocrisy, in a passage perhaps somewhat misunderstood, "Rather give alms of such things as ye have; and, behold, all things are clean unto you."[3] He stops to praise the two mites of the poor widow, not because they were two mites, but because they were all her living, a point very frequently missed by those who think they can imitate her in the smallness of the amount rather than in the completeness of the surrender. "I will give my mite," if it means anything in our mouth, means, "I will give all my living," not the smallest sum that I can grudgingly spare.[4]

And so, passing on to Apostolic times, we find that rules on the subject are gradually being formulated by the Church. S. Paul says, "Upon the first day of the

---

[1] S. Matt. vi. 3.   [2] S. Matt. xix. 21.
[3] S. Luke xi. 41. Τὰ ἐνόντα, of those things that are within, *i.e.* give alms of the food and drink which are within the cup and platter.
[4] S. Luke xxi. 1–4.

week let every one of you lay by him in store, as God hath prospered him, that there be no gatherings when I come;"[1] a rule which finds its counterpart now very generally in the weekly offertory; until we find that it is the custom of many Christians to put by a tenth of whatever God has given them, to be devoted to good purposes—partly to the Church, partly to various good works, or to those organized societies for doing good which need their help. And this they look upon as a *debt* to God, after which, and not before, almsgiving, properly so called, may be said to begin.

II. Now, underlying this universal law as to almsgiving, in its necessity, efficacy, and Divine approval, we may recognize two principles. First, almsgiving would seem to follow as a necessity from God's government of the world. And, secondly, it is adapted to meet some peculiar defect of the human soul, from which fact it derives its power and moral efficacy. In the first place, then, God has notoriously, and as far as we know, of deliberate purpose, distributed unequally the possession of worldly goods here in this life. Some are rich, some are poor, and as far as we can see, this will always be the case, " The poor shall never cease out of the land."[2] Some have power, some have none; some have much influence, some have little; some have wealth, some have poverty. There is a priesthood of influence, a priesthood of power, a priesthood of wealth. And if a man takes the riches, or the power, or the influence, which God

[1] 1 Cor. xvi. 2.   [2] Deut. xv. 11.

has given him, laid up in him, as it were, as in a centre, or store, from which he may minister to the need of others, and spends them to his own aggrandizement—then, he is an unfaithful steward. He is diverting to himself that which God meant to be distributed in good to others. Therefore, if, after making a liberal allowance for our own life, its needs, its necessities, its enjoyments, if you will, we forget our public duties; we are as if we had been entrusted with Government money, for some famine-stricken district of the empire, and as if apart from the liberal salary which Government has given us, we also appropriated public money, and left the people to starve, whose famine we were sent to alleviate. And so you will trace another meaning in the warnings, in the almost threats, which accompany the possession of riches, "Woe unto you that are rich!"[1] "How hardly shall they that have riches enter into the kingdom of God. . . . It is easier for a camel to go through the eye of a needle, than for a rich man to enter into the kingdom of God!"[2]—a rich man being one who bows himself down, vanquished, before his special temptation, who lays up treasure for himself, and is not rich toward God, and forgets his solemn stewardship and duties.[3]

And do not let us push away the thought as if it were one which we could lay on the broad shoulders of the rich. Every one to whom God has given a competency is entrusted by God with so much for the spread of His kingdom. Even the very poor should

[1] S. Luke vi. 24.   [2] S. Mark x. 23, 25.   [3] S. Luke xii. 21.

try to minister in some way to the general good of the world. The poor widow in the Gospel had a home, a life to maintain, yet God was pleased to see her remember the temple out of her needs. God, Who supports all things by the word of His power, throws yet a certain portion of the management of the world upon us; its poor, its manifold wants, with the almost equally manifold means of ministering to them. He makes *Himself* poor. He asks our alms, our offerings, our self-sacrifice. He condescends to accept our help, that we may be "workers together with Him,"[1] Who giveth all.

And yet another principle still underlies almsgiving. Almsgiving is that which almost more than anything else is adapted to correct a sinful tendency in man;[2] that love of money, which is the root of all evil.[3] And it is that practice of virtue which more than any other tends to make a man like God, "that giveth to all men liberally, and upbraideth not."[4] How difficult it is to overcome that selfish feeling, that love of getting, that love of having, that avarice and selfish indulgence We see it in the history of many a past sin; we see it day by day; we can trace it in our own hearts. Selfishness is at the bottom of almost all sin. A wedge of gold and a Babylonish garment quite outweighed in the mind of Achan the

---

[1] 2 Cor. vi. 1.
[2] In Adams' beautiful allegory of "The Old Man's Home," one sign of the old man's supposed weakness of intellect is that, being sufficiently well off, he invariably asks people for alms. His explanation is, he does it for their sakes, not his own.
[3] 1 Tim. vi. 10.   [4] S. James i. 5.

possibility of a national disgrace.[1] Thirty pieces of silver were dearer to Judas[2] than the companionship of Him Whose wisdom "cannot be gotten for gold, neither shall silver be weighed for the price thereof."[3] Material possession of land and moral possession of the credit of a good deed together shut out all view of lying and sacrilege from Ananias and Sapphira.[4] Luxury and ease make our hearts gross, so that we cannot love God. Love of the world shuts our ears to the voice of God and to the Gospel precepts.[5] Well, to all this, the practice of almsgiving is a corrective. It makes us think of others; it makes us deny ourselves; it enlarges our sympathies; it widens our sphere of usefulness; above all, it makes us like God. Think of God, the great Father of all, giving to us our daily bread, sending His rain on the just and on the unjust, kind to the thankful and unthankful alike, in the never-failing Providence of His far-seeing Goodness. Think of our Blessed Lord while on earth, ever ready to give up His leisure, to rise from His meals, to attend to every want, to heal the sick, to be disturbed in His repose, to be at the beck and call of all. The Saviour of mankind! Think of the Holy Spirit, Whose blessed influence spreads

---

[1] Josh. vii. 21. [2] S. Matt. xxvi. 14, 15.
[3] Job xxviii. 15. [4] Acts v. 1, 2.
[5] In relation to the subject of almsgiving, there is a saying of our Blessed Lord quoted by S. Paul—the only one, be it remembered, outside the Gospels—and which we may therefore well take, as having been preserved by tradition in the early Church, as one of immense practical importance in the Christian life—"It is more blessed to give than to receive" (Acts xx. 35). How many of us, alas, in effect turn the text upside down!

everywhere, like the very air we breathe, in the ordinances of the Church, in the pages of the Bible, in the sensitive warnings of conscience! God giveth to all men liberally. Almsgiving was surely meant to correct our tendency to selfishness. It was meant to make us like Him, upon Whom the eyes of all are waiting. It was meant to make with the mammon of unrighteousness very friends hereafter in heaven above to welcome us.

III. As a practical deduction from this, then, dear friends, I would appeal for a few plain rules to guide us on the subject.

(1) Let us make almsgiving a part of our religion. People have got in the way of viewing it as an excrescence, as an addition to the income-tax, instead of being what it is—part of our religion. God gives us all we have. Some of it is to be spent on our own needs, some on Him, some on the needs of others. Almsgiving is a religious act, without which any true religion must fail.

(2) Then I would plead for some method in almsgiving. Would it not be possible to have a certain sum which we would contribute each year to good purposes; and besides this, at special times, give something more which we might *feel?*

(3) Then as to ways and modes of giving. The weekly offertory seems to be a primitive, right, and proper channel for our alms. In it we may give to the worship of God, to the poor, and to other good works, as they are brought before us. This is an opportunity open to all. Do we make the most of

it? Could we not make a point of giving so much a week, of laying by a little more than we do, of giving according to our means? This surely would command a direct blessing from the Lord. And then there are all the opportunities which come to us in the appeals for help from various quarters, where men are wrestling with evil and striving to bring God's Son out of Egypt.[1] Here we may help where we can; and if we cannot, simply say so. But whatever we offer, and whenever we offer, our offering should be characterized by these three things. First, it should be offered unto the Lord; secondly, it should be offered readily; thirdly, it should be offered in a spirit of self-denial. But, alas! what is the general character of our offerings? They are offered too often with some inward grumbling as to perpetual begging. They are offered grudgingly, after every attempt to depreciate the object to which they are to be devoted. They are offered in this spirit—"What is the least sum which I can respectably give?"—not, "What is the sum which will test my earnestness by the self-denial which it must inflict?" I have known before now of a poor person who, having no money to bestow on charitable objects, has given a day's work out of a hard life; that was a real offering. I have heard of a munificent donor whose only lament about his princely gift to God was that he did not feel it. I have heard of a poor woman, almost destitute and bedridden, who actually went without a light in the long winter evenings, and who thereby (and it was

[1] Hos. xi. 1.

only found out after much pressing) contrived to give sixpence a quarter to foreign missions; and when she died, her next quarter's sixpence was found wrapped up and ready. Almsgiving, alas! is a Christian duty which is terribly rare. Rare in its performance at all, rare in the Christ-like spirit which recommends it, rare without a pompous list of subscriptions and a hold over the money when it has been given. It is the most unwelcome business which devolves upon the clergy, that of collecting money for the various purposes of religion and charity. Many clergy in our large towns are beaten down by it simply because there is so little thought in those who might give, so little method, so little will, simply because almsgiving has dropped out as a duty, and has to be collected as an unwelcome tax.

An old writer says,[1] a certain man had three friends, whom he asked to lead him into the presence of the king. The first took him half-way, and could go no further; the second took him to the gate of the palace, unable to do any more; the third took him into the presence of the king, and pleaded his cause for him. The first is abstinence, which helps a man to start towards God; the second is chastity, which brings us where we may see God; the third is mercy and almsgiving, because it brings us into God's very presence, Who is ever calling from His throne of mercy, "Gather My saints together unto Me, those that have made a covenant with Me with sacrifice."[2]

[1] Quoted in Coleridge, "Public Life of our Lord."
[2] Psa. l. 5.

SERMON XXIV.

Prayer.

"*Lord, teach us to pray.*"—S. LUKE xi. 1.

PRAYER is a subject of such great importance that we should never be afraid of considering it too often, or of overrating its value. And it follows to-day in a natural sequence upon the consideration of fasting and almsgiving, which subjects have lately occupied our attention, inasmuch as it forms a part of the main teaching of the great Sermon on the Mount. Fasting and almsgiving go together, yet both are incomplete without prayer. We may keep our bodies in subjection, our appetites in control, and yet be little more than respectable ascetics; we may do our duty in almsgiving, and yet not rise beyond the height of philanthropy. But by prayer we are brought into union with powers high and great, and infinitely above us. Prayer exercises an effect upon a man's soul such as nothing else can. It lifts him up into a higher and purer atmosphere. Prayer supplies the strength and the material of a noble and lofty morality such as no mere earthly precepts could command. Prayer is a fertilizing stream, whose waters overlap the channel of a man's soul, and spread life and health all around him. And so when our Blessed Lord, in answer to His disciples' request, taught them to pray, He was consecrating to their use a weapon of vast spiritual power, to be wielded by all, and at the same time a necessity for all. For prayer is at once man's highest duty and his greatest blessing.

I. Now what is prayer? Prayer is a petition for temporal or spiritual good addressed to a living God. And notice that when our Blessed Lord taught the necessity and efficacy of prayer, as in fasting and in almsgiving, so in this, He was inculcating no new thing. The heathen, in the longing of the inmost soul for intercourse and communion with what was Divine, breathed forth their prayer to the sun and moon and stars, which could not answer them; or they thought in fierce beasts, or strange forms, or hideous idols, to find the God whom their soul desired to love. On the top of some wave-beaten rock, or in some lonely island in the dark forest shade, or by the trickling fountain, we find the ruins still of temples and the altars raised to gods who heard not, neither regarded the frantic cries of man's despair. And so within the pages of Holy Scripture; sacrifice begins at the gate of Eden; the patriarchs and the prophets walk with God. In the law and ritual of Moses God is brought very near to the children of Israel; in the Gospel He is brought nearer still, "He that hath seen Me hath seen the Father;"[1] all prayer offered unto the Father in His name will be granted;[2] until

[1] S. John xiv. 9. [2] S. John xvi. 23.

every little child is taught among us, that in prayer he has a ready means of access to Almighty God, Who dwells amidst the glories and riches of heaven; that, just as in the mystery of some delicately balanced machinery some huge ship, with its mass of wood and iron, can be launched into the water by the mere twist and motion of a slender handle, so prayer, little in itself, is linked by all the machinery of Heaven to the great powers of the universe, so that we may say to this mountain, " Be thou removed, and be thou cast into the sea," and it shall be done.[1]

But, perhaps, already an objection has occurred to us. God is Almighty and All-loving and Irresistible. He orders everything by His power; He predestinates. If, then, He is All-loving and All-powerful at the same time, He will do what I wish without any asking on my part. Further, it is useless for me to ask, for my petition may involve a contradiction of, or even an opposition to, His great plans. For instance, many of our bishops are at the present time urging us to ask God to send fair weather instead of this prolonged rain, and to avert from us what we think to be a threatening and impending calamity. And people say, or think, if they do not always say, that if God interferes exceptionally about the weather at all, as He is Omnipotent and All-loving, He will surely do what I want, and what is good for me, without any asking on my part; and, further, they will say, does it not unduly elevate man's importance to think that he should presume to ask God Almighty to take a certain course,

[1] S. Mark xi. 23.

dictating thereby to Him the line of action which He is to assume? To these objections it is sufficient surely to say that, first of all, God is a living God; that He has not abdicated His power in favour of any law, however good and uniform in its action; secondly, that all prayer is conditioned, as in the Lord's Prayer, by these three limitations, "Hallowed be Thy Name:" grant my prayer only if it be to Thy glory; "Thy kingdom come:" grant my prayer only on condition that it be to the spread of Thy great empire of justice and truth; "Thy will be done:" hear my prayer only so far as it coincides with Thy great plan. Grant me my wishes only so far as they are in accordance with Thy great will. And, thirdly, we may say (and this is a truth which we need to note very carefully), that when God asks us to pray, He is merely asking us to do that which He requires of us at every stage of our life, as a condition of every blessing; namely, to work together with Him, to do our part in contributing to our own needs before He extends to us His bounty. The labour of man must meet the produce of the earth, to prepare it for human food; science and skill must extract from a bountiful universe the gifts which it has in store for the advantage of men. In the spiritual life, Sacraments and Ordinances are deprived of their full efficacy unless they are met on the part of man with repentance and faith. Salvation itself waits for man to do his part, to work out his own salvation,[1] in union with the atoning blood of Christ. God will not force

[1] Phil. ii. 12

man; in everything he must choose. Even in the most common gifts of His daily Providence it is the ordinary principle of His Divine working. God helps those who help themselves.

And so prayer becomes a necessity, if the earth is to bring forth her fruit, if God's wrath is to be averted, if the soul is to receive her proper nourishment. Prayer is a duty laid upon all, more especially upon those who have leisure and opportunity, just as almsgiving is a duty, especially to those to whom God has entrusted wealth. God expects us to bring down blessings from Heaven which we may give to our fellow-men; blessings on those who are toiling in the mission-field abroad; blessings on those who are struggling with heathenism at home, health to the sick, strength to the weak, succour to the tempted, help to the poor, perfecting to the soul. All these blessings God expects us to gather from Him by our prayers, that we may distribute them among others.

Have we, then, learnt to pray? Remember it is one thing to say our prayers, and another thing to pray. Apart from all the manifold imperfections and distractions which disfigure our prayers, have we learnt really to pray? Have we got beyond a system of prayer which resembles the mechanical prayer-wheel of the heathen? Have we got beyond the mere soothing sound of good words, preached at us on Sunday, or coming before our eyes with a certain feeling of unreality in the pages of a book? Have we learnt that prayer is an asking for something which we want, from One who has it in His power to give? From

One who is in Heaven, surrounded by a great crowd of brilliant courtiers, while we are on earth? From One who is apparently as hard sometimes as an unjust judge;[1] as unyielding as a tired-out man, who has gone to rest;[2] so severe as to class His petitioners sometimes with the dogs;[3] so lingering that the child whom He is asked to heal, dies while He is coming;[4] so delaying that hours and miles intervene between the granting of the request and the assurance of its fulfilment.[5] Have we learnt that prayer is a struggle, an effort, an exercise worthy of a strong man? This is what prayer is represented as being in the Bible; this is the asking to which is attached the promise of receiving.

III. What do we need, then, that we may pray as we ought? First of all, prayer requires *time*. We must give time to prayer, time sufficient for its greatness and importance. Can we say that we give time enough to prayer, as we use it day by day, and week by week? Has each day its tithe of prayer? Has Sunday its full share of holy devotion? It is not unfrequently said that it does us no good to come to church, unless we come with hearts ready and prepared. Are we quite right in saying "*no good*"? It is better, it is right so to come, it is suitable to God's dignity and honour, and to our own edification. But surely to come at all, is so far better than to stop away. It is a recognition of God. It is something,

[1] S. Luke xviii. 1.   [2] S. Luke xi. 5.
[3] S. Matt. xv. 26.   [4] S. Mark v. 35.
[5] S. John iv. 50.

even to go through the form of prayer day by day. It is something publicly to acknowledge God before and after our meals. It is something to gather the family together day by day for prayer. As the prince in the fairy story is saved by the pressure of the magic ring, still on his finger, in the midst of his misfortunes, although he had forgotten its efficacy, so oftentimes old forms and habits which have been retained through a careless life,[1] help us because they are there. The old strength returns, the old vigour rekindles the bare form, and there is life. Yes, it is something, even to give time to prayer, for God requires our time as a recognition of His Majesty, Who gives us this opportunity in which we may serve Him.

And then, as I have already anticipated, prayer demands that *trouble* should be expended upon it. Prayer is not an easy matter. And just as we shall always find, that nothing is more insipid than that which we do not understand, and do not thoroughly enter into, so prayer requires an exercise of our faculties if it is to be of real good to us.[2] Even games, and recreations, much more intellectual pursuits, if they are taken up hastily, and are only imperfectly understood, become dull and tasteless; so with prayer, it does require trouble; it does need an effort to find God, at home in the quiet of our own room, amid the surroundings of our daily toil and pleasure; to lift

---

[1] As an instance of this, the author of "Five Years' Penal Servitude" mentions that one-fifth of the prisoners in one of the association rooms in Dartmoor prison knelt down to say their prayers.

[2] "Of all mental exercises, earnest prayer is the most severe."
—COLERIDGE.

up our soul to Him, away from the thoughts of the world, and the associations of our earthly life. It does need an effort, even here in church, amid the manifold distractions of the place, in the assembly of our friends, in the highly pitched form of devotion, in the prolonged effort which worship implies,— through all this to reach Him! This requires an effort, this requires a concentration of the will, a bracing up of the faculties, a determination to break through obstacles, a discipline of the powers of our mind. It is something to give time to prayer, and to the service of God; but it is even more to give that vigorous, earnest effort, which, longing to reach God, breaks through every obstacle, until it finds Him.

And then, lastly, prayer requires preparation. God does not merely ask "*when?*" and "*how?*" but also He asks "*whence?*" It will be a feeble prayer, and one which cannot hope to reach the ear of Almighty God, which comes out of worldliness, or carelessness, or selfishness, or sin. If we pray out of a sinful heart, we are beating against a fast closed door; there is no sound, no voice, no answer to our cry. Sin produces that weakness of the soul which prevents it from rising on the wings of prayer. Sin shuts out the sight of God. "The heart of this people is waxed gross, and their ears are dull of hearing, and their eyes have they closed."[1] Sin in the heart is a dumb and deaf spirit. It prevents us from speaking to God, it prevents us from hearing any reply. Our life must prepare us for prayer, lest He say to us,

[1] Acts xxviii. 27.

"I will not hear."[1] Earnestness of heart, a longing for God, purity of purpose, repentance, faith, holiness, these are the vestments of preparation, which we must put on if our prayers are to mount up before the throne of Grace.

God's mercies, then, are waiting for us; all the stores of Heaven are waiting for us. But we must *ask*. "Ask, and it shall be given you; seek, and ye shall find; knock, and it shall be opened to you."[2] And prayer is worth little which does not involve a journey to the court of Heaven; which does not take time, and a definite place amidst the business of life; which is not pressed home with the full force of our being; which is not recommended by a holy life.

Let us pray God to defend our cause against the ungodly people,[3] the deceitful and the wicked man, to beat back those enemies within and without, which would intercept our prayer. Let us beg of Him to send out His light and His truth that they may lead us, and bring us unto His holy hill, and to His dwelling. And may He help us to cast away that heavy soul, and that disquieted heart, that we may put our trust in Him, Which is the help of our countenance and our God; through Whom alone we have access to the Father, in Whose name, whatsoever we ask in faith, believing we shall receive.

[1] Isa. i. 15. [2] S. Matt. vii. 7. [3] Psa. xliii.

SERMON XXV.

The Sword of the Lord.

"*The days shall come upon thee, that thine enemies shall cast a trench about thee, and compass thee round, and keep thee in on every side, and shall lay thee even with the ground, and thy children within thee; and they shall not leave in thee one stone upon another; because thou knewest not the time of thy visitation.*"—S. LUKE xix. 43, 44.

OUR Blessed Lord, in the awful secrets of His Divine foreknowledge, is weeping over the city, which He sees doomed to one of God's secret punishments, the scourge of war. He was probably just crossing the ground on which, a generation later, the tenth Roman legion would be encamped, as part of the besieging force destined to lay all the splendour before Him into ashes;[1] and in all the bitterness of "a sorrow's crown of sorrow," which is "remembering happier things," seeing what was to be, and knowing what might have been, He wept at the prospect before Him. And yet are we to say that Titus was wrong—I will not say in the details of that awful siege, but—in asserting the majesty of the Roman arms? Do we not see in him a terrible minister of God's judgment, bearing not the

[1] See Geikie's "Life of Christ," the description of Palm Sunday.

sword in vain,[1] sent to enforce justice, and to execute wrath, in the dreadful counsels of the vengeance of Almighty God? As the dispenser of justice to a revolted province, as the executor of plans beyond the keenest range of the ambition of his imperial instincts, he is the instrument in the hands of an Unseen God, a magistrate in the assize of nations, allowed by Almighty God to punish the holy city, with that mysterious and dreadful scourge of war.

And this is a subject very much in our thoughts to-day, as we are plunged at this moment in a war,[2] whose duration may be short or long, its intensity great or little—we cannot tell. We are watching the political anxiety in the counsels of Europe; the bustle and turmoil of armed preparation. Already there is sickening fear in many hearts; yes, there are some whose homes are even now darkened by the shadow of death; there are some who are carried away by the mere excitement of stirring times; there are some who are elated with the dreams of military ambition; some who are puzzled and perplexed, as at an item which will not be reconciled with their calculations of human improvement. Many are asking, where is the time of promised peace? When is to come that time when "nation shall not lift up sword against nation, neither shall they learn war any more."[3] Was it in mockery that the angels sang at the birth of Christ, "On earth peace, good will toward men"?[4]

---

[1] Rom. xiii. 4.
[2] Preached at the commencement of the Egyptian campaign of 1882.
[3] Isa. ii. 4.   [4] S. Luke ii. 14.

Have men learnt nothing better than to bite and devour one another? Is Christianity one more religion among the many that have been paralyzed by the persistency of human passions? But war is a mystery which will not be accounted for on hasty generalizations, or banished by the magic of a few isolated texts of Holy Scripture. In fact, it is possible to be misled by such phrases as "the horrors of war," and to forget its awful judicial character. As far as we can see, while the world is constituted as it is at present, there will be always the possibility of war. And further, war is not always the unmixed evil that we might think it to be. Further still, war is some part of the mighty scheme of God's justice, wherein nations are playing out the great game of life, moved by His Almighty Will, as if they were living, moving, thinking, individual lives.

Is this so? Did not Christianity profess to do away with war? Are we not to look for such a thing in the progress of humanity?

The facts would seem to be this, Christianity did not enter the world as a revolutionary power. There were great masses of evil in the world, in all the miserable surroundings of heathenism, more particularly in the dreadful and crying curse of slavery; but there was no violent onslaught on these things, no sudden and convulsive upheaving of society. No, Christianity trusted to its own principles as a quiet solvent in all these matters. The Christians, although men of yesterday, as they said, began to occupy everything, cities, islands, castles, . . . the very camp.[1] As Christianity spread, Christian masters had to deal with Christian slaves, and the spread of a purer light overthrew the vast scheme of ancient slavery sapped at the foundation. So, too, with the outward setting of life—the family, the city, the community, the nation—Christianity recognized all these, while elevating them to a higher level by the gradual spread of its purer morality. It recognized parental authority, without the sternness of the old Roman discipline; it recognized the sacredness of law, and judicial settlement between man and man, between community and community; and so by a similar process it was bound to recognize the authority of war, as an ultimate appeal between nations, while gradually and by degrees doing away with those wars of rapine, plunder, greed, and ambition, which are most hateful, and reserving the authority of war as the ultimate appeal of justice between nations.[2]

In accordance with this estimate the military profession occupies an honoured place in the New Testament. In fact, more than once centurions are put before us for our honour and respect, without any hint as to their calling being a dishonourable one. S. John the Baptist tells the soldiers who come to him, not to leave their profession, but shows them how they may guard against temptations incident to that profession.[3] War in its high judicial aspect is but

[1] "Hesterni sumus et vestra omnia implevimus, urbes insulas castella municipia, conciliabula, castra ipsa."—Tertull. Apolog. ch. 37.
[2] For this, and several other thoughts in this sermon, see Dr. Mozley's University Sermons, "War," p. 97, etc.
[3] S. Luke iii. 14.

capital punishment on a large scale. The same state which bears not the sword in vain to protect itself from the murderer at home, may also wield the sword against the oppressor, the tyrant, the murderer abroad, and claim in so doing to be wielding the power of the Almighty vengeance of God.[1]

Such is war, perhaps, viewed in its principle. And who shall say that amidst the terrors, and dangers, and bloodshed, and disease, and anguish, the blackened walls, and roofless houses, and shattered hopes, and desolated hearts, there is evil all round, and nothing but evil? War is a scourge of God on those on whom it falls; it is a scourge in the hand of those who wield it; but is there not often a bright harvest of good growing up from, and out of, the storm-cloud of war which sweeps over the land? Is there not, for instance, a beauty and glory in that spirit of patriotism, which throws to the winds its lesser jealousies to fight for the common life and glory of the nation? Is there not a virtue in the unselfish dedication of fortune, or child, or life to the great cause, which ceases to think of money-getting and indolent ease and luxury, to gird itself for the hardships of war?

"The higher aims
Of a land that has lost for a little her lust of gold,
And love of a peace that was full of wrongs and shames,

---

[1] See Dr. Forbes, XXXIX. Articles, vol. ii. p. 181. Gibbon taunts the early Christians with a supposed aversion to war, as making a pretended principle coincide with a coward indolence (see chap. xv. of his history). That this is not a fair account the quotation given above from Tertullian will show—*implovimus, ca stra ipsa;* or, again, *navigamus et nos vobiscum, et militamus.*

Horrible, hateful, monstrous, not to be told ;
And hail once more to the banner of battle unroll'd !
Tho' many a light shall darken, and many shall weep
For those that are crush'd in the clash of jarring claims,
Yet God's just wrath shall be wreak'd on a giant liar;
And many a darkness into the light shall leap,
And shine in the sudden making of splendid names,
And noble thought be freer under the sun,
And the heart of a people beat with one desire;
For the peace, that I deem'd no peace, is over and done."[1]

And who shall say that there is no virtue in gallant deeds and acts of heroism, adding to the treasures of a nation's history, which coming ages shall be ashamed to betray by baseness and treachery? Who can say that "more sin is not committed every day in every capital of Europe than on the largest battle-field?"[2] War is an awful thing, but so are the sins which produce it. The government of the world in the hand of God is a stupendous mystery; and it is a charge of dread, when God puts the sword into the hand of any nation, and bids it strike for justice, freedom, and the right.[3] War, then—just

[1] Tennyson, "Maud."   [2] Mozley.
[3] In reading Holy Scriptures we read, as it were, the history of the world with the curtain up, and the machinery of its scenes exposed to view. We, therefore, learn the causes on account of which the Almighty and Most Merciful God permitted the existence of war, and the purposes of divine retribution and loving mercy which He wrought out by its means in His earlier dispensations. But He is the same, yesterday, to-day, and for ever. Shall we not, then, be assured that in these latter days also His all-wise and benign Providence fulfils itself, even in events apparently the most disastrous, and presenting to our finite views problems the most difficult of solution? And if it be urged, how is it consistent with divine goodness to allow great misery to fall upon men in the execution of His will, the answer would seem to be threefold : (1) Man is free, though God is Omni-

war—is a solemn judicial act, carrying with it the awful judgment of God, but scattering also blessings from its hand to the hearts of nations which have to be ruled with a rod of iron, while it is a hard teacher of grand virtues.

But let us remember, also, that every man in his own life has a war to wage with evil around him. It is possible to pay too high a price for peace. There are wars of just aggression, and wars of just defence all around us, in which sooner or later every Christian has to take his part. It is not likely, for instance, that the great and precious gift of a Revelation from God to man should be allowed to remain unassailed. It is not likely that the Church, that great instrument for doing good, should be allowed to carry out her mission unmolested. It is not likely that in an evil world, we should be allowed to work out the pure morality of the Gospel without a struggle.

potent; (2) God, in the new creation of all things in Christ Jesus, a creation present to Him from all eternity, turns even man's sins into channels of ultimate blessing; (3) We reason as if this world were all. We forget that "it is appointed unto men once to die, but after this the judgment;" that God sends to each of us His summons at the very moment, and in the exact way which He judges to be best. We do not realize that to some who fall in war, the prolongation of life would have been no benefit, to others the great change is the greatest blessing; that the sufferings of the wounded are, after all, but a part—presenting no greater difficulty than any other—of the great mystery of pain itself, whether arising from disease, accident, or violence; that suffering may be the forerunner of repentance unto life, or a cross borne after the giver of the crown; and that the keen sorrow of the company of mourners may be God's gracious discipline leading them to a higher life and a closer nearness to Him, it may be to their conversion from darkness to light.

And there are evils all around us, and evils within our own hearts—crime, oppression, misery—against which we must wage war. We are citizens of Heaven, "citizens of no mean city," and there is a patriotism here, too, which animates the free sons of " Jerusalem which is above." There are difficulties to try our courage, there are hardships to try our self-discipline, there are obstacles to try our constancy. Oh, let us not shrink from wielding the sword of the Lord, constantly speaking the truth, boldly rebuking vice, and patiently suffering for the truth's sake;[1] for at our Baptism we were enlisted as soldiers of the cross, that we might manfully fight under Christ's banner against sin, the world, and the devil.[2] God has given to us that feeling of resentment which resists evil and wrong, which enables us to pursue, punish, and destroy what is bad. God grant that we may always use it in a good cause, and never unsheath the sword save in the battle of truth and right. And if we are perplexed at the sound of war in a Christian nation, or frightened at the warfare of Christian life, let us remember that justice and truth have to be upheld both in nations and in individuals. And justice and truth are contrary to corrupt human nature, so that sometimes we must needs "earnestly contend"[3] for that which is intimately connected with our truest welfare.

And yet how can we but weep with our Blessed Lord, at the awful severity of the punishment of war?

---

[1] Collect for S. John Baptist's Day.
[2] Baptism Service.
[3] S. Jude 3.

It is terrible to think of the money lavished, the skill expended, the strength devoted, for the purposes of destruction. It is grievous to think of the violence and fury of the battle-field, of passions unloosed, and the fever of blood-shedding, and the pain and the suffering and the anguish. It is piteous to think of the desolated homes, and the blighted lives, and the strong arms which tended them paralyzed, and the light which illuminated them quenched in death! What shall we do? What can we do? Let us pray that God will defend the right; let us do all we can to alleviate the horrors of war; but, above all, let us be true to those principles of justice, and truth, and honour, in our individual lives, which are the prop and stay of a nation's cause. And never for fear of man, or love of ease, through fear of consequences, or want of true patriotism, let us tolerate in ourselves and others, what is unbecoming in a citizen of Heaven, but ever be ready to strike a blow in the cause of progress, freedom, and truth.

SERMON XXVI.

Wisdom and Folly.

"*Ye suffer fools gladly, seeing ye yourselves are wise.*"—2 Cor. xi. 19.

S. PAUL in these words, which form the opening sentences of the epistle for to-day,[1] is addressing himself to the Corinthian Church, with thinly veiled severity, because they had been disposed to listen to false teachers, whose sole aim and object it was to disparage his authority. He calls them by their true name, "false apostles, deceitful workers, transforming themselves into the apostles of Christ."[2] And he is saying, "I do not like boasting, boasting is a fool's argument; I do not like talking about myself" (three times over he approaches this difficulty): "I do not like talking about myself, it is vain, it is foolish, it is unworthy, it is contrary to Christian humility. But," he says, "if I am systematically disparaged, if my sufferings in the cause of truth are apparent failures, if they are held up as a mark of the falsity of my mission, if these false teachers ask who I am, and what I have done, and so shake your faith, they

[1] Sexagesima Sunday.   [2] 2 Cor. xi. 13.

compel me to use the fool's argument, and to boast about myself, and to tell you who I am, and what I have done. But," he adds with a touch of irony, "*you are too wise to be upset by my folly;* you Corinthians, who are so wise that you can afford to put up with fools, you will not be disgusted by my foolish way of arguing. You have put up with too much already from these false teachers to be annoyed at my boastful way of talking; you have allowed the teachers who disparage me, to fetter your liberty—'ye suffer if a man bring you into bondage;' to devour your substance—'ye suffer if a man devour you, if a man take of you;' to exalt themselves into a post of preeminence—'ye suffer if a man exalt himself;' to treat you with the rudeness of insolent familiarity—'ye suffer if a man smite you on the face;' and therefore you can put up with one insult more, in having to listen to a poor foolish creature like me. I am assuming now that I really am what they say that I am, a poor weak creature, 'I speak as concerning reproach, as though we had been weak;' but, at the same time, I have plenty to boast of, if boasting were not so foolish: 'Are they Hebrews?'—pure Jews, not foreigners?—'so am I.' 'Are they Israelites?'—belonging to the general Jewish family—'so am I.' 'Are they the seed of Abraham?'—children of the promise—'so am I.' I am of the tribe of Benjamin, I speak the Jewish language, I have been a follower of the Jewish religion, I am a descendant of the great father of the race. 'Are they ministers of Christ? I am more.' I will tell you what I have suffered, rather than what I have done. For he conquers who suffers."

Now S. Paul, in the opening words of this passage, seems lightly and incidentally to introduce a great principle in morals and religion when he says, "Ye suffer fools gladly, seeing ye yourselves are wise." A wise man, that is, can put up with, is not disturbed by a fool, or, in other words, wisdom is the true and best defence against the mischief of folly. It is introduced, as you will see, once more in this way, "I am said to be a fool; very well. At least, then, you will not mind hearing what I have got to say, even although it seems very foolish, because you are of the number of those who are too wise to be upset by folly."

And out of this I wish to gather, as a general principle, that wisdom is the soul's protection against the mischief of folly.

Now, first of all, you will have noticed how constantly and how earnestly Holy Scripture speaks about folly and the fool, where we should talk of wickedness and the sinner. The impiety and madness of atheism, for instance, is described in this way, "The fool hath said in his heart, There is no God." [1] Worldliness and irreligion are condemned by Almighty God in these terms, "Thou fool, this night thy soul shall be required of thee." [2] The danger of forgetting God is set forth in a parable which describes the difference between good and bad, between prepared and unprepared, as the difference between wise and foolish virgins.[3] And it would seem that it is with

[1] Psa. xiv. 1. [2] S. Luke xii. 20. [3] S. Matt. xxv. 1.

religion, just as it is with every trade and profession—it is surrounded and beset by false principles and false methods, which justify wickedness and condone error, and can only be described by the term folly; that, just as there is quackery, as we call it, which threatens the profession of medicine, or dishonest speculation, which disfigures commerce, or adulteration, which disgraces trade, or empiricism or mere experimenting, which injures science, or impostures of every kind, which surround what is true, genuine, and good, so it is with religion. It is beset with wild speculations, imposture, adulteration, fanaticism, unbelief, misbelief, no belief. Men are bound in the name of religion, devoured in the name of religion, degraded, smitten on the face, a prey too often to foolish and designing people, all in the name of religion.

And what is the remedy? Who are those that are most readily taken in, in the things of the world? They are the young, the inexperienced, and the foolish. The experienced, the well-taught, the clear-headed, subtle-minded, can put up with these foolish theories. They can hear them, read of them, talk of them, and smile at them. It is certainty and knowledge that give confidence. And it is just the same in religion. Why is it that we are so soon led astray, so soon upset, "carried about with every wind of doctrine, by the sleight of men, and cunning craftiness, whereby they lie in wait to deceive?"[1] Why are we so fidgety, so perplexed and troubled, fretting

[1] Eph. iv. 14.

ourselves because of the ungodly, chafed by the last scientific book, which the next age finds to be completely in the wrong, annoyed at the pointed jest, vexed by the persistence of evil, disturbed by the delay of Christ's kingdom, deafened by the contending cries all around us? Is it not because we have not that confidence in our position which comes from certainty and experience? Surely our true protection is *wisdom*. If we were wise, we should put up with fools; they would not disturb us; if we were certain, we should be confident; if we were confident, we should not be perplexed. Just as Noah built his ark in the certainty of faith, unmoved by the unbelief around him, unshaken by the apparent delay of God's threatened judgment, building in a clear sky, among an incredulous and scoffing race, but suffering fools gladly, because he himself was wise in the confidence which certainty brings.[1] Or just as the children of Israel surrounded Jericho in the procession of weakness, strong in faith, enduring the folly of fools, because they were confident in the faith of God's promise;[2] or just as S. Paul, in the passage before us, is unmoved by the taunts and disparagement of his adversaries, because he was bold in his integrity and strong in the power of truth—so it must be with us. We know we are right; we may read God's word quite undisturbed by atheistic criticisms. We know we are right; we may come to church quite regardless of the numerous cries which reach our ears on the outside. We know we are right; we may live

[1] Heb. xi. 7.   [2] Heb. xi. 30.

for another world, confident in the truth of God's promise. But still, alas! there are many who can be laughed out of religion by any one, however foolish; there are many who miss their way amidst the converging paths, distracted by the numerous cries which beset their road; there are many who are at the mercy of any controversialist and of the loudest talker. And this ought not so to be. We should seek a remedy for it, and the remedy is wisdom, the soul's protection against folly.

Have we, then, based and rooted our religious faith on wisdom? Religious truth does not come to us by the light of nature; we cannot master it by a mere attendance at church, any more than we can master the principles of art by visiting a picture-gallery. If we will study and think, and pray over the truth, if we will receive instruction, and try to enter into the doctrines and teaching of the Church, then we shall have some of the confidence which arises from certainty. But if we hang loosely to the skirts of religion, picking and choosing here and there according to our fancy, or refusing to enter into, or not seeking to understand Christian truths, then we shall stand at the mercy of every blast, timid, distrustful, wavering, uncertain, disquieted by every rumour. Wisdom is the stability of the soul, wisdom, which is a gift of God, but working with the co-operation of man.

And besides this wisdom, which is able to give an answer to them that ask a reason for the hope that is in us, with meekness and fear,[1] there is a

---
[1] 1 S. Pet. iii. 15.

practical wisdom as well, which comes from long habituation, long familiarity with the truth; that sort of wisdom which says, I cannot explain the method, but this is the result; which will be unable, it may be, to meet that scientific objection which would dethrone prayer with skilful retort, or nicely-balanced argument, but from a long acquaintance with prayer, and long experience of its power and efficacy, can bring to bear the testimony of practical results against the visionary theories of the clever sceptic; which may be unable to prove to demonstration that the Bible is the Word of God, but from long experience has no practical doubt upon the matter; which may be unable to demonstrate by philosophical theories that the Body and Blood of Christ are "verily and indeed taken and received by the faithful in the Lord's Supper,"[1] but yet is convinced, in a confidence that cannot be shaken, of the truth and reality of the sojourn of the Heavenly Guest; which cannot meet an antagonist, armed with invincible proofs as to the holiness and mission of the Church of Christ, but which from long membership and long acquaintance with her privileges and deep respect, cannot be shaken from its integrity, even if beaten in argument. This is a practical wisdom, such as our Blessed Lord described, when He said, "If any man will do His will, he shall know of the doctrine, whether it be of God."[2]

And then, lastly, there is a kind of religious instinct which will guide a man aright if his heart is alive unto God. It is one great blessing which is the

[1] Church Catechism. [2] S. John vii. 17.

privilege of those who live close to God, that He guides them with His eye;[1] that they do not depend on abstract precepts entirely, or upon man's guidance, but are directed by an unerring religious intuition, as the voice of God breathes across the exquisitely sensitive conscience, or as they receive God's commandments in the holy mount of prayer, or wait for the descending cloud to lead them, and the settling cloud to give them rest.[2] Here is a wisdom different to the other two, a religious sensibility, an inner appreciation of the presence of God, which can suffer the folly of fools itself unshaken and unmoved, because it is wise in the wisdom of God's Countenance.

So, dear friends, while folly is unusually foolish, while unbelief and fanaticism make demands upon their votaries, such as the Church would never make upon her members, let us not be disturbed. Let us suffer fools gladly, if we are wise, and know what we believe, and what we are aiming at. Let us know what we believe, and why we believe, and how to act upon our belief, and then no foolishness of fools will disturb or molest us.

[1] Psa. xxxii. 9.   [2] Num. ix. 17-19.

SERMON XXVII.

The Rejected of Men.

"*And one shall say unto Him, What are these wounds in Thine hands? Then He shall answer, Those with which I was wounded in the house of My friends.*"—ZECH. xiii. 6.

WE can trace in the prophecies which foretold the coming of the Messiah two distinct lines of prediction, mingling the one with the other. Mixed up with the promise of glory, dominion, and power, there runs the darker thread of future suffering, degradation, and death. And these two lines of Messianic prophecy, of a glorified and a suffering Messiah, running parallel in the Psalms, take a clearer development still in the prophets; He shall reign, but He shall suffer; He shall be glorified, but also He shall be "the outcast of the people;"[1] He shall be "the desire of all nations,"[2] but He shall also be "despised and rejected of men."[3] And so marked is this double character, imputed prophetically to the Christ Who was to come, that the Jews in later ages, driven by the exigencies of a desperate unbelief, were forced to invent the theory of a double Messiah—One who should reign and

[1] Psa. xxii. 6.   [2] Hag. ii. 7.   [3] Isa. liii. 3.

be the temporal King of the Jews, the Other who should suffer and be rejected, and fill up the measure of prophetic woe. And Zechariah is one of those prophets who, with the prophecy of the righteous Branch,[1] and of the peaceable kingdom, and of the glorious Advent, mingles the prophecy of rejection and gloom; and he is even quoted, as you will remember, by our Blessed Lord Himself in the hour of His Passion, when He says of His terrified and affrighted followers, "I will smite the Shepherd, and the sheep of the flock shall be scattered abroad,"[2] in words taken from this prophecy. And this passage before us is one of those presages of sorrow which lie scattered up and down through the pages of the prophets, "And one shall say unto Him, What are these wounds in Thine hands? Then He shall answer, Those with which I was wounded in the house of My friends," a warning of what was to come, of blessings too easily forfeited, of opportunities too easily lost, of wounds too lightly given. And so it came to pass, as the prophet foretold. The Holy Child was born in David's city, in the house of His friends. There were wounds in those little hands uplifted to bless; "He came unto His own, and His own received Him not."[3] His glory drew to His cradle the eastern kings. They tracked the desert; they sought Him by the guiding of the star; they fell down in wondering adoration: still there were wounds in His hands, for His friends had only pointed out the way to strangers, or had helped Herod in his mission of destruction. The

[1] Zech. iii. 1.   [2] S. Matt. xxvi. 31.   [3] S. John i. 11.

Desire of all nations came to His temple, the First-born of the human race, to be presented unto the Lord in the substance of our flesh, and there are wounds in those hands, which Simeon reverently lifts, the wounds of rejection and neglect. He sits as a teacher in the house of His friends. By parable, by discourse, by words of wisdom, He proclaims the unsearchable riches of His truth. His blessings, His gifts are cast back; and wounded, He prepares His Apostles for the time when they must turn to the Gentiles. Yes, even among the twelve Apostles whom He chose to be near Him there is one who wounds deeply the hand that had blessed him, and guided him, and ordained him. As He hangs on the cross, keener and sharper than the nails which pierce Him are the taunts and words of hatred which smite upon His ear, while He is pleading before the world His atoning Sacrifice. "He is despised and rejected of men," and the wounds which pierce those hands are the treacherous wounds of friends.

And are there no wounds in those hands now? We are His friends; we claim that title now; we shall claim it more eagerly hereafter, as we cry out in our fear and dread, "Lord, Lord, ... we have eaten and drunk in Thy presence, and Thou hast taught in our streets."[1] But what if we are wounding Him? What if those hands are pierced and bleeding in the house of those who call Him their friend?

I. And I would ask you to notice carefully what they are that are said to be wounded in this prophecy; they are *His hands*. Now we are accustomed to look

[1] S. Luke xiii. 26.

upon the hands as symbolical, in the first place, of a man's *work;* the outward administrators of the scheming brain and planning mind. We speak by a bold anthropomorphism of the *hand* of God, meaning His all-creating power. "Thy hands have made me and fashioned me; O give me understanding, that I may learn Thy commandments."[1] When the soldiers nailed those hands to the Tree, they were enacting mystically the complete rejection of God's sovereignty over His people. They refused to yield to Him His vineyard; his right was set aside and rejected; He had no authority over the work of His hands. And so it is now. He sends a soul into a body prepared to receive it; He plants in it all the powers of life; He builds within it His tower of reason; He hedges it with religious instinct, with conscience, with discipline, and He lets it out to the owner for a season. He sends His servants back for fruit at the proper season—something for God. He sends in childhood; but He is told then that there is nothing ready; "Do not seek for fruit in a young unformed mind; young people do not know their responsibilities." He sends in the bright hey-day of youth; they stone His prophets with ridicule, beating some and killing some. He sends in advancing age; His title is disputed; His authority is despised; "the vineyard is not Yours, but *mine.*" He comes Himself in some supreme moment to claim all, to seize all; there is the frantic rejection, the killing, the wounding, the death of righteousness; and Christ is killed out of the

[1] Psa. cxix. 73.

soul. Oh, those wounds of *ownership!* He made those savages wallowing in their hideous vices; He made those slavers, trading in the lives of men; He made that murderer, who kills the body; He made that adulterer, who kills the soul; He gave that cunning to the hand, that vigour to the brain, that activity to the life, which is all turned against Him. Ah, in the swift current of life's business, do you stop to think of your *owner?* "It is He that hath made us, and not we ourselves."[1] He comes to ask for fruit, to seek for fruit, to demand fruit. Are you His friends? Then have you wounded those hands, those hands which own you because they made you?

II. And we are accustomed, again, to look at the hands as the outward expression or symbol of *liberality.* We talk of open-handed liberality; for the hand is the instrument with which we give. And Christ comes to give. He holds in His hands His gifts, strange gifts as they often seem to us; at one time He gives us suffering, a share in His cross—a hard cross of rough wood, not the bright and glittering plaything which takes our fancy, not the cross which we should choose were it in our power to do so; or He gives us His poor, as some of the richest treasures of the Church, to tend and to keep; or He gives to us His suffering Church, as, when hanging on the cross, He commended His blessed Mother to the care of His disciple as a mark of His confidence and trust. Do we receive these gifts at His hands, we who claim to be His friends?

[1] Psa. c. 2.

Now, what is friendship? Let two of the greatest thinkers of ancient times tell us. "Friendship," says one, "is kindliness between persons who reciprocate it, the feeling being mutually known."[1] "Friendship," says the other, "is unanimity as to what is honourable and just—deliberate choice of a like course of life—agreement in decision and action—unanimity in mutual life, intercourse and benevolence—equal participation in bestowing and receiving kindness." And they both coincide in this; there is agreement, there is conscious agreement, there is agreement in noble unchanging subjects, in friendship.[2] Have we, then—may we dare to say it with reverence—have we this friendship with Christ? Are His interests our interests? Do we look for and labour for the spread of the Truth, which is the deep longing of His travailing soul? Do we love the poor, among whom He lived, for whom He worked during His sojourn upon earth? Do we long to see the glad news of the Gospel reaching out to the heathen for whom He died? Are we tender, with His tenderness, towards the sinful and ignorant? Have we that love of our fellow-men which moved Jesus of Nazareth, "Who

---

[1] Aristotle, Ethics, viii. ii. 3. εὔνοιαν γὰρ ἐν ἀντιπεπονθόσι φιλίαν εἶναι. *Η προσθετέον μὴ λανθάνουσαν;—Plato, *Οροι.—φιλία ὁμόνοια ὑπὲρ καλῶν καὶ δικαίων· προαίρεσις βίου τοῦ αὐτοῦ· ὁμοδοξία περὶ προαιρέσεως καὶ πράξεως· ὁμονόια περὶ βίου κοινωνίαν μετ' εὐνοίας· κοινωνία τοῦ εὖ ποιῆσαι καὶ παθεῖν.

[2] "But what is it that can bind two friends together in intimate converse for a course of years, but the participation in something that is unchangeable and essentially good; and what is this but religion?" —Dr. Newman, Sermons, vol. ii. p. 59.

went about doing good?" Have we that love of suffering, as the basis of perfection, which He, Who was made perfect through suffering, has given to those who keep closest to Him? Ah, we leave many wounds in those hands—the wounds of a friend, which are the keenest of all, as we dash aside those noble interests, those precious gifts, and those glorious opportunities which He brings with Him. Yes, the wounds in the hands are there now. They are the symbols of rejected blessings from those who call themselves His friends, but lack the true mark of friendship—sympathy.

III. But the hand is also the symbol of training, forming, leading, or guiding. "There is none to guide her among all the sons whom she hath brought forth; neither is there any that taketh her by the hand of all the sons that she hath brought up."[1] Or, God speaks and says, "I took them by the hand to bring them out of the land of Egypt;"[2] or, again, "The Lord upholdeth him with His hand."[3] And Christ makes a distinct offer through His Church to every soul to train, to lead, and to guide. That hand which touched the leper is still uplifted to heal sin; that hand which restored sight to the blind is still ready to open the eyes of those who long to see; that hand which unstopped the ears of the deaf is still ready to open the ears of man to the voice of God; that hand which raised up the dead body is still ready to raise up those who are "dead in trespasses and sins." In the hand which pours out the water of

[1] Isa. li. 18. [2] Jer. xxxi. 32. [3] Psa. xxxvii. 24.

Regeneration we are bidden to recognize the hand of Christ, pouring upon us from on high the cleansing power of the Holy Spirit. In the hand uplifted to pardon we are bidden to recognize the absolving power of Christ. In the hand laid upon the head we are bidden to recognize the strengthening power of Christ in Confirmation, or His separating power in Ordination, or His enriching power and grace in Benediction. Still the Bread of life is put into the hands of the Apostles to give to the multitude; still by virtue of His interceding hands, "steady until the going down of the sun," we may obtain the victory which we seek over our foes.

But what wounds are these? What hideous gaping wounds? The wounds of unreal excuses, the wounds of prejudice, the wounds of controversy, veiling too often the insincere and unwilling heart. We clergy have too often a good deal put upon us which ought not to be laid to our account, because, granted that we are mistaken as to doctrine or practice, any error of man, any unworthiness of the minister does not, and cannot, interfere with the promise of Christ.[1] The man that brought help to the Jew in the parable was a Samaritan, but he did not therefore refuse the proffered oil and wine. A man would not refuse wholesome bread, because he had a quarrel with him who brought it, nor a splendid gift because he despised the messenger who was sent to convey it. No, it is deeper, it must be deeper; the wounds are in *His* hands. The scars are *there*, smitten in, driven in deep,

[1] See Articles of Religion, No. xxvi.

by those who despise His counsel and refuse His correction, who wound the hands that are waiting to bless, by a scornful and contemptuous rejection. As yet He is your friend. Yes, to all eternity He is your friend. But we may turn Him, may force Him to be our adversary. Those are sad words, which our Blessed Lord spake, "Agree with thine adversary quickly, whiles thou art in the way with him."[1] For some have thought that the adversary who is there spoken of is God, our eternal friend, driven to be our enemy, by our sins. If, then, He is our friend, let us avow His ownership. If He is our friend, let Him do with us as seemeth Him good. If He is our friend, let Him guide us and lead us by the hand, for there is a friend that sticketh closer than a brother.[2] And there are no wounds so deep, no scars so terrible, in that form so bruised and marred, as those wounds which pierce the loving hands of our Saviour and friend. For they are wounds of negligence, wounds of ignorance, wounds of rebellious malignity, given in the house of His friends, by those who can wound most deeply because they have been trusted most, and are nearest to His person.

[1] Matt. v. 25.   [2] Prov. xviii. 24.

SERMON XXVIII.

The Proportion of Faith.

"*Whether prophecy, let us prophesy according to the proportion of faith.*"
—Rom. xii. 6.

THE word faith is obviously used in the Bible in, at least, two senses. In one sense, it is that spiritual faculty *with which* we believe, as we read in the great eleventh chapter of the Epistle to the Hebrews, "through faith we understand that the worlds were framed by the word of God."[1] In the other sense, faith is that which is believed, that body of truth which forms the object of our faith, that collection of Christian doctrines and precepts which, put together, we call "*the Faith.*" So we are told, there is "one Lord, one faith, one baptism;"[2] so we are bidden earnestly to contend "for the faith which was once delivered unto the saints."[3] The two meanings of the word faith being briefly these:—Faith, or the power by which we believe—the Faith, or that body of truth which is to be believed. And so you will notice here, that according to a large and influential array of commentators, we should read, "according to the proportion of *the Faith.*"[4] Now in

[1] Heb. xi. 3.   [2] Eph. iv. 5.   [3] S. Jude 3.
[4] In the revised New Testament the reading "'The Faith" is

this particular passage, S. Paul is giving directions to the Christian prophet, a person who, after making several deductions, answers very much to our modern preacher; and he is saying, when you prophesy, observe the due proportion of the Faith; that is, "You, as a preacher, have to set before men, to explain to men, that great body of rules and precepts and doctrines, which is called *the Faith*—see, that in doing so, you observe the due proportion of that Faith! Do not press any favourite doctrine to the exclusion of others; do not put a subordinate doctrine in the place of a leading one; do not put forward what is popular, at the expense of what is unpopular; do not run riot over a few isolated texts of Scripture; but take the Faith as a whole; its spiritual duties; its moral duties; its bearing on God, on man, on ourselves; the duties which belong to the Church, the duties which belong to the soul; set the Faith before the people, as God has set it before you, popular or unpopular, all round, according to its proper proportion, as it comes before you in all its magnificence.

I. Now this is a most important doctrine to be observed by all. How is it that nearly all forms of error, religious, social, moral, including slavery, have claimed to themselves the authority of Scripture? It is because people have taken isolated texts, without

put in the margin, and the text itself runs thus, "According to the proportion of *our* faith." The first interpretation is, however, said to be that of the Latin Fathers, and is followed by Wordsworth and the moderns whom he quotes, while the second is said to be that of the Greek Fathers, meaning that the strength or direction of our faith must "determine the range of the prophetic utterances."

observing what the Bible teaches as a whole; or else have taken difficult passages by the simple light of the knowledge of their own times, forgetting that interpretation which comes down to us from the common consent of the Church, in the earliest and purest ages; an example of which we have in the repudiation of infant Baptism in some quarters, based on an imaginary silence of Holy Scripture, in the teeth of the universal custom of the primitive Church.

And so you will find that all the principal divisions which have rent the Church, have come from pressing one doctrine out of its due proportion. A misconception of the place which Baptism holds at the threshold of the Church, has taken away a large section of Christians here; an undue prominence given to personal religion, has taken away another large body in this direction; while a mistaken estimate of the rights of congregations, has produced a third division. But, more especially, I would venture to put before you, that which immediately concerns ourselves. Do we, as Church-people, keep sufficiently before us in our own lives the proportion of Faith?

Have we no favourite doctrines, no favourite texts? Are there not some doctrines which we do not believe at all, some which we never think about? Are there not many precepts spoken by our Blessed Lord Himself, which we think we can let alone, and do not practise, not seeing that they are lines, delicate lines, but still giving the whole expression to the beautiful countenance and proportion of the Faith? To illustrate what I mean, take the common precept of almsgiving, one of the most simple, prosaic, yet to some irksome, duties, which our Faith puts upon us. How many people give their money, if they give it at all to God and His Church, as a religious duty and high privilege instead of as an unwelcome tax? I am pleading to-day for help to those Diocesan Societies, which have helped us so much, and do so much good in the diocese. Do you welcome the invitation? Do you say, "I am very glad to have an opportunity of paying my tithe to God in a right and proper direction, of contributing to His honour and glory, of helping to bestow spiritual blessings upon my fellow Christians in this diocese": or do you say, "We are always being asked for money; there is always begging"? No, the principle of almsgiving is this: it is not that the Church begs, but she knows the rule of God's requirements, and His revealed teaching in this matter, and inasmuch as almsgiving is just as much a Christian duty as prayer, and is put before us as an inestimable blessing to the giver, she thinks it right to give you the opportunity, to tell you of good and proper channels in which to spend that money which has already been set apart for God, or dedicated to charitable purposes. That is the theory of almsgiving. The practice, alas, illustrates only too plainly the way in which an unpopular precept becomes detached, and a delicate curve of beauty becomes lost for ever to the proportion of the Faith.

II. If it be true, then, that we are apt to hold only parts of the Faith, to practise only parts of the Faith, to care for and attend to only parts of the

Faith, forgetting and omitting that grand proportion which we ought to observe, why is it? What is the reason?

(1) First of all, dear friends, is it not because too often there is a lack of religious knowledge? It is not that we do not hear the truth, or love the truth, but we undervalue the difficulty of it; every one thinks himself a judge of Theology. Of course, if we humbly accept the conclusions of the Church, as they are put before us in the Creed, the Commandments, the Church Catechism, and the Prayer Book generally, then we shall see the proportion of faith set out before us clearly and nobly and in all its fulness. But if we wish to get to the bottom of the premises from which these conclusions were drawn, if we accept some conclusions and reject others, then there is needed considerable knowledge of Holy Scripture, of Theology generally, of Church history, and of much beside that bears upon the subject. Ah, with many of us the Faith has dwindled down to a few bare and stunted doctrines, either because we have neglected the voice of the Church, or because there has been neglect in putting them before us, or because we have forgotten them. But underneath their dry and stern exterior, if you brush past all the accumulation of the dust of conflict which lies around them, the doctrines of the Church, the Faith of the Church, the discipline of the Church, the services of the Church, are worthy of study. Surely this is a reason why many people hang so loosely to the Church, or do not enter into it, or fear it, or despise it, or dislike it—it is because

they do not understand it. What science should we appreciate, if we did not understand it? Would mathematics interest us if we did not know their first principles? Would art please us if we could not enter into the beauty of form and colour? Would even sports or games please if we did not enter into them? Before you condemn the Church, before you cut away her doctrines, or pare down her proportions, be quite sure you understand them. I plead for a more earnest study, a more thorough appreciation of the converging lines of her doctrine and practice, in the grand proportion of the Faith.

(2) And another reason which prevents men from accepting the whole Faith in its integrity, is, alas, very often, dislike. They do not wish it to be true. They do not wish the Faith to assume such gigantic proportions. They do not like to see the Faith sitting at their dinner-table, walking with them in their daily round, checking them in their conversation, putting its fingers on their money, clutching at their time, drawing away their thoughts and imaginations from this knowable scene, to the unseen and unknowable which lies beyond. They do not like to believe that there is a great spiritual world all around us, of which we are barely cognizant; they do not like to believe that there are supernatural agencies in our midst; they do not like to have to own that there is something which cannot be analysed, but can only be spiritually apprehended; they do not like to believe in the awful future as God reveals it to us. So they pick a few portions or lines out of the Faith,

an isolated doctrine here and there, until there remains a hard dull outline, with no beauty of curve, or rounded shape, or well-defined angles, but merely a few bare, lifeless, colourless abstractions, without form and void; a God, elevation of feeling, pointing upwards; a morality, with or without its Christian beauties and additions, pointing inward; a philanthropy, pointing outward, to man around—this is all that remains. Oh, if there are any doctrines which we shrink from, these are just the doctrines about which we should be most anxious. There is no part of our being which is not touched by the Faith. For the Faith is a revelation which comes from above; we receive it not from man, or by man. It is a revelation of truth such as man could never have attained to; and it is not from below, what our fears or inclinations would make it. The Faith is one, holy, indivisible; it is of God.

(3) And then, lastly, want of holiness, want of goodness, sin—these form a terrible barrier, which prevent us from appreciating the full and high proportion of the Faith. A mist, a fog, a dense vapour, rising up out of our sins, distorts, envelops, and hides the glorious features of the truth. You will remember, as illustrating this, how David had lost all sense of justice, tenderness, morality, and honour when Nathan came to him with his mission of penitence.[1] In the same way, ambition and self-will seemed to have cut away the felt presence of God from Saul, driven at length to necromancy and magic in the utter loneliness and dread of a soul which had

[1] 2 Sam. xii.

lost the light.[1] Balaam, again, became a mere tinkling cymbal under the influence of Balak's bribery.[2] It is an awful thought, but nevertheless true, that we *cannot* see some of the features of the faith. "Blessed are the pure in heart: for they shall see God."[3] What is the opposite of this? Cursed are the impure in heart, for they shall not see God. Spiritual things are spiritually discerned.[4] We can make ourselves short-sighted, by impairing our bodily organ of sight; we can also make ourselves short-sighted in spiritual matters. O terrible malice of sin! It prevents us from seeing the glorious proportions of the Faith.

Let us labour, then, dear friends, to put before ourselves the whole Faith, without diminution or addition, without fear or favour or loss. The Faith is a definite body of truth, "One Lord, one faith, one baptism." It is a blessing and privilege to hold it and believe it; it is our loss to reject any portion of it, or to distort any part of it. For the Faith is one grand, noble, harmonious whole; it comes to us from the hands of Almighty God Himself.

[1] 1 Sam. xxviii.
[2] Numb. xxiii.
[3] S. Matt. v. 8.
[4] 1 Cor. ii. 14.

SERMON XXIX.

The Physician of the Body and the Physician of the Soul.[1]

"*Honour a physician with the honour due unto him, for the uses which ye may have of him; for the Lord hath created him.*"—ECCLUS. xxxviii. 1.

WHEN Sakya-Muni, in the Buddhist legend, breaks forth from the gilded captivity of a luxurious court, in which his father had tried to stifle in him the ascetic promise of his earlier life, he is startled by the phenomena of a suffering world, which had hitherto been kept away from him. The sight of an old man tells him that life is no perpetual youth; the sight of a sick man, another unknown phenomenon, speaks to him of the vast possibilities of suffering, as well as the capabilities of pleasure; while at last, the first sight of death, the first confronting with a body from which life had fled—an experience still full of gloom and sadness to us all—decided his course. Men were growing old, were

[1] A sermon preached in substance in S. Paul's Cathedral, before the Guild of S. Luke, on Friday, Oct. 17, the Eve of S. Luke's Day. 1890.

failing in sickness, were dying around him; life was not meant for a gluttonous dream of sensual pleasures; he must first know the causes of so much misery, and help in the disentanglement of the human race:—he breaks away from his surroundings, and devotes himself to the amelioration of humanity.

It is always, I venture to think, an astounding thought to those who pause to think—the infinite sorrows and sufferings of the world. As we passed down to this church to-night, if only we could have known the tragic histories which encountered us in the streets; if only we could have known what was meant by those closely drawn blinds and the silent house; if only we had paused to enter the well-lighted wards of the hospital; yes, if only we had listened as we came up through the country to the inarticulate wail of failure, and incompleteness, and aimless effort going on around us, even in the material world, perhaps we could hardly endure, as has been beautifully said, "that eternal element of tragedy which lies in the very fact of frequency. . . . If we had a keen vision and feeling of all ordinary human life, it would be like hearing the grass grow, and the squirrel's heart beat, and we should die of that roar which lies on the other side of silence." "Nothing but the Infinite Pity is sufficient for the infinite pathos of human life."

And yet men, and whole classes of men, are found, like Gautama—the Buddha in the legend—ready to break out, to cast aside ease, voluptuousness, ambition, pleasure, in the cause of humanity. Nay, it is no longer an impulse, it is a sacred duty which has appealed with mighty force to all those who aspire to be followers of the Crucified—" Who for us men, and for our salvation came down from Heaven, and was incarnate by the Holy Ghost of the Virgin Mary, and was made man. . . . He *suffered.*" It has been a mighty impulse which has never ceased to stir the followers of Jesus of Nazareth, " Who went about doing good." How can I best meet pain and want and degradation, and the manifold ills which leap upon a fallen world? Beneath His gentle eye, little children and feeble old men, the wasted invalid, and the worn slave, steal out to offer suffering, when all other action is denied them, as their contribution to the world's good. And Christ and His followers have welcomed them. In His train has sprung up the hospital—that creation of Christianity—the tenderness and patience for those destined only to circle slowly round the semi-stagnant pool of a suffering life, while the great torrent of activity rushes by them. Oh! it is a grand thing, as you view life's conflict close at hand, beneath the glitter and flash and smoke of the combat, to see the many forms who are moving up and down, regardless of peril, and heedless of life, to minister to those who are hard hit in life's conflict and dragging out a maimed existence in silent suffering.

And I am conscious that I am speaking to-night, on this eve of S. Luke, to a large body of men who appeal to our honour and our respect as pre-eminently the followers of Him, the Good Physician of our race,

Jesus Christ—members of that profession which he,[1] whose loss to this place, and I might say, to all Christendom, has left a yet unhealed scar, called "That noble profession of medicine which ministers with one hand to the progress of advancing science, while with the other it daily lavishes its countless deeds of unknown, unacknowledged generosity and kindness on the sick and poor." Perhaps we may venture to say that there is hardly any body of men which with less ostentation and greater unweariedness of devotion ministers to the suffering of our humanity than does the medical profession. You may see the doctor in the long, dreary country roads, in all weathers, and at all times, speeding on his errand of mercy, with hardly a moment which he can call his own. See him in the densely populated alleys of our large towns, battling with death and disease; see him in the hospitals (and instances are not unknown) sucking out the deadly diphtheric growth, or risking his life amidst the most dangerous infection; bearing the sad news of an impending terrible misfortune to those whose whole life thereby suffers an eclipse; or wrestling with slowly yielding phenomena, in order to add something to the store of human happiness and human relief. This, and much more than this, might be said.

But on an occasion and in a place like this, there are higher thoughts still which suggest themselves. The great saint, whose festival we are keeping,

[1] The allusion is to Dr. Liddon, whose death had taken place five weeks before.

suggests, in his double aspect of Physician and Evangelist, a comparison between the physician of the body and the physician of the soul, between those who minister to two great departments of human life—the physician who ministers to the body and the priest who ministers to the spirit, each having a common meeting-ground in the centre of life.

Just as, my brethren, there are men who meet us in our profession, and put before us low ideals, telling us that we shall best secure our aims by being mere preachers of philanthropy, good men of the world, or, at the best, a body of moral police; so, I doubt not, there are many who put before your profession aims only bounded by the lowest materialism, or the strictest professional views of mere worldly advancement. But if I understand it aright, the aim of this guild is otherwise; it is to recognize in every way the dignity and greatness of the medical profession, its unique opportunities and its immense responsibilities; and therefore bear with me if I ask you to see how, as it seems to me, the work of the priest and of the physician are caught up into the same high level, just as the work of the evangelist and physician are combined in S. Luke.

I. First of all, the main duty of a priest is to God. And I claim that the main duty of a physician points there also. It is no light responsibility to minister so closely to the bodies of men in a world created by Him Who in the beginning saw everything that He had made, and behold it was very good. Nay, further, it is no light dignity to minister to the body, which has been for ever honoured by the Incarnation; it is no light thing to be even a workman employed in repairing the temple of the Holy Ghost.

Apart from its corruption and its degradation, if there was no pain, and no sin, and no disfigurement, we should all agree that what we call the body is one of the most beautiful works of God. The body to a Christian thinker is no "vile body," it is rather what S. Paul calls, with a calmer estimate and a more enlightened view, "the body of our humiliation," capable of being offered a living sacrifice to God, an object for earnest prayer, that with other parts of our composite life it may be presented unimpaired and blameless in the day of the Lord. No vile body, it is true, but subject to humiliation (He does not deny that), like some savage islander gracing the victor's triumph, uncouth yet conquered. To his eyes, who had seen nobler things, not pure beauty, pure strength, a dress for gods and heroes, but a conspicuous part of human nature. And his estimate may well be our estimate to-day. The body is not everything, but it is a part of our being which we would not ignore if we could; it is stored with discipline, it is full of help, subject to humiliation, but not vile; to be pressed into the service of religion, in its wide experience with its ministering senses; to be led, if need be, in chains to grace the victor's triumph, not contemptuously thrust aside as the beast, or despised as the prison house, or feared as the seducer of virtue.

> Let us not always say,
> "Spite of this flesh to-day
> I strove, made head, gained ground upon the whole"!
> As the bird wings and sings,
> Let us cry, All good things
> Are ours, nor soul helps flesh more, now, than flesh helps soul!

I do claim that just as the priest comes much and often before God, while wrestling for the souls which God has given him, so also those who deal with the framework are brought daily and hourly, by the mysteries which they touch, into the very presence of God; that life palpitating beneath your touch is the stamp of His image; that form is honoured by the Incarnate God Himself; those senses and feelings are being played and moved by invisible powers; the wind of the Spirit evokes, as it strikes them, the cry which goes out from their life; the Incarnation, the Atonement, are both shaped out there in human flesh and human suffering. Truly the priest and physician are both alike in this—they move in the midst of mysteries, they are very near to God.

II. Then, the physician also, as well as the priest, has his especial duties to man. It is a happy thing when we go together in our professional rounds, when the doctor lets the priest know those cases of sickness which might otherwise escape him. Yes, in births, in deaths, in hours of sickness, our duties often lie close together. The relation is too obvious to need drawing out. Pardon me, therefore, if I think there are some ways in which you might help us even more than you do now. And first I might venture to say in the awful struggle of youth against sin, How tempting it is to fall back on nature, to say he cannot help himself! It has been well said, "There is a fundamental mistake in the popular excuse for sensual sin—that it is natural. The mistake lies in the idea that man's animal and spiritual natures are separable, that he can live as pure animal in one part of his life, and pure spirit in another. But, as a fact, man's life is only lived according to nature, when every part of it is lived in flesh and spirit. The spiritual motive must control the bodily organ. Only so are his acts really human. If he tries to act as a mere animal he becomes sinful The evidence of this lies in the fact that while the physical natures of animals contain within them the check on sensual indulgence, the check in man centres in his spiritual faculties. You can have a dissipated man, *i.e.* a man whose bodily impulses are uncontrolled by will or spirit. You cannot have a dissipated animal."[1] Ah yes, you can help us so much by telling men that the body never need run riot over the higher self; that this is not nature, but the opposite, that in the fiercest temptation grace is stronger than nature. And you can tell them, with a voice more powerful than we can, that the body is a splendid servant, but a terrible master.

Again, is it not possible for you sometimes to pave the way for spiritual ministrations, when your skill tells you that you have done your best, and that the few days that remain of life are but as nothing in

[1] Rev. C. Gore, "On the Christian Doctrine of Sin," p. 534, note. Appendix to "Lux Mundi," 10th edit.

view of the awful possibilities of eternity? Our paths lie here very close at hand to each other, as we minister to the moral needs and necessities of man.

III. There only remains one last way in which would to God we mutually provoked one another to good works, the priest the physician, the physician the priest, as to who should best realize his own personal responsibility, the solemn lesson of his profession to himself. And I rejoice to see one common meeting ground—that you with us feel the need and the blessings of frequent Communion; that you, as well as we, feel the power and need of prayer and frequent intercessions for others. You know the dignity and value of prayer; but pardon me if I add how tremendously there should be growing upon us the seriousness of our profession in this thoughtless, restless, irreverent age. We are brought face to face with terrible realities. What responsibilities are ours; what confidences are reposed in us; what joys, what sorrows, what hopes, what fears! I suppose especially we ought to be influenced far more than we are by the constantly recurring mystery of death, which we are brought to see who stand frequently by the open door of Paradise, when we catch dim glimpses of glory, and hear faint voices from the other world, and are reminded by disease and accident how near death is to us. These things may harden by an oft repeated impression, if they do not elevate. As we see the despair, the awful separation, the losses of death, there are two lessons which we ought not to be slow in learning. One is

U

detachment, to sit loosely to the things of this world. Here we have no continuing city, but we seek one to come. Another attachment to Him, Who is the Way, the Truth, the Life.

My brethren, the time is short. It is a glorious thing to be allowed to share in the mysterious work of God in the world, in relieving the manifold needs of our fellow-men, in learning for ourselves the deepest lessons which God can teach, which fall unheeded on an unsuspecting world. There is a great work for us. What are we doing? It has been beautifully said by a modern bishop: "When we are close to a cataract we are dazed with the countless, bewildering succession of constant movements, in all variety, vastness, and rapidity of mutation. Myriads of lines of foam, and clouds of spray, and torn masses of ever plunging water. But leave the cataract, and some miles away look back. Far off in the lustrous distance you see a broad white unwavering ribbon or banner, nailed as it were to the steadfast rock of the mountain side. And so our myriad thoughts and actions every day and night are our works, but all the hurry and movement is lost in the retrospect from the awful distance of eternity, when each man's works have become each man's work."

SERMON XXX.

The Valley of Decision.[1]

"*Multitudes, multitudes in the Valley of Decision: for the day of the Lord is near in the Valley of Decision.*"—JOEL iii. 14.

THE prophet summons us in these verses to share with him a great vision of judgment which opens out before him. There, where he is accustomed to look out into futurity; there, where he takes his stand to see what auguries flit across the *templum* of his vision; there, where by long and patient endurance, obedience, and love he has laboured to understand the things of God, comes up before him this troubled vision—"Multitudes, multitudes"; as though, whichever way he looked, there were still tumultuous masses on all sides: one living, surging, boiling sea; throngs upon throngs gathered together blindly, unknowingly, rebelliously, in the valley of sharp and severe judgment. There is a fascination, and even a terror, in the appearance of a great mob. Many of our writers of fiction have spoken of it over and over again: the remorseless sea of turbulently swaying

[1] A Sermon preached in S. Paul's Cathedral, on Sunday afternoon, December 13, being the Third Sunday in Advent, 1891.

shapes, faces hardened in the furnace of suffering until the touch of pity could make no mark on them. The sea, with its roar and its thunderings, with here and there an articulate voice, or distinctive shout, "leaping up into the air like spray." You yourselves, I doubt not, have felt the fascination before now as you have looked out, it may be, from the steps or walls of this great building on some gathering throng of people below—so many souls for whom Christ died—with their lives outlined behind them; each face a history or a prophecy, perhaps both; each life with its portentous gift of freewill, wild and uncontrolled to all appearance, and yet shaped and guided in every movement by a predestinating hand. A crowd like this the prophet bids us contemplate, gathered together in the Valley of Decision, in a valley of judgment, partially realized, no doubt, in every successive judgment of God, fading at last into the great and final judgment of the last day, when we, too, shall form a part of that great multitude gathered together, treading closely one on another, in trembling hope, in patient expectation of the mercy of God.

I. The Valley of Decision—what a thought it is! Decision, something which is sharply, abruptly cut off once for all and remains, once for all determined—a word around which there gathers a sinister meaning, of causes which must carry out their effects, of great laws of being which must be satisfied, of eternal justice and eternal truth, of atonement wrought out, yet waiting to be accepted or rejected, of a crisis no longer to be avoided, a stern, inflexible, final

Decision. There is a sharpness, and severity, and a menace in the very word; a certainty and a definite abruptness which arrests and startles a world which slumbers on, lulled by "to-morrow," and buoys itself on "perhaps." Decision! "My Spirit shall not always strive with man." There is a winding up of the ages; there is an end to the probation of life; God will arrest all this tangled machinery at the right moment, when all influences have done their work, and when once for all the settlement must be made. There will not be for ever this restless ebb and flow of opportunity and chance, but God will assert Himself as the eternal justice, to be justified in His saying, and clear when He is judged. However free we are, however many may be our opportunities, however great may be God's mercy, there is a decision at last, a decision for the multitude of the world, and a decision for each member of it in the Valley of Jehoshaphat.

This Valley of Decision, dear brethren, where is it? I answer, first of all here, here in this world. "Multitudes, multitudes" are stepping into it; while we sit here, "multitudes, multitudes" are passing out of it, over whose lives may be traced "decided." There are souls just entering in their tiny vessels of flesh into all the fierce storms of life, to be moulded and formed by it; some, perhaps, on this very day taking a definite decided line whose issues they cannot foresee. There are some whose course it would seem was being decided for them as they drift here and there, without rudder, without compass, knocked about from one rock to another, in a path shaped by circumstance. The world all unconsciously to its teeming multitudes—this world—is a Valley of Decision in which they gather together to certain ends and work out definite issues. And what is it that is being decided in this valley, where we tread on the monuments of the past, and watch an ever-widening throng gathering in it, to work out the momentous destiny of life?

Many things, dear brethren, are being decided here, and first of all, *character*. Character is being decided, that strange stamp which gives to each one of us his own individuality; that personality which spreads itself over our whole being, our face, our movements, our likes and dislikes; that stamp whereby men can label us and catalogue us, and yet feel at the end that we elude classification; and find, it may be, a Matthew among their publicans and sinners, a Rahab amongst their outcasts, a S. Paul among their misguided fanatics. Yet character is the clue whereby our fellow-men appraise us, and utilize us, and calculate upon our actions, whether in certain circumstances and courses of life we shall act as good or bad, as strong or weak, as helpful or impotent. They judge thereby—by our character—whether we are benevolent, or cruel, or humble, or proud, or worldly, or spiritual, or timid, or brave. Our friends can label us, and place us in our right class, and what they judge by they call character. After the first opening years of childhood this bias, this warp displayed itself, it coloured our actions, and gave what was called an expression to the face, and individuality to our movements.

And what has gone to form this character? I answer at once, habits. And what has gone to form habits? Again I answer without hesitation, single actions done day by day in the same direction, with the same purpose. Just as you may notice on some wind-swept coast the stunted trees spreading out their torn and wild head of branches, all turned in one direction where the violence of the wind from off the sea has bent them day by day in the direction of the strongest and most frequent gale, until they have grown to it; so almost without thinking, as day after day single opportunities in all manner of variety are offered to us, we go on forming habits, habits which gradually decide, cutting away everything else in our moral nature until we go straight at once to the good or bad in the thing, and are bent or strengthened by the blast; and decision forms character. Do not let us blame our surroundings and say that they in the end are responsible, because that is not true. Joseph becomes a viceroy out of temptation and the prison, where David out of the same temptation lost his kingly pre-eminence. Daniel became great in sanctity out of those heathen surroundings which were the curse and the death of many an Israelite of God. Circumstances are the material of life, good or bad. It is we who take up our circumstances, and out of them make habits, and habits decide or form a character in this Valley of Decision which we call human life. And this is not all; besides character, we decide our own *happiness* or *misery*, still in this Valley of Decision. Do not let us be deceived, or led astray in this matter. Life is not an unhappy time to be slurred over in view of a happier future. Life is not a purgatory to be shortened in view of a paradise beyond. Life was meant to be happy. Godliness has the promise of "the life that now is." We must never give up that. "I am come that they might have life, and that they might have it more abundantly." But God places this in our own hands in the tremendous gift of choice and free-will; and so this world is a Valley of Decision to hundreds who make or mar their own happiness.

In hundreds and hundreds of instances to-day Lot is choosing Sodom, because it is a good place for his cattle, and that, to his mind, means prosperity, and prosperity means happiness. And what is the result of his choice? Loss, degradation, and sin. Over and over again Esau is choosing the hunter's life, instead of the home life of quiet duty. The free, open life of the colonies is what he is aiming at, in spite of the long and careful training of home, or the prophecies which went before on him. This shall be his choice, and not the humdrum life of the office, or the weary ladder of the slowly mounting profession; and he does not know that the choice which he made in wilfulness is the beginning of those series of choices which culminate in the lost birthright. He sold it for a mess of pottage. He displeased his father and vexed his mother, and he woke up to find himself disinherited of his blessing, and losing the joy out of life. How many owe their fate in life just to taking the turn either in the right or the wrong direction. How many downfalls begin just with the wrong determination, a false step. No compass, no aim, no direction, and the mist settles down, and the mistake has once been made, and ever since they have been going down. The neglected Sunday; the omitted prayers; the easy acquiescence in bad counsel. These were decisions which we did not realize at the time. And so you will notice God's efforts for our salvation seem to be in this direction—to help, as it were, our decision, that is, to fortify the will within us. At Baptism He regenerates it, at Confirmation He strengthens it, at each Holy Communion He tries to determine it. His word is to inform it, conscience is to guide it, prayer is to help it. Ah! how momentous, dear brethren, are the decisions of everyday life— "multitudes, multitudes in the Valley of Decision," making or marring their happiness day by day with terrible persistency. Either life to them is getting clearer, or it is getting darker; either they are getting more in view of the great peaks of holiness, or else the blinding, drifting mist terrifies them, and daunts them as they stand still, dazed, and bewildered. They have decided, and day after day seems to make it more impossible to alter their decision.

And yet another thing is being decided in this Valley of Decision, and that is *eternity*. The great decision is not, after all, the sudden thing we suppose it to be, except in very rare cases; it is not the one convulsive "Lord, remember me!" which is all of a sudden to reverse the decision of a lifetime, and to turn the thief into a saint. It is not, as a rule, one mighty burst of light, and glorious vision and overwhelming voice which is to separate them from the past in the throes of conversion. Such things are, such things may be; but as a rule men are quietly taking their places, one by one, in the decisions of life for the decisions of eternity. Gradually the face gets set one way by a series of unnoticed decisions. God does not, as a rule, work in sudden unexpected ways, suspending laws, stultifying causation, bringing figs from thistles, or grapes from thorns. If we could only see the inner springs which bring about these great changes, we should often find that it was only a higher decision asserting itself, that life had been reared up in great purposes, and that it was only the change of the building from a profane to a sacred use, the basilica becoming the church, or the melody in its minor key of worldliness, turned only by a slight modification into the major key of holiness. Just as a more comprehensive knowledge of God's laws would eliminate much that now seems miraculous, so a more complete knowledge of His dealings would eliminate much that now seems arbitrary and strange. It is here in this world, by deliberate act and free choice, that we make our decision, a decision on which hangs eternity.

II. But here in this world it is quite true the decision may alter; it may not, after all, be final. A man, as we have seen, may turn round and gather together all the broken fragments of happiness and goodness which he has thrown away and reconstruct his life. But the prophet looks on to another day, the final day of decision—" multitudes—multitudes in the Valley of Decision," where all nations shall be gathered together before their Judge at the great day of judgment at the end of the world. " He hath appointed a day, in the which He will judge the world in righteousness." Dear brethren, is this a belief which is still a living and a practical one to you? Is it any longer our belief, as we gaze out into the world, ever discovering some new wonder, brighter, stronger, clearer, healthier, more refined, that the fruit is becoming scantier on the tree, and the leaves more shrivelled, and the blasts more keen, and that there will come a day when the last fruit will fall, and the last flower will close, and winter arrest all the brightness of the world with a sharp judgment?

> "Sure, if our eyes were purged to trace
>   God's unseen armies hovering round,
> We should behold, by angel grace,
>   The four strong winds of Heaven fast bound.
>
> "Their downward sweep a moment stayed
>   On ocean cove, and forest glade,
> Till the last flower of autumn shed
>   Her funeral odours on her dying bed."

Is it a spectacle of a world more and more unchristian, until at last the fire dies out, and then the end? Is it this that we expect, or rather the development more and more in perfect beauty of a world strong in its own great resources, of a world strong in the power and faith of Jesus Christ, when at last He will come and take His power and reign? Surely His own words lead us to think not of a development into a consummation, but rather of a sudden arrest by an unlooked-for crisis, like a thief in the night, as the flood on the prosperous world, like the fires on unconscious Sodom, as a snare on the unsuspecting bird. We can hardly conceive, for instance, one of our public journals at the present day, while making all possible allowance for the passing away of generations, making any reservation such as "if the world should last so long." "Until Doomsday" means with us practically "for ever." Yet it is just this which God seems to keep ever before us—a day of decision; a day known to Him; a day of which God the Son said in His humanity, in words so strangely misunderstood, that He was ignorant; not because He did not know it, but because it is one of those secrets involving not a date in coming history, but all the complicated windings of predestination, the bringing together of lines which our human understanding as they pass us can only regard as parallel, predestination and free-will; involving the determination of mysteries which could not be translated, so to speak, into the capacity of human nature, or be made intelligible to a human audience. Such a day, however, we are led to expect, not to be arrived at by the usual scientific processes, not to be reached at the end of a series, but a cloud suddenly developing itself out of that dim horizon where the strongest telescope fails to reach, out of that margin of uncertainty which still remains, when fact after fact and phenomenon after phenomenon has been analysed, reduced, and classified, until the unknown becomes a strip. Still in this strip faith works. Here it is her turn to observe, to reduce, to compare, to examine the revelations which have been made, to watch the signs of the times, to take note of this very certainty and security, to notice the very clearness and brightness of the horizon as an indication of an approaching storm. And faith has never altered her voice. God hath appointed a day. The Lord will come. "Multitudes, multitudes in the Valley of Decision," of sharp irreversible judgment, for which this Advent bids us prepare ourselves; for it will be a day of decision for the world. There are certain great crises, dear brethren, when we realize the unity of the world. It is so when we stand at the foot of the Cross and read the inscription which Pilate hung there in letters of Hebrew, Greek, and Latin. The monotheism of God's people, the Jews; the intellect and language of Greece; the power and discipline of Rome, join hands and link the world together on Calvary. Great calamities, great needs, or the development of human kindliness bring out again that one touch of nature which makes the whole world kin. The communion of nations in commerce which God brings about by the varied distribution of His material gifts, is but an image or picture of the communion of saints which God brings about by the distribution of His spiritual gifts. And so at the day of judgment we shall be allowed to be present at the decision of the world. We shall understand passages of history now dark to us; foundations without visible superstructure; lines which seemed to mean nothing, lives of patriarchs, and records of obscure kings, which we should have left out; little glories of colour and form which we had never noticed while we were absorbed in some glaring daub, or were wondering at the picture-frames of history. It will be a day of terror and of sharp decision, but it will be a day of unveiled mysteries and of solved riddles.

My brethren, in view of that day, ought we not to be content to work our work betimes, to do the very best we can for our generation, to build, and labour, and go on laying stone upon stone, knowing that some day we shall see the design and meaning of our work; why we were forced to toil on in that uncongenial work, unknown, unnoticed, obscure; why we were crippled in our means, and feeble in our health, and bowed down with a cross; why we had no joy in the work, and so little encouragement; why life to us was so singularly unlike this great cathedral, almost unique in its history, designed and finished by one man, by one master-builder, in his lifetime and during one episcopate? No; as the multitudes throng in, each bringing his fragment of work, when the idle and the wicked see how even they were used by God's wonderful power, their broken work and their brilliant ornaments, useful for foundations, carted into the pit —then for the first time we shall see the proportions and the design of the new city rising phœnix-like out of the ruin of the world. In view of that day, as again and again we sink back baffled at life's tasks and despair of success, let us rise up and build with fresh vigour, confident in God's strength, and awaiting His decree. We are told that when Sir Christopher Wren commenced to build this cathedral, he had a stone brought to him out of the ruin and rubbish of the fire, on which he found written, to his surprise and thankfulness, the one word, *Resurgam*. So, my brethren, in all the wreckage and failures of life there is written, not in terror, but as an omen of good things, *Resurgam*—" I shall rise again." "The Lord shall judge His people."

And yet God Himself never hesitates to put before us the terrors of the last day, its reversals, its strange unlooked-for contradictions, the shame, the exposure, the anguish, and the doom—in one word, its decisions. Perhaps, as we have already said, we underrate the decisions of life and believe ourselves to be more free than we are. Certainly life, with its daily accumulations, makes it more and more difficult to steer the ship. It answers to the helm, but heavily and with difficulty. But when the great day comes, the final day of decision, we shall then be brought face to face with accounts over which we have lost control. The man who has repented himself will then have to face long accumulations of sin which have passed out through his example or actions right through to a series of generations, like "Jeroboam the son of Nebat, who made Israel to sin." The responsibility of just loosening the pure snow which rolled down through the ages in a gathering avalanche of destruction, the gentle, graceful, unloosing of faith which ended in sweeping away all restraint, and the snapping of all props and the desolation of the Lord's vineyard; and, thank God also, those forgotten words of advice, that brave wrestling with doubt, that hand held out to steady a leader, the post held against overwhelming odds—all these are to be decided and our life with them. We may be selfish now; we cannot be selfish then; for our destiny for weal or woe will have to be disentangled out of all those lives around us, out of those destinies which have crossed our path, those whom we have helped or hindered on the road to Heaven.

Just one word more. If Advent is to be anything more than a yearly scare, a terror, and a time for uttering unpleasant things, do let us keep hold on ourselves. "If we would judge ourselves," says Holy Scripture—" if we would judge ourselves "—that is the secret; if we are to be anything more than debtors who have to face their liabilities, never having kept their accounts, let us examine ourselves and judge ourselves, let us make our spiritual state just as much a matter of business as our worldly affairs. And then, when the great day comes, which may come to us before death, and deprive us of the intermediate state—at least we shall have eliminated some of the elements of surprise here. In view of our communions, in view of our Christianity, in view of the coming festival of Christmas with regard to the final day of decision, we ourselves have gone down into the valley of decision, and judged ourselves that we might not be judged of the Lord.

SERMON XXXI.

The Enthusiasm of the City.[1]

"*In that day shall this song be sung in the land of Judah; We have a strong city; salvation will God appoint for walls and bulwarks.*"
—ISA. xxvi. 1.

THE Prophet Isaiah is gazing to-day on one of those visions of restoration which lightened up the gloom of Judgment, and fringed with glory the smoke and dust of destruction which hang over the track of the hosts of vengeance as they scoured across the plain of history. He appears at times like the solemn figure of Majesty Who, seated on the Mount of Olives and gazing back over the city which had finally rejected Him, sees the ruin of the siege and the convulsion of falling Jerusalem pass through judgment into the calmness of life eternal for the people of God. With Isaiah it never seems far absent; after judgment a remnant; after the catastrophe which levels the tree still a shoot out of the withered stump, still a vision of a restored city and of the eternal purpose which nothing can frustrate, nothing

[1] A sermon preached in S. Paul's Cathedral, on Sunday afternoon, December 17, being the Third Sunday in Advent, 1893.

eventually can overcome, as the omnipotent will of God rides triumphantly on the storm.

But it is the character of the vision which attracts our notice to-day. We have accustomed ourselves so much and so continuously to think of our own individual wants and sins, our own personal salvation and individual assurance, our own comfort, our own joy and peace in believing, that we hardly recognize Redemption under the image of a city, or a salvation which is something more than co-extensive with our own immediate interests. It is a phenomenon which must strike the most casual reader of the Bible,—the indomitable patriotism, the longing for a visible embodiment of a public hope, the establishment of a kingdom or city to which all contribute, and which sheds a return of a fuller life over all. Now it takes a nobler, now it takes a baser, shape. Now, when there is a new tax to be paid, it was a kingdom where there would be no Roman emperor, no procurators, no publican, no taxes; now, when the image of the emperor defiled the choicest traditions, it was the vision of a lawgiver ruling the earth according to the law of God from a purified Jerusalem. Abraham, father of the faithful, had earned it by his faith. In spite of failure, in the hands of selfish judges and petty kings, trampled on by heathen oppressors, still it was there, the city of God, the faithful city. "A king shall reign in righteousness." Nothing could ever eclipse this hope, nothing finally supersede it, no earthly reward could push it away, no cruel disappointment could extinguish it. Look at Nehemiah loaded with honour in a heathen court, yet bewailing with the bitterness of a personal bereavement the ruined state of Jerusalem, so that the sorrow of his heart betrayed itself in his countenance and aroused the suspicions of the king. Look backwards in history, it is the same thing. Personal and domestic calamities fall heavily upon poor old Eli—that weak old man—but it is the news of the national disaster which crushes him to the ground. Look on to the times of the New Testament, where the horrors of crucifixion never drew forth a groan, the coming fate of Jerusalem causes the incarnate God to weep. In that Psalm which we still sing at a most solemn moment of life when the Church is strengthening with her blessing that mysterious bond which signifies the mystical union betwixt Christ and the Church, it rings out almost in irony across the selfishness of our joy, and the scant limitation of the horizon of our happiness. "Yea, that thou shalt see thy children's children." Yes, all this, the happy home, the name, the good fortune, the place in the world, the grip on history. But more than all these to a Jew—and why not to a Christian?—more than these, without which the fulness of marriage blessings would seem incomplete— "and peace upon Israel." "The Lord from out of Sion shall so bless thee that thou shalt see Jerusalem in prosperity all thy life long." How it lingers upon us with reproachful cadence, this unselfish longing for the public good, the commonweal, a life of which our own little life, with its joys and sorrows, is but a part, a life, which it were treachery to enjoy without a thought of the greater and fuller interests of the city, of the kingdom of Messiah's reign of joy, and peace, and an equable government. "Why should not my countenance be sad, when the city, the place of my fathers' sepulchres, lieth waste"? Ichabod, Ichabod, the glory of God is departed from Israel, because the ark of God is taken.

I. Is this a pathetic emotion which has passed away—a city sentiment, a kingdom motive, which sighs in on the music of the world and dies away in the march of the Overture, to give place to plaintive solos and deeper music of the soul? Is it an old Jewish craze which we bury in the lumber-room of Utopias, or Republics, or Cities of God, in which men have thought they saw a way to bridge over the selfishness of humanity and discover a sentiment which was not based on utility, or the struggle for existence, or the rule of self-preservation, or the pitiless logic of economic laws which know neither mitigation or equity at the hands of humanity? No, this sentiment is still alive in the heart of Christianity. It culminates in the Creed which is at once the profession of faith, the conviction, and the hymn of praise of the Christian. The Creed which begins with "I," loses itself in "The Catholic Church," the Creed which cements the personal union of the soul with God widens out into the "communion of saints." No, it is with this as with so many other things in Judaism—the thing which the Jew saw indistinctly, although he knew it was there, is focussed in

Christianity into a definite, a real object. That which Jerusalem could never be, in its fulness, to the Jew, the Church has become to the Christian— the abode of God's presence, the centre of unity, a city which hath foundations, whose gates are salvation, and whose walls are praise, while, as we look, still there is an indis'inct outline beyond all this, still there is an upper city quivering in the hazy distance of which this is but a suburb, an outer line of defence. A clearer view, a more extended vision, an unclouded spiritual eyesight, will see an abode beyond, which is not a mere palisade of security for saved individuals, but a city with a constitution, a government, and a king—the Heavenly Jerusalem.

"We have a strong city." The city, as Isaiah saw it, was as yet empty, waiting for the righteous nation which keepeth truth to enter in. The Church is not what man has made it, nor an invention of human wisdom, nor an incorporated society of those who think alike on religious matters with a government which on the whole is best, a constitution which may be stretched to breaking point of elastic and comprehensive principles. Just as God designed a kingdom with laws, a constitution for His people Israel, so He has designed for us His holy Church, to break down, as it were, with His own hands that selfish individualism which thinks only of personal salvation, to set up the glory of God as an object of worship, and to give to us all the aid of mutual co-operation and help. "One Lord" gives us a common enthusiasm, "one faith" gives us a common object, "one baptism" makes us a common family. A city with laws, and privileges, and obligations where, if one member suffer, all the members suffer with it, where we can march on through the hostile world in all the safety of a formation which offers a front on each side to the enemy—here is an idea which at once gives a nobler aspect to life and to the world. The soul of man is not a mere wayfarer from Jerusalem to Jericho, who falls among thieves, where every one is bad, or at least suspicious, who must simply put his back against the wall, and fight until he is rescued; he is, on the contrary, in the midst of a world full of capacity, full of beauty, full of goodness, because redeemed by God Himself—in a world where he can reverently look up and adore God for His great glory; where the lilies in their royal robes are part of the ritual of the earth which perpetually does Him homage; where "the heavens declare the glory of God; and the firmament showeth His handy-work"; where men in their worship are not ashamed to invite the angels to join with them; where the liturgy of the altar in heaven is linked with the altar on earth, and the one great act of Atonement claims the adoration of earth and heaven; where men are endowed with spiritual powers, and spiritual excellences are displayed in the new field of humanity; where God speaks to man, and man speaks to God, and prayer and sacraments oppose a barrier to sin, bulwarks and walls of salvation within which rises up the life of a fuller humanity.

I plead, therefore, for the Church for some of that

enthusiasm which must ever cling as a glorious tradition round the battlements of the city of God There are questions which from time to time stir to its very depth the heart of the true patriot. He looks out on the vast world of heathenism in its forlorn state—"aliens to the commonwealth of Israel," losers in the rich blessings of life, a break in the plan of salvation offered to the world by Jesus Christ, tracts of dominion torn from His empire—and as he sees the missionary host sweeping by him "to the help of the Lord against the mighty," he shouts for the battle. He sees a great nation nominally still owning allegiance to Jesus Christ, yet, by some strange and extraordinary weakness, hesitating, under the sacred name of liberty, to give the children their lawful heritage of true religion, venturing to bring forward that very name of our salvation with fear and suspicion under the protection of a "conscience clause," and as the result of a precarious majority of a controversial committee, to be named as cautiously as you would in a Mahommedan mosque, or to be assigned a place in a pantheon of distinguished heroes as one whom it would be impolitic to omit, but sectarian to adorn with his full titles. And his spirit is stirred within him for the honour of the city of God, for a question larger than his own salvation— the honour of Jesus Christ Himself; or in the circle of his friends and relations that worthy name is blasphemed, or the sacred cause of truth and holiness is betrayed, and he hears that dread reproach, "Whosoever therefore shall be ashamed of Me and of My words, ... of him also shall the Son of man be ashamed when He cometh in the glory of His Father with the holy angels." And he is emboldened to speak a word for Christ. He stands out as the citizen of no mean city of which he would be ashamed to feel ashamed, and fear to be afraid to own his enthusiasm.

There are hundreds and hundreds of souls—thank God!—to-day who feel as keenly as did Israel of old the patriotism of the city of God, who are Churchmen first and individuals afterwards, who cherish her creeds with personal devotion, who reverence her altars with an undying enthusiasm, whose spirit stirs to the voices of her worship, and whose blood mounts high in the ardour of her service. It is a sign of approaching death when the members once alive with Christ cease to feel even pain, or a passing interest in the great Church questions of the day. God has never left Himself without witness in the quiet lives of simple devotion, only to be detected by their fragrance, and hidden by the leaves of their humility —waiting for the consolation of Israel. Still we look, in times like these, we look out anxiously for more Church laymen fired with the spirit of Nehemiah, wide in their sympathies as the prophet Isaiah, devoted to the service of the city of God, men whose love and whose zeal can find no other expression than this the language of youthful love, "As a young man marrieth a virgin, so shall thy sons marry thee."

"We have a strong city." You will say: "The language of enthusiasm, after all, does not carry us far." But the language of enthusiasm subsides, if you look at it, into a strong, underlying principle of duty. Members of a city are not left entirely to their enthusiasms as motives of action. They are reminded of the obligations of duty. The freedom purchased by a stable government, the benefits procured by the public vigilance, have a right to demand corresponding duties from the individual in contribution, in service, in regulation of life. And to-day we are reminded by the Ember Collect that those of us who are spared on Sunday next will be seeing in this church the spectacle of young men in the prime of life devoting themselves to be public servants in the city of God, going forth endowed with the Holy Ghost to enlarge Jerusalem, if it may be to take in more ground for God, to widen the temple enclosure, and to take in more of the language of the world into songs of the temple, and to realize on earth that heavenly idea where the apostle sees no temple in heaven, because it was all temple, and no one spot was more sacred than another spot, where it was all full of the glory of God. The sight of men thus obeying a vocation, and enlisting themselves in the service of God, and their fellow-men, may well quicken in us all the sense of duty. When I was sent into the world, God deliberated and God willed that another human being should take his place on this little ledge called "life," with the abyss of eternity around it, whose storms shake and shatter. It must come at times before any thinking man: "Why has God placed me here? Is it simply to browse on the pasture beneath my feet, to snatch a patch of herbage from my fellow-man, to enjoy, to die, and be as if I had never been, and leave room for another life as uneventful and as uninteresting as my own"? There are two sad sayings, grim in their cynicism, merciless in their truth. The one describes the man to whom life had been simply a narrow circumference centred in himself. "He was born a man, but he died a grocer," *i.e.* his manhood was swallowed up in his trade. The other speaks of the dying out of enthusiasm and the loss of individuality, under the deadening contact of the world, and the drab of its unrelieved monotony: "We are born originals, and we die copies." To lose all sense of the city spirit, to lose all sense of duty to a great cause, or of participation in a public life, is to degrade our humanity and to mistake the object of our existence. What those ordained men hope to do for God's Church in the power of the Holy Ghost, each earnest individual life which recognizes what is meant by duty must be prepared to do in his capacity and his station, with the opportunities which God has given him. It has been said with great truth, that vocation is a call to God and not merely a call to labour. When our blessed Lord Jesus Christ was showing His disciples the pattern of humble service we read, " When Jesus knew that His hour was come that He should depart out of this world to His Father, having loved His own which were in the world, He loved them unto the end. And . . . knowing that the Father had given all things into His hands, and that He was come from God, and went to God; He riseth from supper and laid aside

His garments; and took a towel, and girded Himself. After that He poureth water into a basin, and began to wash the disciples' feet, and to wipe them with the towel wherewith He was girded." So the mystery of the Incarnation, the counsels of eternity, the greatness of the Atonement, are bound down, in the person of our Lord Jesus Christ, to the simple basin, and the washing of the feet of twelve poor peasants. Do not we want ordained tradesmen, men who will bring to business the same sense of duty, the same *esprit de corps* of the heavenly citizenship, the same imperial traditions, the same sense of service to a present God that forms the atmosphere of the sacred ministry, and the peculiar consecration of the priesthood? Do we not need ordained heads of families, men who bring to the service of God armed bands of children and servants, trained in purity, obedience, gentleness, and true religion, who in the onslaught of sin and in the furious assaults which batter the Church from time to time can throw into the breach the sanctity of family life, and the priceless defence of a Christian household—men and women who build up the walls of Jerusalem opposite their own houses? Do we not want ordained men among the clerks of our large warehouses whose life shall be a rallying point for all that is good and true, on whose shield is blazoned the device of the archangel, as they leap down into the arena, flashing back the proud legend, "Who is like God?" We need to feel it more and more on each side of us, to touch that ninefold line of defence which links us on to heaven, to be in touch with the great past, to feel the pulses of life which breathed through the splendid faith of our forefathers, and which mounts up again and again in unquenchable ardour in the true members of a city.

"We have a strong city," no poor kingdom of broken-backed toilers grubbing up the unyielding earth to eat a crust in sullenness, to die unheeded and unmissed, but citizens of the heavenly city, waiting to go up higher. Ah! dear brethren, it is true, the aspect of that city which most attracts us, which most catches the eye, and most arrests our thankful adoration, is salvation, defence, protection. We know something of that dark cloud which lowers over the plain. We can see beneath its brown ripples and stifling folds the glitter of steel, and some wound smarts the keener and some pain shoots the stronger through the limbs as we remember the contest. But here is salvation. Beautiful is the font, but its water is salvation; beautiful is the altar, but its Presence is salvation; beautiful are the feet of them that preach the Gospel of peace, but their message is salvation. The city of God is, after all, a camp here below, its glorious services are but *Te Deums* on the field of battle. But here, at all events, is something which dignifies life, and gives a fresh aspect of glory to its drudgeries, a fresh relief to its pains. Here we are learning to take our place in the golden city, where no thief approacheth, neither moth corrupteth; where God is the conscious object of every prayer, of every word that is said, every action that is done; where every place, even the lowest, is heaven; where some rule without pride, and others are ruled without jealousy; where one star differeth from another star, and yet the glory of one is the glory of all; where we shall be able to praise God among much people in the great company of the redeemed. "Who are these, and whence came they?" Do we still ask this question? My brethren, our blessed Lord gave us the answer when He spoke of the children of the kingdom—those who, born to be kings and priests, have crushed out selfishness and overcome self, and learned the lesson of the city spirit sheltered under the protection of those bulwarks of salvation.

"Jerusalem, Jerusalem!
God grant that I may see
Thy endless joys, and of the same
Partaker aye may be.

"Thy houses are of ivory,
Thy windows crystal clear,
Thy tiles are made of beaten gold;
O God, that I were there!"

THE END.

December 1901.

A Selection of Works
IN
THEOLOGICAL LITERATURE
PUBLISHED BY
MESSRS. LONGMANS, GREEN, & CO.
London: 39 PATERNOSTER ROW, E.C.
New York: 91 and 93 FIFTH AVENUE.
Bombay: 32 HORNBY ROAD.

Abbey and Overton.—THE ENGLISH CHURCH IN THE EIGHTEENTH CENTURY. By CHARLES J. ABBEY, M.A., Rector of Checkendon, Reading, and JOHN H. OVERTON, D.D., Canon of Lincoln. *Crown 8vo. 7s. 6d.*

Adams.—SACRED ALLEGORIES. The Shadow of the Cross —The Distant Hills—The Old Man's Home—The King's Messengers. By the Rev. WILLIAM ADAMS, M.A. 16*mo*. 3*s. net*.
The four Allegories may be had separately, with Illustrations. 16*mo*. 1*s. each*.

Aids to the Inner Life.
Edited by the Venble. W. H. HUTCHINGS, M.A., Archdeacon of Cleveland, Canon of York, Rector of Kirby Misperton, and Rural Dean of Malton. *Five Vols.* 32*mo, cloth limp*, 6*d. each; or cloth extra*, 1*s. each*.
OF THE IMITATION OF CHRIST. By THOMAS À KEMPIS.
THE CHRISTIAN YEAR.
THE DEVOUT LIFE. By ST. FRANCIS DE SALES.
THE HIDDEN LIFE OF THE SOUL.
THE SPIRITUAL COMBAT. By LAURENCE SCUPOLI.

Arbuthnot.—SHAKESPEARE SERMONS. Preached in the Collegiate Church of Stratford-on-Avon on the Sundays following the Poet's Birthday, 1894-1900. Collected by the Rev. GEORGE ARBUTHNOT, M.A., Vicar of Stratford-on-Avon. *Crown 8vo. 2s. 6d. net.*

Bathe.—Works by the Rev. ANTHONY BATHE, M.A.

A LENT WITH JESUS. A Plain Guide for Churchmen. Containing Readings for Lent and Easter Week, and on the Holy Eucharist. 32mo, 1s.; *or in paper cover*, 6d.

AN ADVENT WITH JESUS. 32mo, 1s., *or in paper cover*, 6d.

WHAT I SHOULD BELIEVE. A Simple Manual of Self-Instruction for Church People. *Small 8vo, limp*, 1s.; *cloth gilt*, 2s.

Bathe and Buckham.—THE CHRISTIAN'S ROAD BOOK. 2 Parts. By the Rev. ANTHONY BATHE and Rev. F. H. BUCKHAM.
Part I. DEVOTIONS. *Sewed*, 6d.; *limp cloth*, 1s.; *cloth extra*, 1s. 6d.
Part II. READINGS. *Sewed*, 1s.; *limp cloth*, 2s.; *cloth extra*, 3s.; *or complete in one volume, sewed*, 1s. 6d. *limp cloth*, 2s. 6d.; *cloth extra*, 3s. 6d.

Benson.—Works by the Rev. R. M. BENSON, M.A., Student of Christ Church, Oxford.

THE FOLLOWERS OF THE LAMB: a Series of Meditations, especially intended for Persons living under Religious Vows, and for Seasons of Retreat, etc. *Crown 8vo*. 4s. 6d.

THE FINAL PASSOVER: A Series of Meditations upon the Passion of our Lord Jesus Christ. *Small 8vo*.

Vol. I.—THE REJECTION. 5s.
Vol. II.—THE UPPER CHAMBER.
Part I. 5s.
Part II. 5s.

Vol. III.—THE DIVINE EXODUS. Parts I. and II. 5s. each.
Vol. IV.—THE LIFE BEYOND THE GRAVE. 5s.

THE MAGNIFICAT; a Series of Meditations upon the Song of the Blessed Virgin Mary. *Small 8vo*. 2s.

SPIRITUAL READINGS FOR EVERY DAY. 3 *vols. Small 8vo*. 3s. 6d. *each.*
I. ADVENT.   II. CHRISTMAS.   III. EPIPHANY.

BENEDICTUS DOMINUS: A Course of Meditations for Every Day of the Year. Vol. I.—ADVENT TO TRINITY. Vol. II.—TRINITY, SAINTS' DAYS, etc. *Small 8vo*. 3s. 6d. *each*; *or in One Volume*, 7s.

BIBLE TEACHINGS: The Discourse at Capernaum.—St. John vi. *Small 8vo*. 1s.; *or with Notes*. 3s. 6d.

THE WISDOM OF THE SON OF DAVID: An Exposition of the First Nine Chapters of the Book of Proverbs. *Small 8vo*. 3s. 6d.

THE MANUAL OF INTERCESSORY PRAYER. *Royal 32mo*; *cloth boards*, 1s. 3d.; *cloth limp*, 9d.

THE EVANGELIST LIBRARY CATECHISM. Part I. *Small 8vo*. 3s.

PAROCHIAL MISSIONS. *Small 8vo*. 2s. 6d.

IN THEOLOGICAL LITERATURE.   3

Bigg.—UNITY IN DIVERSITY: Five Addresses delivered in the Cathedral Church of Christ, Oxford, during Lent 1899, with Introduction. By the Rev. CHARLES BIGG, D.D., Regius Professor of Ecclesiastical History in the University of Oxford. *Crown 8vo. 2s.6d.*

Bickersteth.—YESTERDAY, TO-DAY, AND FOR EVER: a Poem in Twelve Books. By EDWARD HENRY BICKERSTETH, D.D., late Lord Bishop of Exeter. 18mo. 1s. *net.* With red borders, 16mo, 2s. *net.*

The Crown 8vo Edition (5s.) may still be had.

Blunt.—Works by the Rev. JOHN HENRY BLUNT, D.D.

THE ANNOTATED BOOK OF COMMON PRAYER: Being an Historical, Ritual, and Theological Commentary on the Devotional System of the Church of England. 4to. 21s.

THE COMPENDIOUS EDITION OF THE ANNOTATED BOOK OF COMMON PRAYER: Forming a concise Commentary on the Devotional System of the Church of England. *Crown 8vo.* 10s. 6d.

DICTIONARY OF DOCTRINAL AND HISTORICAL THEOLOGY. By various Writers. *Imperial 8vo.* 21s.

DICTIONARY OF SECTS, HERESIES, ECCLESIASTICAL PARTIES AND SCHOOLS OF RELIGIOUS THOUGHT. By various Writers. *Imperial 8vo.* 21s.

THE REFORMATION OF THE CHURCH OF ENGLAND: its History, Principles, and Results. 1574-1662. *Two Vols. 8vo.* 34s.

THE BOOK OF CHURCH LAW. Being an Exposition of the Legal Rights and Duties of the Parochial Clergy and the Laity of the Church of England. Revised by the Right Hon. Sir WALTER G. F. PHILLIMORE, Bart., D.C.L., and G. EDWARDES JONES, Barrister-at-Law. *Crown 8vo.*

A COMPANION TO THE BIBLE: Being a Plain Commentary on Scripture History, to the end of the Apostolic Age. *Two Vols. small 8vo. Sold separately.* OLD TESTAMENT. 3s. 6d. NEW TESTAMENT. 3s. 6d.

HOUSEHOLD THEOLOGY: a Handbook of Religious Information respecting the Holy Bible, the Prayer Book, the Church, etc., etc. *Paper cover,* 16mo. 1s. *Also the Larger Edition,* 3s. 6d.

Body.—Works by the Rev. GEORGE BODY, D.D., Canon of Durham.

THE LIFE OF LOVE. A Course of Lent Lectures. 16mo. 2s. *net.*

THE SCHOOL OF CALVARY; or, Laws of Christian Life revealed from the Cross. 16mo. 2s. *net.*

THE LIFE OF JUSTIFICATION. 16mo. 2s. *net.*

THE LIFE OF TEMPTATION. 16mo. 2s. *net.*

THE PRESENT STATE OF THE FAITHFUL DEPARTED. *Small 8vo. sewed,* 6d. 32mo. *cloth,* 1s.

Book of Private Prayer, The. For use Twice Daily; together with the Order for the Administration of the Lord's Supper or Holy Communion. *Revised and Enlarged Edition.* 18mo. *Limp cloth,* 2s.; *Cloth boards,* 2s. 6d.

Book of Prayer and Daily Texts for English Churchmen. 32mo. 1s. *net.*

Boultbee.—A COMMENTARY ON THE THIRTY-NINE ARTICLES OF THE CHURCH OF ENGLAND. By the Rev. T. P. BOULTBEE, formerly Principal of the London College of Divinity, St. John's Hall, Highbury. *Crown 8vo.* 6s.

Bright.—Works by WILLIAM BRIGHT, D.D., late Regius Professor of Ecclesiastical History in the University of Oxford.

THE AGE OF THE FATHERS. Two Vols. 8vo. [*In the Press.*

SOME ASPECTS OF PRIMITIVE CHURCH LIFE. *Crown 8vo.* 6s.

THE ROMAN SEE IN THE EARLY CHURCH: And other Studies in Church History. *Crown 8vo.* 7s. 6d.

WAYMARKS IN CHURCH HISTORY. *Crown 8vo.* 7s. 6d.

LESSONS FROM THE LIVES OF THREE GREAT FATHERS. St. Athanasius, St. Chrysostom, and St. Augustine. *Crown 8vo.* 6s.

THE INCARNATION AS A MOTIVE POWER. *Crown 8vo.* 6s.

Bright and Medd.—LIBER PRECUM PUBLICARUM ECCLESIÆ ANGLICANÆ. A GULIELMO BRIGHT, S.T.P., et PETRO GOLDSMITH MEDD, A.M., Latine redditus. *Small 8vo.* 7s. 6d.

Browne.—WEARIED WITH THE BURDEN: A Book of Daily Readings for Lent. By ARTHUR HEBER BROWNE, M.A., LL.D., Vicar of Kempsford, Gloucester. *Crown 8vo.* 4s. 6d.

Browne.—AN EXPOSITION OF THE THIRTY-NINE ARTICLES, Historical and Doctrinal. By E. H. BROWNE, D.D., sometime Bishop of Winchester. *8vo.* 16s.

Campion and Beamont.—THE PRAYER BOOK INTERLEAVED. With Historical Illustrations and Explanatory Notes arranged parallel to the Text. By W. M. CAMPION, D.D., and W. J. BEAMONT, M.A. *Small 8vo.* 7s. 6d.

Carpenter and Harford-Battersby.—THE HEXATEUCH ACCORDING TO THE REVISED VERSION ARRANGED IN ITS CONSTITUENT DOCUMENTS BY MEMBERS OF THE SOCIETY OF HISTORICAL THEOLOGY, OXFORD. Edited with Introduction, Notes, Marginal References, and Synoptical Tables. By J. ESTLIN CARPENTER, M.A. (Lond.) and G. HARFORD-BATTERSBY, M.A. (Oxon.). *Two vols.* 4to. (*Vol. I. Introduction and Appendices; Vol. II. Text and Notes*). 36s. *net.*

Carter.—Works by, and edited by the Rev. T. T. CARTER, M.A., late Hon. Canon of Christ Church, Oxford.

UNDERCURRENTS OF CHURCH LIFE IN THE EIGHTEENTH CENTURY. *Crown 8vo.* 5s.

NICHOLAS FERRAR: his Household and his Friends. With Portrait. *Crown 8vo.* 6s.

THE SPIRIT OF WATCHFULNESS AND OTHER SERMONS. *Crown 8vo.* 5s.

THE TREASURY OF DEVOTION: a Manual of Prayer for General and Daily Use. Compiled by a Priest.
18mo. 2s. 6d.; *cloth limp,* 2s. Bound with the Book of Common Prayer, 3s. 6d. Red-Line Edition. *Cloth extra, gilt top.* 18mo. 2s. 6d. net. Large-Type Edition. *Crown 8vo.* 3s. 6d.

THE WAY OF LIFE: A Book of Prayers and Instruction for the Young at School, with a Preparation for Confirmation. 18mo. 1s. 6d.

THE PATH OF HOLINESS: a First Book of Prayers, with the Service of the Holy Communion, for the Young. Compiled by a Priest. With Illustrations. 16mo. 1s. 6d.; *cloth limp,* 1s.

THE GUIDE TO HEAVEN: a Book of Prayers for every Want. (For the Working Classes.) Compiled by a Priest. 18mo. 1s. 6d.; *cloth limp,* 1s. *Large-Type Edition. Crown 8vo.* 1s. 6d.; *cloth limp,* 1s.

THE STAR OF CHILDHOOD: a First Book of Prayers and Instruction for Children. Compiled by a Priest. With Illustrations. 16mo. 2s. 6d.

SIMPLE LESSONS; or, Words Easy to be Understood. A Manual of Teaching. I. On the Creed. II. The Ten Commandments. III. The Sacrament. 18mo. 3s.

MANUAL OF DEVOTION FOR SISTERS OF MERCY. 8 parts in 2 vols. 32mo. 10s. Or separately:—Part I. 1s. 6d. Part II. 1s. Part III. 1s. Part IV. 2s. Part V. 1s. Part VI. 1s. Part VII. Part VIII. 1s. 6d.

SPIRITUAL INSTRUCTIONS. *Crown 8vo.*

THE HOLY EUCHARIST. 3s. 6d.
THE DIVINE DISPENSATIONS. 3s. 6d.
THE LIFE OF GRACE. 3s. 6d.
OUR LORD'S EARLY LIFE. 3s. 6d.
OUR LORD'S ENTRANCE ON HIS MINISTRY. 3s. 6d.
THE RELIGIOUS LIFE. 3s. 6d.

A BOOK OF PRIVATE PRAYER FOR MORNING, MID-DAY, AND OTHER TIMES. 18mo, *limp cloth,* 1s.; *cloth, red edges,* 1s. 3d.

THE DOCTRINE OF THE PRIESTHOOD IN THE CHURCH OF ENGLAND. *Crown 8vo.* 4s.

THE DOCTRINE OF CONFESSION IN THE CHURCH OF ENGLAND. *Crown 8vo.* 5s.

Coles.—Works by the Rev. V. S. S. COLES, M.A., Principal of the Pusey House, Oxford.
   LENTEN MEDITATIONS. 18mo. 2s. 6d.
   ADVENT MEDITATIONS ON ISAIAH I.-XII. : together with Outlines of Christmas Meditations on St. John i. 1-12. 18mo. 2s.

Company, The, of Heaven : Daily Links with the Household of God. Being Selections in Prose and Verse from various Authors. With Autotype Frontispiece. *Crown* 8vo. 3s. 6d. *net.*

Conybeare and Howson.—THE LIFE AND EPISTLES OF ST. PAUL. By the Rev. W. J. CONYBEARE, M.A., and the Very Rev. J. S. HOWSON, D.D. With numerous Maps and Illustrations. LIBRARY EDITION. *Two Vols.* 8vo. 21s. STUDENTS' EDITION. *One Vol. Crown* 8vo. 6s. POPULAR EDITION. *One Vol. Crown* 8vo. 3s. 6d.

Creighton.—Works by the Right Hon. and Right Rev. MANDELL CREIGHTON, D.D., late Lord Bishop of London.
   A HISTORY OF THE PAPACY FROM THE GREAT SCHISM TO THE SACK OF ROME (1378-1527). *Six Volumes. Crown* 8vo. 5s. *each.*
   THE CHURCH AND THE NATION : Charges and Addresses. *Crown* 8vo. 5s. *net.*

Day-Hours of the Church of England, The. Newly Revised according to the Prayer Book and the Authorised Translation of the Bible. *Crown* 8vo, *sewed*, 3s. ; *cloth*, 3s. 6d.
   SUPPLEMENT TO THE DAY-HOURS OF THE CHURCH OF ENGLAND, being the Service for certain Holy Days. *Crown* 8vo, *sewed*, 3s. ; *cloth*, 3s. 6d.

Edersheim.—Works by ALFRED EDERSHEIM, M.A., D.D., Ph.D.
   THE LIFE AND TIMES OF JESUS THE MESSIAH. *Two Vols.* 8vo. 12s. *net.*
   JESUS THE MESSIAH : being an Abridged Edition of 'The Life and Times of Jesus the Messiah.' *Crown* 8vo. 6s. *net.*

Ellicott.—Works by C. J. ELLICOTT, D.D., Bishop of Gloucester
   A CRITICAL AND GRAMMATICAL COMMENTARY ON ST. PAUL'S EPISTLES. Greek Text, with a Critical and Grammatical Commentary, and a Revised English Translation. 8vo.

GALATIANS. 8s. 6d.	PHILIPPIANS, COLOSSIANS, AND PHILEMON. 10s. 6d.
EPHESIANS. 8s. 6d.	
PASTORAL EPISTLES. 10s. 6d.	THESSALONIANS. 7s. 6d.

   HISTORICAL LECTURES ON THE LIFE OF OUR LORD JESUS CHRIST. 8vo. 12s.

English (The) Catholic's Vade Mecum: a Short Manual of General Devotion. Compiled by a PRIEST. 32mo. *limp*, 1s. ; *cloth*, 2s.
   PRIEST's Edition. 32mo. 1s. 6d.

IN THEOLOGICAL LITERATURE.   7

Epochs of Church History.—Edited by Right Hon. and Right Rev. MANDELL CREIGHTON, D.D., late Lord Bishop of London. *Small 8vo.* 2s. 6d. *each.*

THE ENGLISH CHURCH IN OTHER LANDS. By the Rev. H. W. TUCKER, M.A.

THE HISTORY OF THE REFORMATION IN ENGLAND. By the Rev. GEO. G. PERRY, M.A.

THE CHURCH OF THE EARLY FATHERS. By the Rev. ALFRED PLUMMER, D.D.

THE EVANGELICAL REVIVAL IN THE EIGHTEENTH CENTURY. By the Rev. J. H. OVERTON, D.D.

THE UNIVERSITY OF OXFORD. By the Hon. G. C. BRODRICK, D.C.L.

THE UNIVERSITY OF CAMBRIDGE. By J. BASS MULLINGER, M.A.

THE ENGLISH CHURCH IN THE MIDDLE AGES. By the Rev. W. HUNT, M.A.

THE CHURCH AND THE EASTERN EMPIRE. By the Rev. H. F. TOZER, M.A.

THE CHURCH AND THE ROMAN EMPIRE. By the Rev. A. CARR, M.A.

THE CHURCH AND THE PURITANS, 1570-1660. By HENRY OFFLEY WAKEMAN, M.A.

HILDEBRAND AND HIS TIMES. By the Very Rev. W. R. W. STEPHENS, B.D.

THE POPES AND THE HOHENSTAUFEN. By UGO BALZANI.

THE COUNTER REFORMATION. By ADOLPHUS WILLIAM WARD, Litt.D.

WYCLIFFE AND MOVEMENTS FOR REFORM. By REGINALD L. POOLE, M.A.

THE ARIAN CONTROVERSY. By the Rev. Professor H. M. GWATKIN, M.A.

Eucharistic Manual (The). Consisting of Instructions and Devotions for the Holy Sacrament of the Altar. From various sources. 32mo. *cloth gilt, red edges.* 1s. *Cheap Edition, limp cloth.* 9d.

Farrar.—Works by FREDERIC W. FARRAR, D.D., Dean of Canterbury.

TEXTS EXPLAINED; Or, Helps to Understand the New Testament. *Crown 8vo.* 5s. *net.*

THE BIBLE: Its Meaning and Supremacy. *8vo.* 6s. *net.*

Fosbery.—VOICES OF COMFORT. Edited by the Rev. THOMAS VINCENT FOSBERY, M.A., sometime Vicar of St. Giles's, Reading. *Cheap Edition. Small 8vo.* 3s. *net.*
The Larger Edition (7s. 6d.) may still be had.

Fuller.—IN TERRÂ PAX; Or, The Primary Sayings of Our Lord during the Great Forty Days in their Relation to the Church. Sermons preached at St. Mark's, Marylebone Road. By MORRIS FULLER, B.D. *Crown 8vo.* 6s. *net.*

Gardner.—A CATECHISM OF CHURCH HISTORY, from the Day of Pentecost until the Present Day. By the Rev. C. E. GARDNER, of the Society of St. John the Evangelist, Cowley. *Crown 8vo, sewed,* 1s. ; *cloth,* 1s. 6d.

Geikie.—Works by J. CUNNINGHAM GEIKIE, D.D., LL.D., late Vicar of St. Martin-at-Palace, Norwich.

THE VICAR AND HIS FRIENDS. *Crown 8vo. 5s. net.*

HOURS WITH THE BIBLE: the Scriptures in the Light of Modern Discovery and Knowledge. *Complete in Twelve Volumes. Crown 8vo.*

OLD TESTAMENT.

CREATION TO THE PATRIARCHS. *With a Map and Illustrations.* 5s.

MOSES TO JUDGES. *With a Map and Illustrations.* 5s.

SAMSON TO SOLOMON. *With a Map and Illustrations.* 5s

REHOBOAM TO HEZEKIAH. *With Illustrations.* 5s.

MANASSEH TO ZEDEKIAH. *With the Contemporary Prophets. With a Map and Illustrations.* 5s.

EXILE TO MALACHI. *With the Contemporary Prophets. With Illustrations.* 5s.

NEW TESTAMENT.

THE GOSPELS. *With a Map and Illustrations.* 5s.

LIFE AND WORDS OF CHRIST. *With Map.* 2 vols. 10s.

LIFE AND EPISTLES OF ST. PAUL. *With Maps and Illustrations.* 2 vols. 10s.

ST. PETER TO REVELATION. *With 29 Illustrations.* 5s.

LIFE AND WORDS OF CHRIST.
Cabinet Edition. With Map. 2 vols. *Post 8vo.* 10s.
Cheap Edition, without the Notes. 1 vol. 8vo. 6s.
A SHORT LIFE OF CHRIST. *With 34 Illustrations. Crown 8vo.* 3s. 6d.; *gilt edges*, 4s. 6d.

Gold Dust: a Collection of Golden Counsels for the Sanctification of Daily Life. Translated and abridged from the French by E.L.E.E. Edited by CHARLOTTE M. YONGE. Parts I. II. III. Small Pocket Volumes. *Cloth, gilt, each* 1s. Parts I. and II. in One Volume. 1s. 6d. Parts I., II., and III. in One Volume. 2s. net.

*** The two first parts in One Volume, *large type*, 18mo. *cloth, gilt.* 2s. net. Parts I. II. and III. are also supplied, bound in white cloth, with red edges, in box, price 2s. 6d. net.

Gore.—Works by the Right Rev. CHARLES GORE, D.D., Lord Bishop of Worcester.

THE CHURCH AND THE MINISTRY. *Fourth Edition, Revised. Crown 8vo.* 6s., *net.*

ROMAN CATHOLIC CLAIMS. *Crown 8vo.* 3s. net.

Goreh.—THE LIFE OF FATHER GOREH. By C. E. GARDNER, S.S.J.E. Edited, with Preface, by RICHARD MEUX BENSON, M.A., S.S.J.E., Student of Christ Church, Oxford. With Portrait. *Crown 8vo.* 5s.

IN THEOLOGICAL LITERATURE.   9

Great Truths of the Christian Religion. Edited by the Rev. W. U. RICHARDS. *Small 8vo.* 2s.

Hall.—Works by the Right Rev. A. C. A. HALL, D.D., Bishop of Vermont.

CONFIRMATION. *Crown 8vo.* 5s. (The Oxford Library of Practical Theology.)

THE VIRGIN MOTHER: Retreat Addresses on the Life of the Blessed Virgin Mary as told in the Gospels. With an appended Essay on the Virgin Birth of our Lord. *Crown 8vo.* 4s. 6d.

CHRIST'S TEMPTATION AND OURS. *Crown 8vo.* 3s. 6d.

Hall.—THE KENOTIC THEORY. Considered with Particular Reference to its Anglican Forms and Arguments. By the Rev. FRANCIS J. HALL, D.D., Instructor of Dogmatic Theology in the Western Theological Seminary, Chicago, Illinois. *Crown 8vo.* 5s.

Hallowing of Sorrow. By E. R. With a Preface by H. S. HOLLAND, M.A., Canon and Precentor of St. Paul's. *Small 8vo.* 2s.

Hanbury-Tracy.—FAITH AND PROGRESS. Sermons Preached at the Dedication Festival of St. Barnabas' Church, Pimlico, June 10-17, 1900. Edited by the Rev. the Hon. A. HANBURY-TRACY, Vicar of St. Barnabas', Pimlico. With an Introduction by the Rev. T. T. CARTER, M.A., of Clewer. *Crown 8vo.* 4s. 6d. net.

'Worship'—The Very Rev. the DEAN OF CHICHESTER. 'The Intellectual Obligations of Love'—The Rev. H. S. HOLLAND, Canon of St. Paul's. 'Parochial Organisation'—The Rev. H. M. VILLIERS, Vicar of St. Paul's, Knightsbridge. 'Religious Education'—The Rev. B. REYNOLDS, Prebendary of St. Paul's. 'Devotion'—The Rev. W. C. E. NEWBOLT, Canon of St. Paul's. 'Penitence'—The Rev. E. F. RUSSELL, St. Alban's, Holborn. 'The Sanctification of Individual Life'—The Rev. V. S. S. COLES, Principal of Pusey House. 'The Revival of the Religious Life'—The Rev. R. M. BENSON, S.S.J.E. 'The Blessed Sacrament'—The Rev. DARWELL STONE, Principal of Dorchester College. To which are appended 'Prayer for the Departed' and 'Eucharistical Adoration'—Two Sermons by the Rev. the Hon. A. HANBURY-TRACY.

Harrison.—PROBLEMS OF CHRISTIANITY AND SCEPTICISM. By the Rev. ALEXANDER J. HARRISON, B.D. Incumbent of St. Thomas the Martyr, Newcastle-upon-Tyne. *Crown 8vo.* 7s. 6d.

Hatch.—THE ORGANIZATION OF THE EARLY CHRISTIAN CHURCHES. Being the Bampton Lectures for 1880. By EDWIN HATCH, M.A., D.D., late Reader in Ecclesiastical History in the University of Oxford. *8vo.* 5s.

A 2

Holland.—Works by the Rev. HENRY SCOTT HOLLAND, M.A., Canon and Precentor of St. Paul's.

GOD'S CITY AND THE COMING OF THE KINGDOM. Crown 8vo. 3s. 6d.
PLEAS AND CLAIMS FOR CHRIST. Crown 8vo. 3s. 6d.
CREED AND CHARACTER: Sermons. Crown 8vo. 3s. 6d.
ON BEHALF OF BELIEF. Sermons. Crown 8vo. 3s. 6d.
CHRIST OR ECCLESIASTES. Sermons. Crown 8vo. 2s. 6d.
LOGIC AND LIFE, with other Sermons. Crown 8vo. 3s. 6d.
GOOD FRIDAY. Being Addresses on the Seven Last Words. Small 8vo. 2s.

Hollings.—Works by the Rev. G. S. HOLLINGS, Mission Priest of the Society of St. John the Evangelist, Cowley, Oxford.

THE HEAVENLY STAIR; or, A Ladder of the Love of God for Sinners. Crown 8vo. 3s. 6d.
PORTA REGALIS; or, Considerations on Prayer. Crown 8vo. limp cloth, 1s. 6d. net; cloth boards, 2s. net.
CONSIDERATIONS ON THE WISDOM OF GOD. Crown 8vo. 4s.
PARADOXES OF THE LOVE OF GOD, especially as they are seen in the way of the Evangelical Counsels. Crown 8vo. 4s.
ONE BORN OF THE SPIRIT; or, the Unification of our Life in God. Crown 8vo. 3s. 6d.

Hutchings.—Works by the Ven. W. H. HUTCHINGS, M.A. Archdeacon of Cleveland, Canon of York, Rector of Kirby Misperton, and Rural Dean of Malton.

SERMON SKETCHES from some of the Sunday Lessons throughout the Church's Year. Vols. I and II. Crown 8vo. 5s. each.
THE LIFE OF PRAYER: a Course of Lectures delivered in All Saints' Church, Margaret Street, during Lent. Crown 8vo. 4s. 6d.
THE PERSON AND WORK OF THE HOLY GHOST: a Doctrinal and Devotional Treatise. Crown 8vo. 4s. 6d.
SOME ASPECTS OF THE CROSS. Crown 8vo. 4s. 6d.
THE MYSTERY OF THE TEMPTATION. Lent Lectures delivered at St. Mary Magdalene, Paddington. Crown 8vo. 4s. 6d.

Hutton.—THE SOUL HERE AND HEREAFTER. By the Rev. R. E. HUTTON, Chaplain of St. Margaret's, East Grinstead. Crown 8vo. 6s.

IN THEOLOGICAL LITERATURE. 11

Inheritance of the Saints; or, Thoughts on the Communion of Saints and the Life of the World to come. Collected chiefly from English Writers by L. P. With a Preface by the Rev. HENRY SCOTT HOLLAND, M.A. *Ninth Edition. Crown 8vo. 7s. 6d.*

Jameson.—Works by Mrs. JAMESON.

SACRED AND LEGENDARY ART, containing Legends of the Angels and Archangels, the Evangelists, the Apostles. With 19 Etchings and 187 Woodcuts. 2 *vols. 8vo.* 20s. *net.*

LEGENDS OF THE MONASTIC ORDERS, as represented in the Fine Arts. With 11 Etchings and 88 Woodcuts. *8vo.* 10s. *net.*

LEGENDS OF THE MADONNA, OR BLESSED VIRGIN MARY. With 27 Etchings and 165 Woodcuts. *8vo.* 10s. *net.*

THE HISTORY OF OUR LORD, as exemplified in Works of Art. Commenced by the late Mrs. JAMESON; continued and completed by LADY EASTLAKE. With 31 Etchings and 281 Woodcuts. 2 *Vols. 8vo.* 20s. *net.*

Jennings.—ECCLESIA ANGLICANA. A History of the Church of Christ in England from the Earliest to the Present Times. By the Rev. ARTHUR CHARLES JENNINGS, M.A. *Crown 8vo. 7s. 6d.*

Johnstone.—SONSHIP: Six Lenten Addresses. By the Rev. VERNEY LOVETT JOHNSTONE, M.A., late Assistant Curate of Ilfracombe. With an Introduction by the Rev. V. S. S. COLES, M.A., Principal of the Pusey House, Oxford. *Crown 8vo.* 2s.

Joy and Strength for the Pilgrim's Day: Selections in Prose and Verse. By the Editor of 'Daily Strength for Daily Needs,' etc. *Small 8vo.* 3s. 6d. *net.*

Jukes.—Works by ANDREW JUKES.

THE NEW MAN AND THE ETERNAL LIFE. Notes on the Reiterated Amens of the Son of God. *Crown 8vo.* 6s.

THE NAMES OF GOD IN HOLY SCRIPTURE: a Revelation of His Nature and Relationships. *Crown 8vo.* 4s. 6d.

THE TYPES OF GENESIS. *Crown 8vo.* 7s. 6d.

THE SECOND DEATH AND THE RESTITUTION OF ALL THINGS. *Crown 8vo.* 3s. 6d.

Kelly.—A HISTORY OF THE CHURCH OF CHRIST. By the Rev. HERBERT H. KELLY, M.A., Director of the Society of the Sacred Mission, Mildenhall, Suffolk. Vol. I. A.D. 29-342 *Crown 8vo.* 3s. 6d. *net.* [*Vol.* 2 *in the press.*

Knox Little.—Works by W. J. KNOX LITTLE, M.A., Canon Residentiary of Worcester, and Vicar of Hoar Cross.

HOLY MATRIMONY. *Crown 8vo.* 5*s.* [The Oxford Library of Practical Theology.]

THE PERFECT LIFE: Sermons. *Crown 8vo.* 7*s.* 6*d.*

THE CHRISTIAN HOME. *Crown 8vo.* 3*s.* 6*d.*

CHARACTERISTICS AND MOTIVES OF THE CHRISTIAN LIFE. Ten Sermons preached in Manchester Cathedral, in Lent and Advent. *Crown 8vo.* 2*s.* 6*d.*

THE MYSTERY OF THE PASSION OF OUR MOST HOLY REDEEMER. *Crown 8vo.* 2*s.* 6*d.*

THE LIGHT OF LIFE. Sermons preached on Various Occasions. *Crown 8vo.* 3*s.* 6*d.*

SUNLIGHT AND SHADOW IN THE CHRISTIAN LIFE. Sermons preached for the most part in America. *Crown 8vo.* 3*s.* 6*d.*

Law.—A PRACTICAL TREATISE UPON CHRISTIAN PERFECTION. By WILLIAM LAW, M.A. Edited by L. H. M. SOULSBY. 16*mo*, *red borders*, 2*s. net.*

Lear.—Works by, and Edited by, H. L. SIDNEY LEAR.

FOR DAYS AND YEARS. A book containing a Text, Short Reading, and Hymn for Every Day in the Church's Year. 16*mo.* 2*s.* 6*d.* Also a Cheap Edition, 32*mo*, 1*s.*; *or cloth gilt*, 1*s.* 6*d.*; *or with red borders*, 2*s. net.*

FIVE MINUTES. Daily Readings of Poetry. 16*mo.* 3*s.* 6*d.* Also a Cheap Edition, 32*mo.* 1*s.*; *or cloth gilt*, 1*s.* 6*d.*

WEARINESS. A Book for the Languid and Lonely. *Large Type. Small 8vo.* 5*s.*

CHRISTIAN BIOGRAPHIES. *Nine Vols. Crown 8vo.* 3*s.* 6*d. each.*

MADAME LOUISE DE FRANCE, Daughter of Louis XV., known also as the Mother Térèse de St. Augustin.

A DOMINICAN ARTIST: a Sketch of the Life of the Rev. Père Besson, of the Order of St. Dominic.

HENRI PERREYVE. By PÈRE GRATRY.

ST. FRANCIS DE SALES, Bishop and Prince of Geneva.

THE REVIVAL OF PRIESTLY LIFE IN THE SEVENTEENTH CENTURY IN FRANCE.

A CHRISTIAN PAINTER OF THE NINETEENTH CENTURY.

BOSSUET AND HIS CONTEMPORARIES.

FÉNELON, ARCHBISHOP OF CAMBRAI.

HENRI DOMINIQUE LACORDAIRE.

[continued.

IN THEOLOGICAL LITERATURE. 13

Lear.—Works by, and Edited by, H. L. SIDNEY LEAR.—*continued.*

DEVOTIONAL WORKS. Edited by H. L. SIDNEY LEAR. *New and Uniform Editions. Nine Vols.* 16mo. 2s. *net each.*

FÉNELON'S SPIRITUAL LETTERS TO MEN.

FÉNELON'S SPIRITUAL LETTERS TO WOMEN.

A SELECTION FROM THE SPIRITUAL LETTERS OF ST. FRANCIS DE SALES. Also *Cheap Edition*, 32mo, 6d. *cloth limp ;* 1s. *cloth boards.*

THE SPIRIT OF ST. FRANCIS DE SALES.

THE HIDDEN LIFE OF THE SOUL.

THE LIGHT OF THE CONSCIENCE. Also *Cheap Edition,* 32mo, 6d. *cloth limp ;* 1s. *cloth boards.*

SELF-RENUNCIATION. From the French.

ST. FRANCIS DE SALES' OF THE LOVE OF GOD.

SELECTIONS FROM PASCAL'S 'THOUGHTS.'

Lepine.—THE MINISTERS OF JESUS CHRIST. By J. FOSTER LEPINE, Vicar of Lamorbey, Kent. Parts I. and II. *Crown 8vo.* 5s. *each.*

Liddon.—Works by HENRY PARRY LIDDON, D.D., D.C.L.,LL.D.

SERMONS ON SOME WORDS OF ST. PAUL. *Crown 8vo.* 5s.

SERMONS PREACHED ON SPECIAL OCCASIONS, 1860-1889. *Crown 8vo.* 5s.

CLERICAL LIFE AND WORK : Sermons. *Crown 8vo.* 5s.

ESSAYS AND ADDRESSES : Lectures on Buddhism—Lectures on the Life of St. Paul—Papers on Dante. *Crown 8vo.* 5s.

EXPLANATORY ANALYSIS OF PAUL'S EPISTLE TO THE ROMANS. 8vo. 14s.

EXPLANATORY ANALYSIS OF ST. PAUL'S FIRST EPISTLE TO TIMOTHY. 8vo. 7s. 6d.

SERMONS ON OLD TESTAMENT SUBJECTS. *Crown 8vo.* 5s.

SERMONS ON SOME WORDS OF CHRIST. *Crown 8vo.* 5s.

THE DIVINITY OF OUR LORD AND SAVIOUR JESUS CHRIST. Being the Bampton Lectures for 1866. *Crown 8vo.* 5s.

ADVENT IN ST. PAUL'S. *Two Vols. Crown 8vo.* 3s. 6d. *each. Cheap Edition in one Volume. Crown 8vo.* 5s.

CHRISTMASTIDE IN ST. PAUL'S. *Crown 8vo.* 5s.

PASSIONTIDE SERMONS. *Crown 8vo.* 5s.

EASTER IN ST. PAUL'S. Sermons bearing chiefly on the Resurrection of our Lord. *Two Vols. Crown 8vo.* 3s. 6d. *each. Cheap Edition in one Volume. Crown 8vo.* 5s.

[*continued.*

Liddon.—Works by HENRY PARRY LIDDON, D.D., D.C.L., LL.D.—*continued.*

SERMONS PREACHED BEFORE THE UNIVERSITY OF OXFORD. *Two Vols. Crown 8vo.* 3s. 6d. each. *Cheap Edition in one Volume. Crown 8vo.* 5s.

THE MAGNIFICAT. Sermons in St. Paul's. *Crown 8vo.* 2s. net.

SOME ELEMENTS OF RELIGION. Lent Lectures. *Small 8vo.* 2s. net. [*The Crown 8vo Edition* (5s.) *may still be had.*]

SELECTIONS FROM THE WRITINGS OF. *Crown 8vo.* 3s. 6d.

Luckock.—Works by HERBERT MORTIMER LUCKOCK, D.D., Dean of Lichfield.

THE SPECIAL CHARACTERISTICS OF THE FOUR GOSPELS. *Crown 8vo.* 6s.

AFTER DEATH. An Examination of the Testimony of Primitive Times respecting the State of the Faithful Dead, and their Relationship to the Living. *Crown 8vo.* 3s. net.

THE INTERMEDIATE STATE BETWEEN DEATH AND JUDGMENT. Being a Sequel to *After Death. Crown 8vo.* 3s. net.

FOOTPRINTS OF THE SON OF MAN, as traced by St. Mark. Being Eighty Portions for Private Study, Family Reading, and Instruction in Church. *Crown 8vo.* 3s. net.

FOOTPRINTS OF THE APOSTLES, as traced by St. Luke in the Acts. Being Sixty Portions for Private Study, and Instruction in Church. A Sequel to 'Footprints of the Son of Man, as traced by St. Mark.' *Two Vols. Crown 8vo.* 12s.

THE DIVINE LITURGY. Being the Order for Holy Communion, Historically, Doctrinally, and Devotionally set forth, in Fifty Portions. *Crown 8vo.* 3s. net.

STUDIES IN THE HISTORY OF THE BOOK OF COMMON PRAYER. The Anglican Reform—The Puritan Innovations—The Elizabethan Reaction—The Caroline Settlement. With Appendices. *Crown 8vo.* 3s. net.

THE BISHOPS IN THE TOWER. A Record of Stirring Events affecting the Church and Nonconformists from the Restoration to the Revolution. *Crown 8vo.* 3s. net.

IN THEOLOGICAL LITERATURE. 15

Lyra Germanica: Hymns for the Sundays and Chief Festivals of the Christian Year. *First Series.* 16*mo, with red borders,* 2*s. net.*

MacColl.—Works by the Rev. MALCOLM MACCOLL, D.D., Canon Residentiary of Ripon.

THE REFORMATION SETTLEMENT: Examined in the Light of History and Law. Tenth Edition, Revised, with a new Preface. *Crown* 8*vo.* 3*s.* 6*d. net.*

CHRISTIANITY IN RELATION TO SCIENCE AND MORALS. *Crown* 8*vo.* 6*s.*

LIFE HERE AND HEREAFTER : Sermons. *Crown* 8*vo.* 7*s.* 6*d.*

Marriage Addresses and Marriage Hymns. By the BISHOP OF LONDON, the BISHOP OF ROCHESTER, the BISHOP OF TRURO, the DEAN OF ROCHESTER, the DEAN OF NORWICH, ARCHDEACON SINCLAIR, CANON DUCKWORTH, CANON NEWBOLT, CANON KNOX LITTLE, CANON RAWNSLEY, the Rev. J. LLEWELLYN DAVIES, D.D., the Rev. W. ALLEN WHITWORTH, etc. Edited by the Rev. O. P. WARDELL-YERBURGH, M.A., Vicar of the Abbey Church of St. Mary, Tewkesbury. *Crown* 8*vo.* 5*s.*

Mason.—Works by A. J. MASON, D.D., Lady Margaret Professor of Divinity in the University of Cambridge and Canon of Canterbury.

PURGATORY; THE STATE OF THE FAITHFUL DEAD; INVOCATION OF SAINTS. Three Lectures. *Crown* 8*vo.* 3*s.* 6*d.*

THE FAITH OF THE GOSPEL. A Manual of Christian Doctrine. *Crown* 8*vo.* 7*s.* 6*d. Cheap Edition. Crown* 8*vo.* 3*s. net.*

THE RELATION OF CONFIRMATION TO BAPTISM. As taught in Holy Scripture and the Fathers. *Crown* 8*vo.* 7*s.* 6*d.*

Maturin.—Works by the Rev. B. W. MATURIN.

SOME PRINCIPLES AND PRACTICES OF THE SPIRITUAL LIFE. *Crown* 8*vo.* 4*s.* 6*d.*

PRACTICAL STUDIES ON THE PARABLES OF OUR LORD. *Crown* 8*vo.* 5*s.*

Medd.—THE PRIEST TO THE ALTAR ; Or, Aids to the Devout Celebration of Holy Communion, chiefly after the Ancient English Use of Sarum. By PETER GOLDSMITH MEDD, M.A., Canon of St. Alban's. Fourth Edition, revised and enlarged. *Royal* 8*vo.* 15*s.*

Meyrick.—THE DOCTRINE OF THE CHURCH OF England on the Holy Communion Restated as a Guide at the Present Time. By the Rev. F. MEYRICK, M.A. *Crown* 8*vo.* 4*s.* 6*d.*

Monro.—SACRED ALLEGORIES. By Rev. EDWARD MONRO. *Complete Edition in one Volume, with Illustrations. Crown* 8*vo.* 3*s.* 6*d. net.*

A SELECTION OF WORKS

Mortimer.—Works by the Rev. A. G. MORTIMER, D.D., Rector of St. Mark's, Philadelphia.

THE EUCHARISTIC SACRIFICE: An Historical and Theological Investigation of the Sacrificial Conception of the Holy Eucharist in the Christian Church. *Crown 8vo.* 10s. 6d.

CATHOLIC FAITH AND PRACTICE: A Manual of Theology. Two Parts. *Crown 8vo.* Sold Separately. Part I. 7s. 6d. Part II. 9s.

JESUS AND THE RESURRECTION: Thirty Addresses for Good Friday and Easter. *Crown 8vo.* 5s.

HELPS TO MEDITATION: Sketches for Every Day in the Year.
Vol. I. ADVENT TO TRINITY. 8vo. 7s. 6d.
Vol. II. TRINITY TO ADVENT. 8vo. 7s. 6d.

STORIES FROM GENESIS: Sermons for Children. *Crown 8vo.* 4s.

THE LAWS OF HAPPINESS; or, The Beatitudes as teaching our Duty to God, Self, and our Neighbour. 18mo. 2s.

THE LAWS OF PENITENCE: Addresses on the Words of our Lord from the Cross. 16mo. 1s. 6d.

SERMONS IN MINIATURE FOR EXTEMPORE PREACHERS: Sketches for Every Sunday and Holy Day of the Christian Year. *Crown 8vo.* 6s.

NOTES ON THE SEVEN PENITENTIAL PSALMS, chiefly from Patristic Sources. *Small 8vo.* 3s. 6d.

THE SEVEN LAST WORDS OF OUR MOST HOLY REDEEMER: with Meditations on some Scenes in His Passion. *Crown 8vo.* 5s.

LEARN OF JESUS CHRIST TO DIE: Addresses on the Words of our Lord from the Cross, taken as teaching the way of Preparation for Death. 16mo. 2s.

Mozley.—Works by J. B. MOZLEY, D.D., late Canon of Christ Church, and Regius Professor of Divinity at Oxford.

ESSAYS, HISTORICAL AND THEOLOGICAL. *Two Vols.* 8vo. 24s.

EIGHT LECTURES ON MIRACLES. Being the Bampton Lectures for 1865. *Crown 8vo.* 3s. net.

RULING IDEAS IN EARLY AGES AND THEIR RELATION TO OLD TESTAMENT FAITH. 8vo. 6s.

SERMONS PREACHED BEFORE THE UNIVERSITY OF OXFORD, and on Various Occasions. *Crown 8vo.* 3s. net.

SERMONS, PAROCHIAL AND OCCASIONAL. *Crown 8vo.* 3s. net.

A REVIEW OF THE BAPTISMAL CONTROVERSY. *Crown 8vo.* 3s. net.

IN THEOLOGICAL LITERATURE. 17

Newbolt.—Works by the Rev. W. C. E. NEWBOLT, M.A., Canon and Chancellor of St. Paul's Cathedral.

APOSTLES OF THE LORD: being Six Lectures on Pastoral Theology, delivered in the Divinity School, Cambridge, Lent Term, 1901. *Crown 8vo.* 3s. 6d. *net.*

RELIGION. *Crown 8vo.* 5s. (The Oxford Library of Practical Theology.)

THE DIAL OF PRAYER: being Devotions for Every Hour. *Small 8vo.* 2s.

WORDS OF EXHORTATION. Sermons Preached at St. Paul's and elsewhere. *Crown 8vo.* 5s. *net.*

PENITENCE AND PEACE: being Addresses on the 51st and 23rd Psalms. *Crown 8vo.* 2s. *net.*

PRIESTLY IDEALS; being a Course of Practical Lectures delivered in St. Paul's Cathedral to 'Our Society' and other Clergy, in Lent, 1898. *Crown 8vo.* 3s. 6d.

THE GOSPEL OF EXPERIENCE; or, the Witness of Human Life to the truth of Revelation. Being the Boyle Lectures for 1895. *Crown 8vo.* 5s.

COUNSELS OF FAITH AND PRACTICE: being Sermons preached on various occasions. *Crown 8vo.* 5s.

SPECULUM SACERDOTUM; or, the Divine Model of the Priestly Life. *Crown 8vo.* 7s. 6d.

THE FRUIT OF THE SPIRIT. Being Ten Addresses bearing on the Spiritual Life. *Crown 8vo.* 2s. *net.*

THE MAN OF GOD. *Small 8vo.* 1s. 6d.

THE PRAYER BOOK: Its Voice and Teaching. *Crown 8vo.* 2s. *net.*

Newman.—Works by JOHN HENRY NEWMAN, B.D., sometime Vicar of St. Mary's, Oxford.

LETTERS AND CORRESPONDENCE OF JOHN HENRY NEWMAN DURING HIS LIFE IN THE ENGLISH CHURCH. With a brief Autobiography. Edited, at Cardinal Newman's request, by ANNE MOZLEY. 2 *vols. Crown 8vo.* 7s.

PAROCHIAL AND PLAIN SERMONS. *Eight Vols. Crown 8vo.* 3s. 6d. *each.*

SELECTION, ADAPTED TO THE SEASONS OF THE ECCLESIASTICAL YEAR, from the 'Parochial and Plain Sermons.' *Crown 8vo.* 3s. 6d.

FIFTEEN SERMONS PREACHED BEFORE THE UNIVERSITY OF OXFORD. *Crown 8vo.* 3s. 6d.

SERMONS BEARING UPON SUBJECTS OF THE DAY. *Crown 8vo.* 3s. 6d.

LECTURES ON THE DOCTRINE OF JUSTIFICATION. *Crown 8vo.* 3s. 6d.

⁎⁎ *A Complete List of Cardinal Newman's Works can be had on Application.*

Osborne.—Works by EDWARD OSBORNE, Mission Priest of the Society of St. John the Evangelist, Cowley, Oxford.

THE CHILDREN'S SAVIOUR. Instructions to Children on the Life of Our Lord and Saviour Jesus Christ. *Illustrated.* 16mo. 2s. net.

THE SAVIOUR KING. Instructions to Children on Old Testament Types and Illustrations of the Life of Christ. *Illustrated.* 16mo. 2s. net.

THE CHILDREN'S FAITH. Instructions to Children on the Apostles' Creed. *Illustrated.* 16mo. 2s. net.

Ottley.—ASPECTS OF THE OLD TESTAMENT: being the Bampton Lectures for 1897. By ROBERT LAWRENCE OTTLEY, M.A., Vicar of Winterbourne Bassett, Wilts; sometime Principal of the Pusey House. 8vo. 7s. 6d.

Oxford (The) Library of Practical Theology.—Produced under the Editorship of the Rev. W. C. E. NEWBOLT, M.A., Canon and Chancellor of St. Paul's, and the Rev. DARWELL STONE, M.A., Principal of the Missionary College, Dorchester. *Crown 8vo.* 5s. each.

RELIGION. By the Rev. W. C. E. NEWBOLT, M.A., Canon and Chancellor of St. Paul's. [*Ready.*

HOLY BAPTISM. By the Rev. DARWELL STONE, M.A., Principal of the Missionary College, Dorchester. [*Ready.*

CONFIRMATION. By the Right Rev. A. C. A. HALL, D.D., Bishop of Vermont. [*Ready.*

THE HISTORY OF THE BOOK OF COMMON PRAYER. By the Rev. LEIGHTON PULLAN, M.A., Fellow of St. John Baptist's Oxford. [*Ready.*

HOLY MATRIMONY. By the Rev. W. J. KNOX LITTLE, M.A., Canon of Worcester. [*Ready.*

THE INCARNATION. By the Rev. H. V. S. ECK, M.A., St. Andrew's, Bethnal Green. [*Ready.*

FOREIGN MISSIONS. By the Right Rev. E. T. CHURTON, D.D., formerly Bishop of Nassau. [*Ready.*

PRAYER. By the Rev. ARTHUR JOHN WORLLEDGE, M.A., Canon and Chancellor of Truro. [*In the press.*

SUNDAY. By the Rev. W. B. TREVELYAN, M.A., Vicar of St. Matthew's, Westminster. [*In preparation.*

THE BIBLE. By the Rev. DARWELL STONE, M.A., Joint Editor of the Series. [*In preparation.*

THE CREEDS. By the Rev. A. G. MORTIMER, D.D., Rector of St. Mark's, Philadelphia. [*In preparation.*

THE CHURCH CATECHISM THE CHRISTIAN'S MANUAL. By the Rev. W. C. E. NEWBOLT, M.A., Joint Editor of the Series.
[*In preparation.*

[*continued.*

IN THEOLOGICAL LITERATURE. 19

Oxford (The) Library of Practical Theology.—*continued*.
RELIGIOUS CEREMONIAL. By the Rev. WALTER HOWARD FRERE, M.A., of the Community of the Resurrection, Examining Chaplain to the Bishop of Rochester. [*In preparation*.
INSTITUTIONS OF THE CHURCH. By the Rev. LEIGHTON PULLAN, M.A., Fellow of St. John's College, Oxford.
[*In preparation*
HOLY ORDERS. By the Rev. A. R. WHITHAM, M.A., Principal of Culham College, Abingdon. [*In preparation*.
VISITATION OF THE SICK. By the Rev. E. F. RUSSELL, M.A., St. Alban's, Holborn. [*In preparation*.
CHURCH WORK. By the Rev. BERNARD REYNOLDS, M.A., Prebendary of St. Paul's. [*In preparation*.

Bodington.—Devotional Books, by the Rev. CHARLES BODINGTON, Canon and Treasurer of Lichfield.

Paget.—Works by FRANCIS PAGET, D.D., Lord Bishop of Oxford.
STUDIES IN THE CHRISTIAN CHARACTER: Sermons. With an Introductory Essay. *Crown 8vo. 4s. net.*
THE SPIRIT OF DISCIPLINE: Sermons. *Crown 8vo. 4s. net.*
FACULTIES AND DIFFICULTIES FOR BELIEF AND DISBELIEF. *Crown 8vo. 4s. net.*
THE HALLOWING OF WORK. Addresses given at Eton, January 16-18, 1888. *Small 8vo. 2s.*
THE REDEMPTION OF WAR: Sermons. *Crown 8vo. 2s. net.*

Passmore.—Works by the Rev. T. H. PASSMORE, M.A.
THE THINGS BEYOND THE TOMB IN A CATHOLIC LIGHT. *Crown 8vo. 2s. 6d. net.*
LEISURABLE STUDIES. *Crown 8vo. 4s. net.* [*Ready*.
CONTENTS.—The 'Religious Woman'—Preachments—Silly Ritual—The Tyranny of the Word—The Lectern—The Functions of Ceremonial—Homo Creator—Concerning the Pun—Proverbia.

Percival.—THE INVOCATION OF SAINTS. Treated Theologically and Historically. By HENRY R. PERCIVAL, M.A., D.D. *Crown 8vo. 5s.*

Pocket Manual of Prayers for the Hours, Etc. With the Collects from the Prayer Book. *Royal 32mo. 1s.*

Powell.—CHORALIA : a Handy-Book for Parochial Precentors and Choirmasters. By the Rev. JAMES BADEN POWELL, M.A., Precentor of St. Paul's, Knightsbridge. *Crown 8vo. 4s. 6d. net.*

Practical Reflections. By a CLERGYMAN. With Preface by H. P. LIDDON, D.D., D.C.L., and the LORD BISHOP OF LINCOLN. *Crown 8vo.*

THE BOOK OF GENESIS. 4s. 6d.	THE MINOR PROPHETS. 4s. 6d.
THE PSALMS. 5s.	THE HOLY GOSPELS. 4s. 6d.
ISAIAH. 4s. 6d.	ACTS TO REVELATION. 6s.

Preparatio; or, Notes of Preparation for Holy Communion, founded on the Collect, Epistle, and Gospel for Every Sunday in the Year. With Preface by the Rev. GEORGE CONGREVE, S.S.J.E. *Crown 8vo. 6s. net.*

Priest's Prayer Book (The). Containing Private Prayers and Intercessions; Occasional, School, and Parochial Offices; Offices for the Visitation of the Sick, with Notes, Readings, Collects, Hymns, Litanies, etc. With a brief Pontifical. By the late Rev. R. F. LITTLEDALE, LL.D., D.C.L., and Rev. J. EDWARD VAUX, M.A., F.S.A. *Post 8vo. 6s. 6d.*

Pullan.—Works by the Rev. LEIGHTON PULLAN, M.A., Fellow of St. John Baptist's College.

LECTURES ON RELIGION. *Crown 8vo. 6s.*

THE HISTORY OF THE BOOK OF COMMON PRAYER. *Crown 8vo. 5s.* (The Oxford Library of Practical Theology.)

Puller.—THE PRIMITIVE SAINTS AND THE SEE OF ROME. By F. W. PULLER, of the Society of St. John the Evangelist, Cowley. With an Introduction by EDWARD, LORD BISHOP OF LINCOLN. Third Edition, Revised and Enlarged. *8vo. 16s. net.*

Pusey.—Works by the Rev. E. B. PUSEY, D.D.

PRIVATE PRAYERS. With Preface by H. P. LIDDON, D.D., late Chancellor and Canon of St. Paul's. *Royal 32mo. 1s.*

SPIRITUAL LETTERS OF EDWARD BOUVERIE PUSEY, D.D. Edited and prepared for publication by the Rev. J. O. JOHNSTON, M.A., Principal of the Theological College, Cuddesdon; and the Rev. W. C. E. NEWBOLT, M.A., Canon and Chancellor of St. Paul's. New and cheaper Edition. With Index. *Crown 8vo. 5s. net.*

Pusey.—THE STORY OF THE LIFE OF DR. PUSEY. By the Author of 'Charles Lowder.' With Frontispiece. *Crown 8vo. 7s. 6d. net.*

Randolph.—Works by B. W. RANDOLPH, D.D., Principal of the Theological College and Hon. Canon of Ely.

THE EXAMPLE OF THE PASSION: being Addresses given in St. Paul's Cathedral at the Mid-Day Service on Monday, Tuesday, Wednesday, and Thursday in Holy Week, and at the Three Hours' Service on Good Friday, 1897. *Small 8vo. 2s. net.*

MEDITATIONS ON THE OLD TESTAMENT for Every Day in the Year. *Crown 8vo. 6s.*

THE THRESHOLD OF THE SANCTUARY: being Short Chapters on the Inner Preparation for the Priesthood. *Crown 8vo. 3s. 6d.*

IN THEOLOGICAL LITERATURE.

Rede.—THE COMMUNION OF SAINTS: A Lost Link in the Chain of the Church's Creed. By WYLLYS REDE, D.D., Rector of the Church of the Incarnation, and Canon of the Cathedral, Atalanta, Georgia. With a Preface by LORD HALIFAX. *Crown 8vo.* 3s. 6d.

RIVINGTON'S DEVOTIONAL SERIES.

16mo, Red Borders. Each 2s. net.

BICKERSTETH'S YESTERDAY, TO-DAY, AND FOR EVER.
CHILCOT'S TREATISE ON EVIL THOUGHTS.
THE CHRISTIAN YEAR.
HERBERT'S POEMS AND PROVERBS.
KEMPIS' (À) OF THE IMITATION OF CHRIST.
LEAR'S (H. L. SIDNEY) FOR DAYS AND YEARS.
LYRA APOSTOLICA. POEMS BY J. W. BOWDEN, R. H. FROUDE, J. KEBLE, J. H. NEWMAN, R. I. WILBERFORCE, AND I. WILLIAMS; and a Preface by CARDINAL NEWMAN.
FRANCIS DE SALES' (ST.) THE DEVOUT LIFE.

WILSON'S THE LORD'S SUPPER.
*TAYLOR'S (JEREMY) HOLY LIVING.
*——— ——— HOLY DYING.
SCUDAMORE'S STEPS TO THE ALTAR.
LAW'S TREATISE ON CHRISTIAN PERFECTION. Edited by L. H. M. SOULSBY.
LYRA GERMANICA: HYMNS FOR THE SUNDAYS AND CHIEF FESTIVALS OF THE CHRISTIAN YEAR. *First Series.*
CHRIST AND HIS CROSS: SELECTIONS FROM SAMUEL RUTHERFORD'S LETTERS. Edited by L. H. M. SOULSBY.

* *These two in one Volume.* 5s.

18mo, without Red Borders. Each 1s. net.

BICKERSTETH'S YESTERDAY, TO-DAY, AND FOR EVER.
THE CHRISTIAN YEAR.
KEMPIS' (À) OF THE IMITATION OF CHRIST.
HERBERT'S POEMS AND PROVERBS.

SCUDAMORE'S STEPS TO THE ALTAR.
WILSON'S THE LORD'S SUPPER.
FRANCIS DE SALES' (ST.) THE DEVOUT LIFE.
*TAYLOR'S (JEREMY) HOLY LIVING.
*——— ——— HOLY DYING.

* *These two in one Volume.* 2s. 6d.

Robbins.—AN ESSAY TOWARD FAITH. By WILFORD L ROBBINS, D.D., Dean of the Cathedral of All Saints', Albany, U.S. *Small 8vo.* 3s. net.

Robinson.—STUDIES IN THE CHARACTER OF CHRIST. By the Rev. C. H. ROBINSON, M.A., Canon Missioner of Ripon; Reader in Hausa in the University of Cambridge. *Crown 8vo.* 3s. 6d.

Romanes.—THOUGHTS ON THE COLLECTS FOR THE TRINITY SEASON. By ETHEL ROMANES, Author of 'The Life and Letters of George John Romanes.' With a Preface by the Right Rev. the LORD BISHOP OF LONDON. 18mo. 2s. 6d.; gilt edges. 3s. 6d.

Sanday.—Works by W. SANDAY, D.D., LL.D., Lady Margaret Professor of Divinity and Canon of Christ Church, Oxford.

DIFFERENT CONCEPTIONS OF PRIESTHOOD AND SACRIFICE: a Report of a Conference held at Oxford, December 13 and 14, 1899. Edited by W. SANDAY, D.D. 8vo. 7s. 6d.

THE CONCEPTION OF PRIESTHOOD IN THE EARLY CHURCH AND IN THE CHURCH OF ENGLAND: Four Sermons. Crown 8vo. 3s. 6d.

INSPIRATION: Eight Lectures on the Early History and Origin of the Doctrine of Biblical Inspiration. Being the Bampton Lectures for 1893. 8vo. 7s. 6d.

Sanders.—FÉNELON: HIS FRIENDS AND HIS ENEMIES, 1651-1715. By E. K. SANDERS. With Portrait. 8vo. 10s. 6d. net.

Scudamore.—STEPS TO THE ALTAR: a Manual of Devotion for the Blessed Eucharist. By the Rev. W. E. SCUDAMORE, M.A. Royal 32mo. 1s.

On toned paper, with red rubrics, 2s.: The same, with Collects, Epistles, and Gospels, 2s. 6d.; 18mo, cloth, 1s. net; Demy 18mo, cloth, large type, 1s. 3d.; 16mo, with red borders, 2s. net; Imperial 32mo, limp cloth, 6d.

Simpson.—Works by the Rev. W. J. SPARROW SIMPSON, M.A., Vicar of St. Mark's, Regent's Park.

THE CHURCH AND THE BIBLE. Crown 8vo. 3s. 6d.

THE CLAIMS OF JESUS CHRIST: Lent Lectures. Crown 8vo. 3s.

Songs, The, of Degrees; or, Gradual Psalms. Interleaved with Notes from Neale and Littledale's Commentary on the Psalms. By A. B. B. Crown 8vo. 1s. net.

Stone.—Works by the Rev. DARWELL STONE, M.A., Principal of Dorchester Missionary College.

CHRIST AND HUMAN LIFE: Lectures delivered in St. Paul's Cathedral in January 1901; together with a Sermon on 'The Fatherhood of God.' Crown 8vo. 2s. 6d. net.

OUTLINES OF CHRISTIAN DOGMA. Crown 8vo. 7s. 6d.

HOLY BAPTISM. Crown 8vo. 5s. (The Oxford Library of Practical Theology.)

Strange.—INSTRUCTIONS ON THE REVELATION OF ST. JOHN THE DIVINE: Being an attempt to make this book more intelligible to the ordinary reader and so to encourage the study of it. By Rev. CRESSWELL STRANGE, M.A., Vicar of Edgbaston, and Honorary Canon of Worcester. *Crown 8vo.* 6s.

Strong.—CHRISTIAN ETHICS: being the Bampton Lectures for 1895. By THOMAS B. STRONG, B.D., Dean of Christ Church, Oxford. 8vo. 7s. 6d.

Stubbs.—ORDINATION ADDRESSES. By the Right Rev. W. STUBBS, D.D., late Lord Bishop of Oxford. Edited by the Rev. E. E. HOLMES, formerly Domestic Chaplain to the Bishop; Hon. Canon of Christ Church, Oxford. With Photogravure Portrait. *Crown 8vo.* 6s. *net.*

Tee.—THE SANCTUARY OF SUFFERING. By ELEANOR TEE, Author of 'This Everyday Life,' etc. With a Preface by the Rev. J. P. F. DAVIDSON, M.A., late Vicar of St. Matthias', Earl's Court. *Crown 8vo.* 7s. 6d.

Waggett.—THE AGE OF DECISION. By P. N. WAGGETT, M.A., of the Society of St. John the Evangelist, Cowley St. John, Oxford. *Crown 8vo.* 2s. 6d. *net.*

Williams.—Works by the Rev. ISAAC WILLIAMS, B.D.

A DEVOTIONAL COMMENTARY ON THE GOSPEL NARRATIVE. *Eight Vols. Crown 8vo.* 5s. *each.*

THOUGHTS ON THE STUDY OF THE HOLY GOSPELS.
A HARMONY OF THE FOUR EVANGELISTS.
OUR LORD'S NATIVITY.
OUR LORD'S MINISTRY (Second Year).
OUR LORD'S MINISTRY (Third Year).
THE HOLY WEEK.
OUR LORD'S PASSION.
OUR LORD'S RESURRECTION.

FEMALE CHARACTERS OF HOLY SCRIPTURE. A Series of Sermons. *Crown 8vo.* 5s.

THE CHARACTERS OF THE OLD TESTAMENT. *Crown 8vo.* 5s.

THE APOCALYPSE. With Notes and Reflections. *Crown 8vo.* 5s.

SERMONS ON THE EPISTLES AND GOSPELS FOR THE SUNDAYS AND HOLY DAYS. *Two Vols. Crown 8vo.* 5s. *each.*

PLAIN SERMONS ON CATECHISM. *Two Vols. Cr. 8vo.* 5s. *each.*

Wilson.—THOUGHTS ON CONFIRMATION. By Rev. R. J. WILSON, D.D., late Warden of Keble College. 16mo. 1s. 6d.

Wirgman.—Works by A. THEODORE WIRGMAN, D.D., D.C.L., Canon of Grahamstown, and Vice-Provost of St. Mary's Collegiate Church, Port Elizabeth, South Africa.

THE DOCTRINE OF CONFIRMATION. *Crown 8vo.* 7s. 6d.

THE CONSTITUTIONAL AUTHORITY OF BISHOPS IN THE CATHOLIC CHURCH. *Crown 8vo.* 6s.

Wordsworth.—Works by CHRISTOPHER WORDSWORTH, D.D., sometime Bishop of Lincoln.

THE HOLY BIBLE (the Old Testament). With Notes, Introductions, and Index. *Imperial 8vo.*
   Vol. I. THE PENTATEUCH. 25s. Vol. II. JOSHUA TO SAMUEL. 15s. Vol. III. KINGS to ESTHER. 15s. Vol. IV. JOB TO SONG OF SOLOMON. 25s. Vol. V. ISAIAH TO EZEKIEL. 25s. Vol. VI. DANIEL, MINOR PROPHETS, and Index. 15s.
   Also supplied in 12 Parts. Sold separately.

THE NEW TESTAMENT, in the Original Greek. With Notes, Introductions, and Indices. *Imperial 8vo.*
   Vol. I. GOSPELS AND ACTS OF THE APOSTLES. 23s. Vol. II. EPISTLES, APOCALYPSE, and Indices. 37s.
   Also supplied in 4 Parts. Sold separately.

A CHURCH HISTORY TO A.D. 451. *Four Vols. Crown 8vo.*
   Vol. I. TO THE COUNCIL OF NICÆA. A.D. 325. 8s. 6d. Vol. II. FROM THE COUNCIL OF NICÆA TO THAT OF CONSTANTINOPLE. 6s. Vol. III. CONTINUATION. 6s. Vol. IV. CONCLUSION, TO THE COUNCIL OF CHALCEDON, A.D. 451. 6s.

THEOPHILUS ANGLICANUS: a Manual of Instruction on the Church and the Anglican Branch of it. 12mo. 2s. 6d.

ELEMENTS OF INSTRUCTION ON THE CHURCH. 16mo. 1s. *cloth.* 6d. *sewed.*

THE HOLY YEAR: Original Hymns. 16mo. 2s. 6d. *and* 1s. *Limp,* 6d.
   ,,   ,, With Music. Edited by W. H. MONK. *Square 8vo.* 4s. 6d.

ON THE INTERMEDIATE STATE OF THE SOUL AFTER DEATH. 32mo. 1s.

Wordsworth.—Works by JOHN WORDSWORTH, D.D., Lord Bishop of Salisbury.

THE MINISTRY OF GRACE: Studies in Early Church History, with reference to Present Problems. 8vo. 12s. 6d. *net.*

THE HOLY COMMUNION: Four Visitation Addresses. 1891. *Crown 8vo.* 3s. 6d.

THE ONE RELIGION: Truth, Holiness, and Peace desired by the Nations, and revealed by Jesus Christ. Eight Lectures delivered before the University of Oxford in 1881. *Crown 8vo.* 7s. 6d.

UNIVERSITY SERMONS ON GOSPEL SUBJECTS. *Sm. 8vo.* 2s. 6d.

PRAYERS FOR USE IN COLLEGE. 16mo. 1s.

10,000/12/01.

www.ingramcontent.com/pod-product-compliance
Lightning Source LLC
Chambersburg PA
CBHW031427230426
43668CB00007B/474